Lorenzo D. L. G.

The Kingdoms

Rise of the Shadows

BARKERBOOKS

BARKERBOOKS
THE KINGDOMS: RISE OF THE SHADOWS

Proofreading: Yeni Rodríguez | BARKER BOOKS®
Book Cover Design: Armando Saint-Martin | BARKER BOOKS®
Book Interior Layout: Armando Saint-Martin | BARKER BOOKS®
Cover Illustration: DALL-E

First Edition. Published by BARKER BOOKS®

I.S.B.N. Paperback | 979-8-89558-866-6
I.S.B.N. Hardcover | 979-8-89558-867-3
I.S.B.N. eBook | 979-8-89558-865-9

Library of Congress Copyrights Control Number: **1-14924666922**

Barker Publishing, LLC
Tacoma, WA
https://barkerbooks.com
publishing@barkerbooks.com

INDEX

Dedicated to my mother, whose never-ending encouragement fueled this project. Thank you for always believing in me.

I hope you enjoy reading this as much as I enjoyed writing it.

PART I
THE LANDS

CHAPTER I

Prologue

Fifteen years ago...

Two explorers were finding their way inside a cavern, far away from the lands, and in the middle of the vast ocean surrounding them. The air inside that chamber was scarce, and they knew there was no way back, so they only had themselves to survive. But they kept going, hoping to find the treasure they'd been on the lookout for the last couple of years: the Khan.

"I can't breathe," one of them said, "we should return to the village."

"There's no going back now. We've been out for several days; it can't be for nothing," the other grunted, "this place isn't in the lands' map, so what we find here could be the greatest discovery of all time."

"Or it can be worse than Kumblesgard," the man squeezed through a set of boulders.

"Nothing could ever be worse than Kumblesgard, idiot! It was called the most catastrophic event for a reason. Those damned echoes were surely the deadliest things in these lands," the explorer laughed.

"This cave is on another land," the other man argued, "you even said it."

"You know what I meant. Now stop panting, we don't have much air here."

They kept stepping on the slippery moist rocks as the cave's roof enclosed over their heads, and the explorers' panic rose. They finally managed to reach the end of the cavern by crawling into a tiny hole and leaving their torches in the chamber behind.

"Oh! Damn it!" One of them yelled.

The end of the cave was blocked with boulders. After days of expedition, their journey had led nowhere.

"We did all of this for nothing?" The man roughly placed his arm on the stones blocking the path, "we wasted our entire lives looking for this treasure, and it was all for nothing!"

When the man leaned on the rocks, a strange sound was heard. He flinched and pulled himself apart, noticing as the boulders vanished into thin air, leaving behind blue ashes that blinded them both.

"Hidden passage," the explorer stepped into the mist, "I have never seen this kind of thing in my life."

"Quiet!" The other man shut him up, "we have entered the heart of the beast. What awaits us ahead are traps and other types of sorcery guarding the treasure."

When the blue fog faded away, it revealed the artifact they had been searching for a long time: the Khan. There were dozens of golden piles with treasures stacked on top of each other, but there was one unique relic at the top of one of the stacks. Its shining black diamonds and dismally beautiful crimson lid were finally seen after centuries. The artifact was shaped like a lamp, with a dark cover on top of the gold-like texture, concealing whatever dark force was inside.

"We made it!" The man shouted.

"The Khan..." The other explorer stared directly at it, "imagine how much money we will get by selling this!"

"Sell it?" He asked, "we are going to keep it for ourselves. Imagine how much power we will have! How much respect we will gain from the kingdom!"

"Like if you don't have enough of that," the explorer whispered.

The man walked towards the Khan, climbing over the other treasures and skulls piled up below. When he finally reached it, he couldn't stop staring at its blinding shine.

"This is the time," the man laughed, "I won't be a nobody anymore. Everyone will respect us now—even the Queen..."

"Be careful how you talk about her," the other man warned, "or have you forgotten?"

But before the explorer could respond, he wrapped his hands around the Khan and grinned as the other man stared at him from beneath the pile. Suddenly, the artifact started shaking—the diamonds on each corner popped out one by one, and the lid opened, revealing some sort of dark magic inside. The man tried to look at what was hidden within, but the treasure exploded and launched him away. Black and purple smoke covered the chamber, unleashing something the lands hadn't seen in a very long time.

"Osrov!" The man at the bottom of the pile cried his friend's name, but the smoke was too thick for him to see past it.

He coughed blood and fell to the ground in pain, watching as a strange shadow slowly approached him. It had the same silhouette as Osrov, but he wielded some sort of scythe in his right hand. The outline of the man paced out of the smoke, scratching the blade on the ground and whistling a familiar tune.

"Osrov..." The man coughed, trying to open his eyes.

That was when he realized it wasn't Osrov anymore. It had the same body shape, same clothes, and even the same stupid grin on his face, but his entire figure was darkened. It looked just as if his shadow emerged from the ground and consumed his body.

The shadow grabbed the explorer's throat, lifted him off the ground, and stabbed the scythe into his chest. And before the man could notice, he was already transforming into the same shadowy creature Osrov had become.

*****

Meanwhile, at the castle, the Queen looked outside the window, sensing something evil lurking in the outsides. She was holding her crying newborn baby when the King roughly barged into the room, panting in fear.

"They've awakened," he desperately paced around.

"Send all the forces we have!" The Queen searched the room's drawers, "archers, knights, magical creatures, whatever we have!"

She placed the baby on the bed, grabbed a sword from one of the drawers, and took a deep breath before marching out of the room, ready to fight.

"Lorette, you can't fight!" The King ripped the sword from her hands.

"They are about to destroy our kingdom! The archers aren't powerful enough to set them back!" She yelled, "I have to go out there."

"Stay here and watch our son," the King walked out the door, "I'm sorry, Lorette."

He locked the door behind him and stormed away, making sure there was no possible way his wife could escape.

"Damn you, Henrius!" The Queen screamed and banged on the door, hoping someone would hear her. After no one answered, she rushed towards her bed in panic.

She took her baby and hid him under the bed, looking out the window and noticing the cloud of darkness making its way to the kingdom. Before she knew it, the streets were covered in blood. She hopelessly screamed when the bedroom door was kicked down by an obscure creature.

The Queen simply gasped. She knew her fate.

*****

The kingdom won the war. They managed to trap the shadow creatures in a prison on the edge of the lands with the help of the other forces from the kingdom. Many lives were lost during the battle, and although days had passed without an official announcement, most villagers knew what happened inside the castle. Queen Lorette had been killed.

After weeks of silence from the King, he finally built up the courage to walk over to the balcony of the castle. People stared at him from below, hoping he wouldn't say what they were all afraid to hear.

"The rumors are indeed true," the King gulped, "my wife, Lorette, has been killed by the shadows. Although they are locked far away from here, there are still plenty of dangers in this kingdom."

The villagers watching from below burst into tears.

"Which is why I will demand every guard, warrior, and archer to kill all magical creatures in this kingdom," the King commanded.

Everyone started running away, either to their houses or to the forest behind the kingdom. The guards were confused—they had spent their entire lives with the magical creatures of the lands, and now they were supposed to murder them all? It was outrageous! If they were indeed killed, there would be no light elves to grow crops, no frost creatures to bring water to the kingdom, and most of all, no one to protect the castle in case of an attack by trotters or any other type of deadly creature. Where would they go? Would they even survive the genocide the King was commanding?

"I gave an order!" The King yelled.

The guards had no other choice but to thrust spears at them, shoot arrows in their direction, and swing their swords at their heads. They were separating children from their families, locking them in dungeons, and executing them all. Villagers who fled to the forest were chased and massacred. It was obvious most of them wouldn't survive.

And while it all happened, the King lifted a small grin.

Chapter 2

Present Day

It had been fifteen years since the Shadow War ended—fifteen years since the magical creatures of the lands were hunted down and killed by order of the King. Those who escaped found shelter in different corners of the lands, creating kingdoms with strong barriers to protect them from trotters lurking the outsides or the King's army. The light elves followed the Nature Queen to the southern shore of the lands, where she created a giant barrier made out of thick vines to protect her people. The Frost Queen hid herself inside Trotter Mountain, while the fire creatures followed their King and built a home within the lands' volcano, which is surrounded by a lava lake that could sizzle anyone crossing it. Rumor has it that under the smoldering lake, a mysterious creature lurks. The remaining elves separated themselves into tribes and hid in the outsides of the Main Kingdom. However, life there is harsh, so when they run out of provisions they have to infiltrate the Main Kingdom in search of supplies—it always ends in their deaths. The creatures who started the war—mostly known as *shadows*—were trapped in a magical prison on the northern edge of the lands. They are no longer a threat as the King assures there's no possible way for them to escape that prison. After exiling all the magical creatures, the King ordered the construction of a steel wall around the Main Kingdom to stop any trespassers. Although it might've seemed safe for the villagers, the true danger came from within the kingdom.

*****

I was running through the stone streets of the Main Kingdom, avoiding each guard I saw and dropping golden coins on the sidewalks. I wore a dark blue sweater, a scarlet scarf, and a dark cape that covered my hair. A small piece of cloth was wrapped around my face, hiding my mouth and nose as I jumped from roof to roof. I kept sprinting faster, climbing ladders, landing on haystacks, and ensuring each coin I dropped was caught by a villager. I tried using my handmade grapple hook to make long jumps and reach the higher places, but sometimes it didn't work.

As soon as I launched the grapple to a nearby house, I tripped and fell onto the street below. A guard noticed me and sighed, shaking his head.

"You again," he grunted as I got back up my feet and ran to the first ladder I saw.

I climbed it with ease and kicked it down as soon as the guard began chasing me. And when I thought I was finally safe, the roof of the house I was standing on collapsed beneath me.

A couple of seconds later, I was lying on the floor of *Uncle Bob's store* with several armed guards standing in front of me. When I tried sprinting out of the store, I noticed two more of them waiting outside with brown horses by their side.

"Oh s—" I mumbled before they grabbed my wrists and dragged me to the castle.

It didn't take long for me to arrive at the palace as *Uncle Bob's store* was right beside the castle's main gate. When the velvet doors were opened, the guards yanked me up the stairs and abruptly tossed me to the King's bedroom door, where he awaited in his leather chair.

"I know how to walk!" I freed myself from the guards' hands and sat in front of the King.

"How many times have I told you? How many times!" The King slammed his desk and looked me directly in the eyes, "you are my son, and I prohibit this behavior."

Yes, I was the King's son. I was the child who survived the shadow attack, and I was the one who stole money from his father and gave it to the poor. I am Krell, the Prince and heir to the throne of the Main Kingdom.

"People are dying out there and you are just sitting in your room letting it all happen!" I yelled back.

"I am doing what is possible, and you are not helping!" My father angrily said.

"Mom would've supported me! Mom would've actually helped the kingdom!" I stood up and cried.

"You are the reason your mother is dead!" He screamed, "she gave her life for you, and this is how you talk of her? Go to your room and reflect on everything you've done."

"Reflect...?"

"I gave an order!" He clenched his teeth and said, "go!"

I rolled my eyes and walked out of the room, but my father stopped me soon after by calling my name.

"And take this to your grandfather," he handed me a tray with fruit and bread, "he hasn't eaten today."

I grabbed the tray in annoyance and made my way to my grandfather's room, which was next to mine, almost at the end of the corridor. I gently opened the door and pulled the curtains apart, letting some light into the otherwise gloomy room. I placed the tray on the desk beside his bed and touched his forehead to see if he was sick—he wasn't. I was about to leave the room when I heard him speak with a soft voice.

"Hey, gramps," I leaned over, "I brought you some food in case you're hungry."

"Little boy..." My grandfather innocently smiled, "I haven't seen you in so long. You should come visit more often."

Every single day, I came to check on him, bring him food, and have a small chat, but his old age prevented him from remembering any of it.

"Yes, gramps," I giggled, "I will come visit more often. But right now I'm kinda grounded, so I have to go over to my room."

"Oh, well," he chuckled.

"I'll leave you alone now. Eat well, and if you want to go to the bathroom, call me, alright?" I smiled.

I left his room and entered mine, which was a complete mess. The bedsheets hadn't been changed in months, the wooden walls were rotten and moldy, and there was a loose step next to my bed.

I had no other choice but to lie down and *reflect* on all the things I'd done. However, after just a few seconds, I was bored out of my mind, which meant that I had to sneak out of the castle once again.

As I reached for the door, I realized it was locked from the outside, which would've stopped anyone else, but not me. I kept trying to find a way out, attempting to pick the lock, pry open the window, and even beat the door down, but nothing worked. And just as I was giving up, my eyes caught something outside: a dark figure climbing over the steel wall surrounding the kingdom. As I looked carefully, I realized it was a hooded elf infiltrating the kingdom.

That happened very often, especially when elves ran out of provisions and had no other choice but to steal from our kingdom. Oddly enough, it was only one elf who was sneaking in instead of an entire tribe of them. It was my chance! I could go talk to the elf and he could take me with him and get me the hell out of the Main Kingdom!

I eventually got an idea and broke my room's window by throwing my grapple hook at it. I saw as the elf jumped from one rooftop to another, getting closer to the castle. I stepped out of my window and threw the grapple hook onto the ledge above me. It was obvious the elf was trying to enter the castle through the back door, but I wasn't able to get there. Luckily, the large stained glass window beside it looked like a perfect spot for me to intercept the elf.

"Hope I don't fall," I took a deep breath before jumping.

I gripped the rope with my arms and legs, propelling myself towards the stained glass window, which shattered upon impact. I thought I would arrive in pain, with several cuts and bruises, but surprisingly, I was not the one who got hurt. Yes, I accidentally tackled the elf upon my arrival.

Before I could explain myself, the elf stood up and pulled her hood down, revealing her white hair, emerald eyes, and sapphire paint below her eyes and around her cheeks. I didn't know much about magical creatures, but I was certain she was from the Zumba tribe.

"Don't hurt me, alright! I'm sorry," I tried speaking, but before I could say anything else, she interrupted.

"Where is the King?" The elf asked, "you're the Prince, aren't you?"

"I don't like being called Prince, but yeah," I smirked, but she interrupted again.

"I need you to listen closely," she panted, "we need your help. They are coming, and they won't have any mercy. We need all your forces to assist us."

"What are you talking about?" I tilted my head and noticed the bloodstains on her clothes, "are you okay?"

Before she could answer, a crossbow was fired from afar. Two more shots were heard as the elf tumbled to the floor and curled herself up. More and more arrows flew in her direction, impaling her legs and arms. Then, one last shot was fired, and she fell unconscious.

"Leave her alone!" I screamed, but the guards ignored my words and dragged the elf away.

"Prince Krell!" One of the guards approached me, "the King has prohibited you from exiting your room at any moment! What in the lands' name are you doing?"

"She was trying to tell me something!" I tried running over to her, but the guard stopped me.

"Elves are known for being liars," he leaned over and said, "it's your choice whether you believe them or not."

I was sent to my room for the second time that day, and the guards ensured I had no possible escape. They nailed the windows with wooden planks, barricaded the door, and cemented the pipes shut—as if that was even on my list of escape plans. I was already climbing onto my bed in defeat when I stepped on the loose plank beside it. It made an odd hollow sound as if something was hidden below my room. As a last attempt, I dragged the bed out of the way and noticed all the other loose planks below it. It was a hatch, hidden beneath my feet the whole time. How could I have not noticed it before?

"Prince Krell!" A guard knocked on the door, "I've brought you food."

I had no other choice but to open the mysterious hatch and jump inside. I couldn't see anything; it was all pitch black. All I could do was walk forward, hoping there would be some sort of exit.

"There it goes," I noticed the door at the end of the corridor.

I expected the door to lead to a garden, or the main hall of the castle, but when I opened it, I was pleasantly surprised. It took me directly to the streets of the kingdom, with only one small obstacle preventing my escape: I was still on the second floor of the castle, facing a fifteen-foot drop below. Clearly, I needed to find another way.

When I turned to my right, I noticed my father's balcony, where I could throw my grapple hook and swing to the streets. I launched it and jumped, safely climbing up to the nearest ledge.

However, I didn't know that my father was still in his room, talking to one of the guards.

"Sir, there's an elf intruder," I heard the guard speaking through the half-open balcony door, "we have resolved the issue, and the elf is incarcerated in the dungeons."

"She's alive," I whispered to myself.

"Go on and execute the elf," my father said unemotionally, "after that, throw the body to the other side of the barrier. That will give the Zumba tribe a warning."

The idea was insane. I knew that if the guards actually followed his orders, a war between kingdoms could erupt. I needed to stop him.

"I will go solve some pending issues," my father said to the guard, both of them exiting his room.

That was my chance. My father held the keys to the dungeons in one of his drawers, so I needed to find them before they executed the elf. I climbed to the balcony, opened the door, and stealthily entered his room, searching every drawer on his desk. It wasn't as hard as it might've seemed as my father never stored many things in his drawers. When I saw a bunch of unlabeled keys hanging from one ring, I placed them in my pocket and ran away.

As always, I jumped across the rooftops of all the houses in the kingdom to get closer to the dungeons, where the elf was soon to be executed. I knew I needed to reach her and let her take me away to the outsides. I wanted to see the lands and explore what they had to offer—I needed to escape the Main Kingdom. After a few minutes, I finally made it there, and surprisingly, there were no patrolling guards anywhere around. It was my lucky day.

I jumped down and ran through the moist stone stairs to reach the dungeons' metal door, which was obviously locked. I had to pull out my father's keys and try them one by one.

"No... No... No... No..." I kept going, trying to figure out which was the one, "No... No... No... Wait... This is the one."

I quietly opened the dungeons' door, stepping inside and noticing every single cell that held creatures I didn't even know existed. There was a squid-like creature with tentacles all over its face, a horned monster that looked very much like a person, and a magma creature that had its horns cut off. But I wasn't looking for that—I was looking for the elf, who seemed to be at the end of the lightless corridor.

"You again!" A guard stepped out of the dark with one of the sharpest spears I'd ever seen, "don't think that because you're the Prince, I will have mercy on you."

I tried to run away, but he grabbed my neck and threw me to the ground, attempting to stab me multiple times. I moved out of the way before anything could happen, and when he tried to retrieve the spear from the ground, I kicked his back. I thought he would tumble to the ground, but instead, he pushed the back of his spear at my neck and tossed me against the wall. Before I could defend myself, the guard began to choke me.

"You thought that just because you're the Prince, you wouldn't face any consequences?" The guard laughed, about to kill me, "look where this has led you to."

As he was about to break my neck, something grabbed him from the cell across the corridor. It was the squid-like monster, wrapping its tentacles around the guard's neck and using its sharp teeth to penetrate his throat. I watched as the guard's skin turned gray while the squid creature sucked something out of him. The guard fell to the ground, and I screamed, running through the dungeons in fear. At the end of the narrow hallway, I saw someone in the last cell on the left. It was the elf, sitting on the ground and facing the wall on the other side of the bars.

"Is it time for you to execute me?" She asked, "then just get it over with."

"It's me," I said as she turned around with a bittersweet look in her eyes.

Chapter 3

"The Prince, huh?" The elf laughed after seeing me, "why are you here? Shouldn't you be in your castle, with all the servants giving you everything you want—living the perfect life?"

"I don't like being called *Prince*," I said to her for the second time, "and I came here to ask what you were trying to say back at the castle."

"You actually remember, don't you?" The elf was pleasantly surprised, "my name is Reyna."

"I am Krell," I reached my hand to her cell.

"What are you doing?" She stared at me queerly.

"Trying to shake your hand," I explained.

"Don't. You put me behind bars, and now you're trying to shake my hand? We're definitely not friends."

"Alright, sorry," I awkwardly placed my hand back in my pocket, "now tell me what you came here for."

"The shadows have escaped," Reyna looked at me hauntingly, "I don't know how or why, but they've killed my entire tribe and all the others."

"That's not possible," I nervously laughed, "the shadows are trapped in a magical prison far away from here—my father told me so. He said no one could ever escape that place."

"You really believe what your father says?" Reyna asked, "after the lies he told to the Main Kingdom? After he commanded the execution of all those creatures sixteen years ago?"

"Prove it," I said as she sighed and rolled up her sleeve.

"I don't know if anyone has ever told you this, but the Zumba tribe has tikh bracelets. You put these bracelets on as soon as you turn six years old, and each one represents a member of the tribe. When that member dies, our bracelet falls off, and at their funeral, we all send them flying in a small hot air balloon so that in their next life, they can remember us and we can reunite once more."

Her wrist was empty, which meant all the elves in her tribe had died—she was the last remaining. I didn't hesitate any longer and opened her cell door, setting her free.

"We need to stop them," I said, "where are they heading to now?"

"The shadows are attacking the weaker links to destroy the Main Kingdom by the end," she grabbed her bow from the shelf where all the trespassers' weapons were kept, "they are heading to the Nature Kingdom."

"So then we're going to the Nature Kingdom?" I smiled, ready to leave the Main Kingdom after sixteen long years.

"*We*?" Reyna chuckled, "you are going to stay in your little precious kingdom, having everything you want. Keep doing that while the people who actually care save the lands."

"I'm not like my dad!" I followed her to the dungeons' entrance, "look, I've wanted to leave this kingdom my whole life, and I am finally getting the chance. I'm not going to waste it."

"It will be dangerous," she sighed, "more than anything you could ever imagine. There are going to be thousands of creatures along the way, some good, others evil. It's your choice"

Reyna was about to walk out of the dungeons, but I stopped her once again by tightly grabbing her arm.

"You can't go out there; they'll kill you," I said to her.

She looked around for a couple of seconds and eventually leaned over, grabbing the scarf wrapped around my neck and roughly placing it over her head. Her dark horns and shiny white hair were barely visible.

"This'll do it," she sprinted away and climbed a ladder to one of the rooftops.

She was very fast, and it was very hard to keep up with her pace, but with the help of my grapple hook, it took us only a few minutes to reach the giant barrier surrounding the Main Kingdom.

"We made it," Reyna said, pulling down her hood and glancing at the menacingly tall steel wall, "it looked bigger from the other side."

“How will we climb it?” I asked.

“Don’t you have your little grapple hook?” She asked, and I nodded, “then use it.”

“Do you also have one? Or how will you...?” I started saying, but she interrupted by grabbing her bow and shooting an arrow to the top of the steel wall. The arrow had a rope attached, and upon reaching its destination, it revealed three hooks that anchored themselves at the end of the barrier.

“How did you do that!” I gasped and then smirked.

“Elves have a lot of free time, ” she laughed and pulled the rope a couple of times to ensure it could hold her weight, “let’s just do this quietly, and they will never know that we were even here.”

As she prepared herself and placed both feet on the barrier, she suddenly frowned and turned back to the kingdom, gasping as she stared into the distance. I glanced around curiously and noticed dozens of guards arriving on horses, pointing spears at us.

“First creature to ever escape the dungeons, eh?” The captain of the archers said, menacingly stepping in our direction, “I see you got a little help. I am giving you one last chance, Krell. Go up to the castle, where you are supposed to be, and leave the elf to us.”

“Can’t you understand!” I desperately yelled, “the shadows have escaped, and they are going to destroy all the kingdoms—including ours! We need to work together to stop an incoming war!”

“What have I told you, Krell?” The guard clicked his tongue against the roof of his mouth, “never trust elves; they are known for being liars and killers! You come here right now, or we will open fire and kill you both!”

Reyna didn’t hesitate and rapidly shot an arrow at the guard, killing him in an instant. She ran over to the dead man, ripped the spear from his corpse, and handed it to me.

“Do you know how to use this?” Reyna asked.

"I've never wielded any weapon, but I think I can do it," I said, gulping in fear as I tried lifting the spear, but it was too heavy.

I dragged the weapon and used all my might to knock a couple of guards out. They fell to the ground but then stood up indifferently, running over to Reyna, who was mercilessly killing anyone standing in her path. I distracted the knights by tossing the spear their way, and before I knew it, Reyna had already pierced a hole in their skull.

"Come on!" Reyna shouted, killing the last few guards before turning around, "use your grapple hook."

She shot an arrow to the top of the steel wall, commanding me to follow her lead by launching the grapple hook in the same direction. We tied the ropes around our waist and began ascending vertically.

"You know," I tried not to look down, "I've never been scared of heights until this moment."

"Just go!" Reyna shushed me.

We kept walking up the wall, hoping we wouldn't catch the attention of more guards. Just when I thought we were finally safe, a deep and hollow sound was heard beside me. I immediately turned around and noticed the archers on the highest tower in the kingdom, shooting at us.

"Do they ever give up?" Reyna grunted, dodging the bolts that were being fired at us.

"The guards? Never," I sighed and silently chuckled, but an arrow interrupted my laughter by hitting the grapple hook's rope.

It began tearing apart, and it certainly couldn't hold my weight any longer. I was already reaching the top of the wall when I realized the cord was about to snap in half.

"Jump!" Reyna yelled, raising her hand in my direction, ready to catch me, "what are you waiting for?"

"I can't do it!" I panted, watching the rope shred, "I'm scared."

"I will catch you!" Reyna kept her hand still, "I promise."

Then I jumped. It felt like everything around me froze as the rope snapped, and Reyna reached out her hand to me. We locked eyes for a split second before she snatched my arm and threw me to the top of the steel wall.

"Did you see that?" I panted in excitement, "I jumped, and then the rope tore and I was like, *'no!'* But then you caught me with one hand and..."

"I know," Reyna climbed the wall and caught her breath, "be grateful that I actually grabbed your hand. If it would've been someone else from my tribe, they would've left you there to die."

"What?" I mumbled.

"Oh, crap," Reyna sighed and stared at the distance, "they're still shooting arrows at us!"

"They're not normal arrows!" I explained, "they have cross-bows, which are way more lethal."

"It's literally the same thing," she tried to think of a smart way to escape.

With dozens of arrows flying our way, Reyna had no choice but to hug my waist and leap to the other side of the wall. It was a long fall, and if it weren't for the tall trees and bushes, we would've certainly died upon impact. And although it seemed like an impossible goal, I finally fulfilled my dream and escaped the Main Kingdom—I was on the outsides for the first time in my life!

"Reyna," I said, crawling over to her in pain instead of standing up and appreciating the beauty of the outsides, "are you alright?"

"Yes," she panted in a struggle, "I'm fine."

By staring at her leg, she didn't seem *fine* at all. Blood ran down her knee, and there was some sort of wooden stick impaling her thigh. It took me a couple of seconds to realize she had been struck by an arrow.

"Reyna, your leg!" I tore the scarf from her head and used it as a rag to clean the blood.

"Don't worry, I'm fine," she clenched her teeth.

"I know how to remove arrows from the skin. They taught us that in a class we had at the castle," I rolled up my sleeves, "may I?"

"Be quick."

I cautiously wrapped my hands around the bloody arrowhead penetrating Reyna's leg, snapping it in half so the dart wouldn't cause more damage once it was removed from her body.

"This will probably hurt a bit," I held the arrow with both hands, "who am I kidding? This is going to be the most painful thing you've ever experienced."

"Just get it over with," she breathed heavily.

I managed to pull the arrow out of her leg rather quickly, and before she even noticed, it was already lying by her side. I thought she'd be relieved, but her expression remained unchanged—almost as if her worries somehow increased.

"Ah!" Reyna yelled and then panted in distress.

"It's going to ache for a while, but you'll be fine," I lied.

"I'm going to die," Reyna mumbled, "the arrow was poisoned. The toxin is entering my body slowly, but I will die sooner or later."

"No..." I refused, "you're not going to die! I will find something to heal you! A poison cure!"

"Those can only be found at the Nature Kingdom," Reyna cried, "it's too far away."

"Some magical item! Something that could help you! I don't..." I pondered, "that one healing item the elves had!"

"What?" Reyna used her last few words before fainting, "the novo juice? It could help. But the poison is spreading... Go... Quickly... It's in the Zumba camp... on the desk beside... beside..."

She then closed her eyes and passed out. She was still alive, but if I didn't find that magical healing item—the novo juice—she would die. I started running through the woods, trying to find Reyna's camp and hoping there weren't any shadows left inside it.

PART II
BEYOND THE WALLS

Chapter 4

I ran as fast as I could to the Zumba tribe camp, but time was running out, and the poison was rapidly spreading through Reyna's body. I didn't know the elf very well, but if the toxin killed her, I'd have no other choice but to face the shadows by myself—or, in the worst of cases, return to the Main Kingdom.

"I was told the elf camps were near, so where are they?" I muttered to myself, pushing a branch aside and finding the camp I was searching for, surrounded by wooden barriers, "guess this is it."

The main gate to the camp was securely locked, but I noticed a tall tree that grew even larger than the wooden barriers surrounding it. I placed both feet on a branch and started making my way to the top, searching for a spot where I could enter the camp without getting injured. As soon as I found it, something threw me past the wooden barrier, its sharp claws scratching my skin and tackling me inside the camp. When I opened my eyes and stood up in pain, I noticed the creature's glowing eyes, rocky skin, and sizzling liquid drooling down its chest.

"Trotter!" I screamed as the creature charged at me.

I dodged and tried looking for something to defend myself against the unknown creature, but it didn't seem like the Zumba tribe kept many weapons in storage. That's when I caught a glimpse of a sword just a few feet away from me. It was a small katana placed in some sort of glass container on a wall. I sprinted to the box, but when I tried to break it with my shoulder, nothing happened.

The next time the trotter charged at me, I quickly dodged to the side once again, tricking it into shattering the container behind me. While the creature was stunned, I picked the katana from the ground and stabbed it in its chest, looking away as the monster screeched in pain. I couldn't even believe what I was doing—killing a creature.

I couldn't dwell on it for too long as Reyna was still in danger, waiting for me to arrive with the novo juice. I left the dead trotter behind and scouted the tents—which had arrows, paintings, and berries they stole from our kingdom—until I came across a jar shining with aquamarine light. Inside, there was some blue goo.

"This should be it," I said, noticing a grapple hook lying on a table beside me, "I don't think they'll mind if I take this."

I walked away with the grapple hook on my hands, glancing at the sealed gate, which couldn't be opened even from inside the camp. I tried prying it open, kicking it down, and searching for a lever, but there was no way to get across. Then I had an idea: I launched my grapple hook to the top of the gate, hooked it in place, and pulled.

"Come on...!" I struggled, but the door was eventually flipped open, leading me back to all the beautiful trees and bushes on the other side.

But I didn't have time to appreciate the view. All I needed to do was get back to Reyna as quickly as possible, hoping she wasn't dead by the time I arrived. I rushed to where I had left her, stumbling through the bushes and scratching myself with their spines, but after some time running, I finally found her. She was lying on the ground with pale skin and trembling limbs. Her hands were trying to put pressure on the wound, but she was too weak, so it didn't quite work.

"Reyna," I whispered in her ear, "I'm here, don't worry."

"K-K-Krell?" She muttered in tremendous pain.

"Yes," I smiled, "it's me—I have the juice."

I was about to spill the entire bottle of novo juice on her leg when she stopped me by saying: "only one drop."

I nodded and carefully tilted the flask, watching as a small, thick drop of the liquid reached her thigh. Her blood gleamed with a light blue hue, and after a couple of seconds, the wound started to seal shut. I was so concentrated on the reaction the juice had on her body that I was startled once she woke up with a gasp and began breathing heavily.

"Reyna?" I tried approaching her, but she grabbed her dagger and placed it right under my chin.

"Who are you?" She panted as I raised my hands, "how do you know my name?"

"Reyna... just lower the knife," I gulped, "I'm Krell, remember?"

"Krell?" She repeated, lowering the dagger.

"Do you remember?" I asked.

"Yes," she looked at the ground, "I thought everything was a dream. Is my family... dead?"

"There was no one else inside the camp. I'm sorry," I comforted her.

"Did you really call my dagger a *knife*?" She asked, changing the subject and trying not to cry.

"*Thy* were pointing a dagger at me! I didn't have time to think!"

"*Thy*? Really?" She chuckled, "does all royalty speak that way? It's ridiculous."

"What is wrong with *thy*?" I asked.

"It sounds so weird," Reyna laughed even harder after hearing my response.

"I mean, it does sound kinda weird, but we don't really use that word often! I only say it sometimes, but the King..."

"Your father," she corrected me.

"My father," I sighed, "he uses it every day, so I'm used to hearing it by now."

We both laughed for a short time, getting to know each other a little better. My father always told me that elves were horrendous creatures that lived in the shadows and killed everything that stood in their paths, but in reality, they acted just like us humans. We were very alike—except for the pointy ears and horns.

After some time resting outside the steel barrier, we decided to move east. I didn't ask Reyna where we were going, and I didn't really know anything about the outsides, so I simply followed her lead.

"So, about the shadows..." I tried not to remind her of her deceased family, "how will we stop them? The stories I've heard say they can't be hurt by anything! How can we kill the shadows if we can't even land a hit on them?"

"I know that," Reyna sighed, "but maybe if we convince all the kingdoms to unite and fight those spawns of hell, we could probably forge some sort of cure—something to defeat them."

I was about to contribute to the conversation when she shushed me and slid her hand through the vines in front of us, revealing the Zumba tribe's open gate.

"I kinda missed this place after spending my afternoon in the dungeons," she giggled and then fell to the floor in pain, "ouch! The burn started!"

"Are you okay?" I tried helping her, but she pushed my hands away.

"Yes, it's the juice," she panted, "it has some side effects. It burns... a lot. Quick tip, don't use it on your eyes—it will blind you."

"I wasn't planning to," I giggled, "do you need any help, or...?"

"No, I'm fine, don't worry. I'm going to lay down in my tent; it won't take long. You can go look around the camp if you'd like."

Reyna limped to her tent, holding her leg tightly and cussing in pain. That gave me time to explore the camp for as long as I wanted, but I had one simple item in mind: the katana I used to kill the trotter. I knew that after it saved my life, it had to be my weapon.

"That thing isn't as sharp as you think!" Reyna yelled from inside her tent.

"I killed a trotter with it!" I tried proving her wrong.

"Trotters are easy to kill," Reyna laughed at me, "those bastards can get chopped up by blunt knives."

I dropped the katana in disappointment and started looking for other weapons nearby. I opened the first chest I saw and found a small knife, similar to Reyna's. It looked neat and menacing, but I wanted to wield a larger weapon. I walked over to another chest, which held a bow inside. Even though I wanted to pick it up, I knew I couldn't handle a ranged weapon—I didn't even have the skill to shoot a creature in the head! Then I came upon it: a medium-sized sword—green and black—glowing with phosphorescent light that caught my attention almost immediately. I grabbed the hilt and swung it around, noticing how light and smooth the weapon felt—it was perfect.

"It belonged to the old man of my tribe," Reyna approached me, "you can take it—it's the best sword we have."

"If it's the best sword you have, why don't you grab it?" I asked.

"Because it's a tradition to give your children your weapons. I'm stuck with these daggers for my whole life, or at least until I have a child, which I'm not planning to."

"So, I take it?" I asked one last time before grabbing the weapon.

"Sure," she said.

"Thank you," I smiled, slashing the sword in the air a couple of times, "we've gotta go now. We need to get to the Nature Kingdom before the shadows do."

"Don't worry, we'll get there first—I know a little shortcut," she laughed and started walking away without telling me where to go.

I tried following her out of the camp, but as soon as we exited it, Reyna screamed, "look out!"

I turned to my right and noticed the colossal creature standing beside me. It looked just like a trotter, but ten times bigger, with massive horns emitting smoke. The last thing I noticed before the monster grabbed my body was the boulder on its right hand, used as a weapon. The creature lifted me off the ground and sniffed me.

"Blood," the monster roared.

"Let him go!" Reyna fired arrows at the creature's face, managing to strike one of its eyes.

The trotter-like creature dropped me and stood stunned, but made sure to slam the boulder at Reyna once it regained consciousness. With my only ally injured, the monster started coming at me. I sprinted back inside the camp, and the creature tumbled through the gate and caught up to me.

I confidently held my ground and aimed the sword at the creature, but it didn't quite work as the monster slammed me into one of the tents, which collapsed over my body upon impact. There was no chance I was going to beat that thing without an advantage, which meant I needed to get to the camp's second floor, used as an outlook by the elves.

I immediately got up and limped to the ladder, holding my leg in pain as I evaded the creature. I climbed to the second floor of the camp and stared down at the monster, wondering if I should take the risk and jump on top of him. It was too dangerous, so I looked at the loaded ballista by my side and ran directly to it.

I used all my might to aim the giant crossbow at the monster, and my body recoiled as the first oversized arrow hit its right leg. Then I fired a second arrow at its arm, bringing the creature to the ground. The last thing I needed to do was deliver a final strike to kill the monster.

"Ah!" I yelled, leaping over the ledge with my sword ready.

I landed on the monster's head, impaling my weapon in its chest and killing it. I wanted to admire the creature's deceased body, but Reyna needed my help, so I rushed over to her. She was still lying beside the tree, holding her stomach in pain and trying to stand up.

"Are you okay?" I knelt before her and asked.

"Yeah... I think I only broke a few ribs," she sarcastically said.

I wanted to laugh, but before I could, something grabbed my body and lifted me from the ground. It was the same creature from before—the one I thought I had killed. It only had a small wound in its chest; I hadn't managed to hit the heart. Just when

I thought I was about to get eaten, I heard a voice inside my head telling me to raise my hand.

I don't know why I did it, but I elevated the palm of my hand and shut my eyes, expecting the worst. Then I felt something rubbing against my hand as if a branch fell from a nearby tree and landed on me. I squinted my eyes open and noticed that the sword had magically appeared in my hands. I cut past the giant trotter, slashing my sword at its head and killing it once and for all.

I think it's a good time to mention that trotters aren't living creatures. They have a heart and brain—yes—but they are made of rock. When they're destroyed, the creature loses control of its body and dies. So, no, I'm not a murderer.

"How did you...?" Reyna amusingly asked.

"I don't know what I just did. Something told me to raise my hand—a voice," I explained.

"It must've been the recalling spell."

"The what?"

"A recalling spell is something you place on a certain item so it's never lost. For example, if I cast a recalling spell on my daggers, whenever I lift my hands, they will fly back to me. But I don't know how you just did that if you've never even cast a recalling spell on that sword."

"That's odd. And I also have another question: what the hell was that thing?" I pointed at the dead trotter-like creature.

"A trotter king," she explained, "as you might have noticed, they're bigger than the normal trotters and also way deadlier. Even though it might be hard to believe, they've actually killed some of my people."

"That's terrifying," I gasped and then giggled in disbelief, "and you're telling me I killed one of them? That's insane!"

"Yeah, yeah, I heard you. Stop bragging," Reyna patted my shoulder, "but right now we've got to move east. Hopefully we can warn the Nature Kingdom before the shadows strike."

Chapter 5

After preparing ourselves, we began walking through the shortcut Reyna had mentioned earlier, but she still wouldn't answer the questions I asked along the way, so I had no idea where we were headed. After brainlessly walking for more than twenty minutes, she finally started unveiling useful information about the shortcut. She told me that elves used it frequently, and that it led them near fertile grounds. She also said that it was a useful connecting circuit for all kingdoms.

"And we've arrived," she said, standing in front of a lake with wooden boats docked along its edge.

"A lake?" I asked.

"A river. But not just any river," she said, approaching one of the boats and detaching its rope from a nearby oak tree, "this is the quickest way to reach the Nature Kingdom. It can lead us to that giant vine wall in less than an hour."

"And how will we even cross that wall?" I asked.

"That's a problem for later," she helped me into the canoe and pushed it to the center of the river.

"Isn't it peaceful?" She took a deep breath, passing the oars through the calm current, "being out here with nature surrounding us. No trotters. No danger."

"First time I've felt peace in years," I laughed.

"What is the Main Kingdom like?" She asked.

"Horrible," I sighed, "it's just... poverty everywhere, crimes, murder, and the only man who can fix it is sitting behind his desk the whole day. What is your camp like?"

"I don't know, actually," she said, trying to come up with something, "I've spent my whole life hunting in the outsides that I've never truly experienced how my camp is."

"Listen to me, when all of this is over, I will find you a place to live. Your whole family will have something to eat every day, and even if it means leaving the Main Kingdom forever, I am going to keep you safe," I told her.

"Don't trust me so quickly," Reyna laughed, "you've known me for less than an hour, and now you want to live with me? I appreciate it, but you don't know me, and I don't know you. What if everything I've told you is a lie? Maybe the shadows never existed—maybe I am gaining your trust to get information from the Main Kingdom. You've got to be careful who you trust, or you'll end up getting backstabbed by a person you thought was a friend."

"You're not gonna backstab me, right?" I crawled back and leaned on the boat's edge.

"Maybe, maybe not," she chuckled, "it's your job not to fall into the wrong hands."

I was nervously laughing when I felt a drop of water on my head, trickling down my cheek and eventually splashing onto the boat—it was raining. Then the boat abruptly shook as the fish swam in opposite directions, and muffled growling echoed below us.

"What's happening?" I asked, feeling the boat tremble.

"It's gotta be a sea creature or something," Reyna gulped, "not many live around here, though."

Then something cracked the boat open. It was a giant creature with half its body shaped like a trotter and the other half merged with various animals and sea creatures. The monster leaped and dove back down, launching Reyna and me in different directions. I was trying to hold onto the broken boat, but the current was too strong, pulling me away.

"Krell!" Reyna screamed, managing to swim to shore, "be careful! Waterfall!"

I couldn't hear what she was saying, so I simply let the river take me away, hoping it would eventually lead me to land. The stream propelled me to a boulder, where I hit my head, and lost consciousness for a few seconds. When I finally opened my eyes again, I noticed the waterfall ahead of me. If I didn't do something, I was going to fall to my death.

"I've got you!" Reyna reached her hand out to the river and held me tightly. She tried pulling me out of the violent water, but something in the trees rushed towards her.

"Be-behind you!" I coughed up water.

That same creature was somehow walking on land and following Reyna around. It grabbed her waist and launched her away, leaving me alone with nothing to hold onto. Before giving up, I caught a glimpse of a spiky boulder on the cliff beside the waterfall. I could strap my grapple hook there and make it out alive. I immediately grabbed it from my bag and tossed it to the rock. Before I knew it, I was hanging hundreds of feet from the ground.

"That was close," I laughed and tried climbing the rope.

Unexpectedly, the rock I was hanging from wasn't attached to anything else, and my weight was pulling it off the cliff. I screamed and swung myself back and forth with the grapple hook's rope. With a quick jump, I finally reached land, but as I tried catching my breath, the ground rumbled. Sprinting to the edge of the cliff, I noticed Reyna fighting the creature below me. She was dashing around a circular piece of land just a couple dozen feet above the waterfall.

It took me a while to decide what to do, but when I saw Reyna being dragged across the dirt, my common sense vanished. I jumped down to the monster. While hovering over the merged creature, I raised my sword and struck its back before hitting the ground.

"I thought you were dead!" Reyna tried not to show any emotion, but she still cracked a smile.

The creature ripped the sword from its back and screeched in pain, somehow beginning to dismember itself. The sea animals attached to its left side fell and hopelessly attempted to swim on the ground.

But there were still several other animals left—not to mention the trotter at the center of the malformed monster. I recalled my sword by raising my hand and slashed at the creature's legs. When it tumbled to the ground, Reyna swung her two daggers and cut off one of its arms. There wasn't much the creature could do anymore, so it couldn't defend itself once Reyna stabbed her dagger into its head.

"Reyna," I sighed with a laugh of relief and approached her.

"Don't hug me," she pushed me away, "I'm all covered in blood."

"Oh, sorry, I was just excited," I giggled, "you killed that thing! I mean, what even was it? A trotter? A dolphin? Both? That was insane!"

"That was a mutated creature," she explained, wiping the blood off, "I've never seen one, but my family told me legends about them. I thought they weren't real until now."

"I thought all creatures on the outsides were trotters," I laughed, glancing down at the dead creature.

"Oh, then you know nothing about these lands," she cleaned her face with a nearby puddle.

That was when something caught my attention from afar. There was a dark purple cloud hovering over the trees, corrupting everything in its path. I rubbed my eyes and wondered if it was an illusion, but I could even feel the mystical warm wind blowing in my direction.

"What is that?" I mumbled as she glanced at the cloud's reflection in the puddle.

"We need to get out of here, now!" Reyna grabbed my hand and ran, dragging me with her, "we can't risk being near those things!"

"What are they?" I asked.

"The shadows."

"The shadows?" I repeated with fright.

"Remember? I told you about them a while ago? They're the reason why we're even doing all this in the first place?" Reyna sarcastically said.

"I know, but they're real!"

"Yeah, smartass, they're real," she kept running away, holding my hand, "we're not far from the Nature Kingdom now, we just need to take a path south, and we'll reach the roots of the vine wall."

"Which we still don't know how to cross," I whispered.

We kept running through the tall trees for a while, trying to reach the Nature Kingdom before the shadows got there, and avoiding any trotters we encountered. Within a few minutes, I caught a glimpse of the giant vine covering the kingdom and its village. I couldn't wait to get inside. I mean, I finally knew what the outsides looked like—and honestly, it wasn't quite as pleasant as I expected—but what would a kingdom look like? I imagined stone houses with ivy growing around them, streets covered in flowers, and a beautiful castle in the distance with a glowing light at its center. Before my imagination could go any further, Reyna placed her hand on my chest and stopped me, pointing at the mud puddle in front of us.

"Be careful," she said, "that mud right there can decompose your body as soon as you step on it."

"How could mud ever...?" I laughed, but she shushed me soon after.

"Look at that," she pointed at a simple frog bouncing around the bushes. When the poor thing jumped onto the mud, a hand emerged from the ground and dragged it under.

"How did that happen?" I gasped, looking at my feet to ensure the mud wasn't anywhere near.

"The magic of the outsides!" Reyna laughed, "it's not as beautiful as you might've heard in stories."

I skirted the mud puddle, avoiding the hand that was still searching for more bait. Eventually, I safely reached the other side, where there was a stone bridge.

"You also have to be careful with these bridges," Reyna added.

"What's next? Be careful of trotter poop on the grass?" I chuckled, clearly joking.

"Actually, trotter kings' poop can mutate into another trotter," Reyna said, watching as I looked back at her oddly, "I'm joking, of course."

"Oh," I chuckled.

"But you have to be careful with any bridge you see," Reyna continued, pacing around me, "you've probably heard of the story of a little troll that hides below bridges. Well, *trolems* can turn themselves into stone bridges to capture their prey."

"Is there another way to get across?" I asked, but she shook her head.

Reyna led the way to the other side of the bridge, steadily rushing across and hoping nothing would happen. I thought we were safe until the ground rumbled.

"*Trolem!*" Reyna rolled to the other side of the bridge.

I managed to jump to the ground and crawl away, noticing the monstrosity the bridge was turning into. It was the size of a trotter king, and although both were made of stone, the *trolem* looked like a mountain come to life. It had gems in its eyes as well as rock spikes embedded in its arms and legs.

"*Trolems* have a stone heart! We need to cut our way through its chest to kill it!" Reyna yelled at me as the creature stood on four paws.

The *trolem* swung its arm and tried to smash Reyna, but its moves were too slow to hit her. I guessed the rocks on its body were so heavy that the *trolem* couldn't even control them to move freely. I tried to throw my sword at the creature, but it bounced off and ricocheted back to me. When I raised my hand to recover the weapon, the *trolem* jumped over me and roared in my face. The creature was about to stomp on me when an arrow was fired from behind, killing the *trolem* and giving me the chance to roll away and catch my breath. When the monster collapsed, I noticed many people standing behind it, mounted on horses, holding spears, and coughing behind their silver helms. I recognized them almost immediately: my father's army.

PART III
RECRUITING ALLIES

Chapter 6

"Krell, the Prince of the Main Kingdom, heir to the throne, and son of the beloved King, you are under arrest for violating the established rules of our kingdom. The law clearly states that leaving the kingdom without the King's authorization is prohibited. This violation can—and will—end in a death penalty. Resisting arrest may lead to a worse fate. Surrender at once," the guard stated, surrounded by his steel-armored companions.

"What do we do?" I whispered to Reyna, who was just as shocked as I was.

"I don't know; there are too many," she said.

"Bring out the big guy," the guard chuckled, with all the other men stepping aside, creating a path for someone.

My father's best guard, who had fought alongside him for over thirty years and was considered the strongest in the kingdom, approached us. He wore chucky titanium armor and wielded a weapon made of metal thorns.

"I surrender," I said, "I am faithful to my kingdom, and I accept that I have made a big mistake."

"What are you doing?" Reyna whispered.

"Trust me," I mumbled back, "you shall arrest me now."

"Good boy," the guard laughed, "now put both your hands up in the air."

"If you wish," I grinned, raising my right hand.

When I heard a whooshing approaching, I knew my plan was working. I kept my hand up and surreptitiously glanced at Reyna, who had already realized what was happening.

"Now!" I yelled.

The sword flew back to my hands as Reyna grabbed her bow, and the guards drew their spears, preparing themselves.

"We could've done this the easy way, Krell," the guard roared, "attack!"

The guards rushed at us with their heavy spears and crossbows. Reyna shot them from afar while I carefully attacked from up close. I tried not to kill anyone—aiming to leave them unconscious on the ground—but Reyna couldn't follow those rules and kept slaughtering them all. I broke a guard's armor, and Reyna took that as a signal to impale an arrow in his chest. I was about to tell her that she shouldn't do that when one of the knights tackled me to the ground and tried using his spear to stab me. I immediately recalled my weapon and hit his face. Reyna noticed my struggle and grabbed her two daggers. With no hesitation, she stabbed one guard in the chest, used her other knife to cut another's throat, and kicked the remaining one on the stomach. I was shocked by her brutality. Eventually, Reyna cleared the place up, leaving only one guard alive.

"You killed them all," the remaining knight walked among his companions' bodies, grunting as he raised his greatsword, "but I am Vernan, and I have never known defeat."

Vernan charged at Reyna first, grabbing her neck and tossing her aside. I thought she would stand up and continue fighting, but she laid on the ground in an almost unconscious state.

"Seems like it's only you and me now, huh?" I nervously laughed, walking backwards, "can we wait until she wakes up?"

The guard rammed in my direction, but something dropped from the sky and landed on top of him. It was a creature similar to a bird, but much bigger, with ashes scattered across its body. The strange monster used its long legs to pierce the guard's armor and carried him flying across the sky. I could've run after the creature to see if Vernan was alright, but I was too lazy, so I just walked over to Reyna.

"That guy just got taken by a flying creature!" I approached her and chuckled, "but, anyway, are you alright?"

"Yes," Reyna coughed in pain, "but it feels like I've been pushed by a trotter king again."

That was when an incapacitated guard grabbed my leg and threw me to the ground, crawling over me and raising a tiny knife over my chest. I had my sword at hand, but for some reason, I couldn't kill the man. It was a life-or-death situation, but taking a person's life was something I could never do. When the guard was about to stab me, Reyna fired an arrow at his head, killing him.

"What are you doing?" She asked with the bow at hand, "he could've killed you!"

"Look, I'm not like you!" I pushed the guard away and angrily stood up.

"Yes, because you are a wealthy little boy, and I am an elf who's lived her entire life in a piece of scum," she laughed, "isn't it obvious?"

"I'm not talking about that!" I yelled, "you just killed a dozen men!"

"Yeah, that's what elves do."

"Don't you realize that those people have a life of their own? Even if they tried to kill us, was it necessary to take their lives?"

"Look, Krell," she sighed, "I don't know how things are inside the Main Kingdom, but out here we don't have any mercy. It's either *kill or get killed*."

"I'm not asking you to change your elf traditions, okay? I'm just telling you that if I have the opportunity to kill someone, I won't do it. You can do whatever you want, but I will never kill anyone in my entire life."

"It's none of my business," Reyna said, "but even though you might've not noticed, you are the Prince of the Main Kingdom, which means that you're loved by many people but also hated by others. So when anyone comes here and tries to kill you, I wish you luck. You won't survive in the outsides without killing. But enough of this; we need to focus on getting inside the Nature Kingdom before the shadows do."

"How are we going to get up there?" I ignored her sermon and glanced at the giant, green, thick vine covering the Nature Kingdom.

Reyna shot a grapple arrow at the vine, but when the three claws tried to impale it, the arrow bounced off the structure. She clicked her tongue with the roof of her mouth and grabbed her two daggers, stabbing them into the vine.

"That's our way in."

"By climbing it?"

"Yeah."

"Can't we find another way?"

"If you have a better idea, be my guest."

"But I only have one sword," I said, "it's impossible to climb that wall with one weapon."

Reyna looked around for a few seconds and eventually stepped on top of a dead guard. She grabbed his spear and used her knee to break it in half.

"How did you do that so easily?" I asked.

"They're made out of cheap wood, not metal. They just used some silver paint to make them look more expensive," Reyna giggled, "here it goes."

She handed me the broken spear, and we both began ascending the vine. The one thing I didn't understand was what we were going to do when we got up there. We couldn't just jump to the other side—we'd die! It would be ten times harder to climb down, so how were we going to do it?

"This is... very high," I gulped, ripping my sword from the vine, supporting my weight with the spear, and stabbing it higher up.

"Don't worry, we're getting there."

But as I glanced up, the vine seemed eternal. I couldn't see its end due to the clouds obstructing my view, and looking down wasn't reassuring at all. It was a long fall, and if I ever let go of my sword and spear, I'd plummet into what appeared to be an endless void.

"We're already entering the clouds!" Reyna—a few feet above me—said, "this is when things get foggy and dangerous."

Then I heard a distant cry. It was similar to a trotter's, but it couldn't be one as we were too high up, and trotters cannot growl so loudly—not even trotter kings. Then I noticed a blurry figure hidden within the clouds. It was some sort of flying creature—like a trotter with wings. The monster charged at me, causing me to lose grip of my sword, but I held the spear tightly with both hands.

"Krell! Be careful!" Reyna yelled, climbing down to where I was by stabbing her daggers into the vine, "did it hurt you?"

"I'm fine!" I looked back, "what was that thing?"

"I don't know," Reyna gulped, "but it was the same monster that attacked the guard some minutes ago. It looked like a trotter."

Then many of them started growling at us, hidden in the fog.

"Oh no," Reyna mumbled, "more of them are coming. We have to get to the top as fast as we can!"

I tried to do what she said, but it was impossible to concentrate with the growling getting closer. Reyna gave up after a few seconds, stopped climbing, and yelled something I couldn't hear because of the screeching around us. She then purposefully leaped back and plunged. Luckily, I grabbed her legs with one hand before she fell.

"What are you doing!" I screamed, but she couldn't listen to me.

"Hold me tight! I have a plan!" Despite being upside down, Reyna grabbed her bow and began shooting arrows at the flying creatures, landing every single shot she fired.

"I can't hold you much longer!" I panted, gripping my sword with all my might to ensure Reyna wouldn't slip off.

But she couldn't hear me, and instead of helping, she just kept firing more arrows. As I expected, I eventually couldn't hold on any longer, and we both began plummeting. However, as always, Reyna was two steps ahead—she fired a grapple arrow into the sky, hooking it to the other side of the vine and catching me with her other hand before we started ascending.

"We were about to die!" I panted, "how did you do that?"

"Elves have skills," was her only response.

While we climbed the rope, the creatures were still screaming at us from a distance, but surprisingly, they didn't attack anymore. It was as if they were chanting—screaming in unison, like a ritual.

"We have to get out of here, quick!" Reyna screamed, climbing the rope as I followed at a slower pace.

"What is happening!" I yelled as hard as I could, but my voice was still muffled by the screams.

"They're summoning someone! Or something... We have to reach the top before their summoning comes to life!"

And then we heard a roar. It was loud enough to drown out the creature´s chanting, but we still couldn't figure out where it came from. Then a pair of wings flapped, and something emerged from the other side of the vine. It was a dragon, slowly agitating its wings as it flew over the creatures and stopped their summoning. That made them furious, but when they tried attacking the dragon, it swung its tail around and knocked all of them back.

"Come on! We don't have a lot of time!" Reyna screamed, but I was still captivated by the dragon.

We finally reached the vine's peak, but as we observed the other side, it was completely shrouded in fog. It wouldn't stop us, though, and as soon as we started descending, we realized that the dragon had killed every single creature and had directed its attention to us.

"Stay still, and it won't see us," Reyna whispered with a trembling voice. It was the first time I had seen her scared.

The dragon's nose started smoking, and as it opened its mouth to breathe fire on us, I wrapped my arms around Reyna and threw us both to the other side of the vine. The only problem was that we didn't have a way to save ourselves once we fell to our deaths, and as I checked on Reyna, I noticed she wasn't even conscious at the moment. I panicked, looking at my surroundings and noticing there was absolutely nothing to help us. But that wouldn't stop me—I raised my hand and recalled my sword. As soon as it arrived, I stabbed it into the vine beside us, holding Reyna tightly and hoping it would stop our fall. I heard as the weapon scratched the giant liana, slowing us down as we eventually reached the ground.

"Reyna! Reyna! Reyna!" I gently slapped her face, "wake up, Reyna! Quick!"

Then I heard a chuckle.

"Did you really think I was unconscious?" She laughed.

"What? Reyna!" I pushed her away, "I thought we were going to die! If it weren't for my idea, our guts would be splashed all over the ground right now!"

"I knew you were going to save me anyway."

"What if I didn't have that idea?"

"I would've figured out something."

"In those two seconds we had left before we hit the ground?"

"As I already told you, *elves have skills.*"

She then walked away like nothing had happened, and I had no other choice but to follow her. I had completely forgotten that we were inside the Nature Kingdom, so once I stepped on a fluffy pile of mud, I was unpleasantly surprised. It was like standing on a cloud, only dirtier, grosser, and full of little insects that bit me dozens of times.

"Get used to it," Reyna said, "this whole kingdom will be like this."

"I'm already hating this place."

When Reyna saw a small liana blocking our path, she cut through it, revealing something more shocking than anything I would've expected. The Nature Kingdom wasn't a place full of mud and life. No fairies were flying around the stone houses, no light elves singing in the streets, and the Queen wasn't atop her vine, accepting gifts from the citizens. It was the complete opposite. The houses were made out of concrete, the streets were filled with clash centers—people betting on who'd win each fight—and in the middle of the kingdom stood a giant steel castle with small golden rays. It was obvious that the Queen lived there, but it seemed almost impossible for someone to call that place *home*.

"What is this?" Reyna gasped, "it wasn't like this last time I came here."

"So this is the kingdom of life and peace... Makes sense," I laughed.

"They probably remodeled it after the Trotter War," Reyna said to herself, passing her tongue over her upper teeth.

"The what?"

"The Trotter War. It's a hard story to tell."

"What happened during it?"

"Basically, the trotters got mad and attacked the Nature Kingdom, almost destroying everything inside it."

"Who won?"

"Neither of them. The Trotter God decided that the fight wasn't worth their time and they just returned to Trotter Mountain."

"There is a Trotter God?"

"I mean, it's a legend, but there have been many sightings of him. But enough chit-chat, let's get to the castle."

"Through that hell of a street? Yeah, I think I'll pass."

"We're obviously not going through the streets, dummy. We don't want to attract the unwanted attention of the light elves. That's why we'll use our skills to our advantage," Reyna pointed at the nearby houses.

"We jump across the rooftops until we reach the castle? That's a good idea."

"Each house has a ladder inside that leads to the roof. We just have to sneak inside and get up top," she noticed a house with the lights off, "c'mon."

Reyna jumped down to the streets and quietly walked to the house. It seemed like we were doing a great job until we heard some light elves approaching. Reyna grabbed my wrist before I could say anything and threw me through the window beside us, climbing inside right after.

"Don't make a sound," Reyna whispered as the light elves walked past the house.

I stood quietly without moving a muscle or making a sound. I wasn't even breathing to ensure the light elves wouldn't notice us. After all, we were breaching their kingdom, and who knew how friendly they were to outsiders.

"They're gone," Reyna sighed.

"For a second I thought we'd get caught!" I laughed.

I wasn't so wrong after all.

Chapter 7

"Yuh-yuh-you're not f-from here," said someone inside the house.

It was a light elf, cooking in his kitchen. He had pointy ears, small horns, and was definitely scared judging by how much he stuttered when he spoke.

"Not this again," Reyna grabbed her daggers and slowly approached the elf.

"No! P-please don't ki-kill me!" The defenseless elf covered his face with his hands, "I-I won't tell anyone!"

"Reyna! Don't kill him," I tried reasoning with her.

"We can't leave loose ends," she looked at me and then glanced back at the elf, "if we leave him alive, he will snitch on us!"

"D-d-don't worry! I won't s-sn-snitch on anyone!" He breathed heavily.

"Fine!" Reyna stopped for a few seconds and then tilted her head, visibly annoyed.

"You-you-you're a dark elf, aren't you?" The elf trembled.

"No, buddy, I think you're wrong. I'm a light elf just like all the others," Reyna laughed nervously.

"No-no... But I'm sure that dark elves have the s-s-same skin tone as you. And-and you have those marks on your left hand! Th-those are dark elf marks!"

"Reyna..." I started speaking.

"He clearly doesn't know anything about elves! These marks are from the Zumba tribe, and they are a tradition among us!" She angrily interrupted.

"B-but I know those marks! I am c-certain that they're from the dark el-el—!"

"Oh, shut up," Reyna tried to play it off.

"B-but they are!"

"I told you to shut up!" Reyna screamed, clutching her daggers again and charging at the light elf in rage.

"Help! Help, someone!" The poor guy screamed, running away.

Reyna chased him with her knife, but the elf was surprisingly agile and evaded each swing. Unfortunately, he eventually tripped and fell. As he tried crawling backwards, Reyna grabbed his foot and pulled him closer.

"Stop!" I intervened, "what are you doing?"

"P-please do not kill me!" The elf cried.

"Are you a dark elf, Reyna?" I asked, stepping between the elf and her.

"Yes!" She rolled her eyes and ranted, "God, why does it even matter? It's just a race; it doesn't define your whole personality!"

"Weren't dark elves dangerous?" I took a step back.

"Who told you that? Your father? The same person who lied to you all these years? Are you really gonna believe him?"

"I never told you I believed him! But the dark elves tried to enslave the Main Kingdom all those years ago, and—"

"The *dark elves*?" Reyna repeated, "*all* the elves tried to start a revolution, but only the dark elves were exiled from the Main Kingdom! We were hunted down by your father's army and became a *threat* to humankind! The only dark elves remaining were the Zumbas, but we had to live in the shadows to avoid being murdered."

"B-but I thought the d-dark elves had all died. Yuh-you are one of a kind!" The light elf smiled, examining her closely.

"And now that my family is dead, I'm the last dark elf in the lands."

"I'm so sorry Reyna," I said, "I didn't mean to make you feel different for being a dark elf. I just wanted to—"

"If I may interrupt... w-w-what happened to your marks on your ears a-and on your f-fingertips?"

"It's a long story..." Reyna sighed.

"I mean, w-w-we have all day, d-d-don't we?" The light elf laughed.

"Actually, we don't—the shadows are about to reach the kingdom and destroy everything inside it," Reyna said with a sarcastic smile.

"S-shadows?" The elf muttered.

"That is also a long story," she sighed.

"I think we have plenty of time, Reyna," I said, clenching my teeth and hoping she wouldn't get angry or annoyed.

"Are you really siding with him?" She was indeed annoyed.

"I'm just saying..." I leaned against the wall, "it's pretty intriguing how you've camouflaged as a light elf this whole time, you know?"

Reyna looked at me for a couple of seconds, then rolled her eyes.

"It all started long ago..." She began, "my mother was pregnant with me when the elf revolution started. Almost no one sided with the Dark Elf King, but he still fought to become the new leader of the Main Kingdom. As we all know, it ended in war. The battle concluded rather quickly, and the troops from the Main Kingdom killed the Dark Elf King after some days. Although we had nothing to do with it, the dark elves were exiled from the kingdom and forced to live on the outskirts. My parents tried sneaking back in, but nothing worked, so they had to resort to their last option: Renna, the witch."

"R-Renna!" The light elf shouted, surprised, "l...l-like t-t-the almighty Renna?"

"Excuse me, who's Renna?"

"I'm trying to tell a story; question until the end, please," Reyna laughed, but just a second later, her smile dropped.

"Anyway," she continued, "my parents sought Renna the witch and asked if she could cast a spell that could transform all dark elves to light elves. She told them she wasn't able to do that, but she could erase every single inner trait that differentiated us from the other elves. The only thing she couldn't remove were the skin marks, so we had to figure out a way to take care of them ourselves."

"What did you do?" I asked.

"We peeled our skin off," she said.

At first, I thought it was a joke, but her face remained serious.

"Oh, you're not joking."

"Why would I be?"

"I... I don't... You know what, just continue with the story."

"Thank you," Reyna sighed, "all dark elves peeled their own skin off: first the back of their ears, then their fingertips, and lastly their whole arms. We managed to sneak back inside the kingdom, but the Shadow War occurred not long after, and we were exiled from the Main Kingdom once again, forced to live on the outsides. When I was just seven years old, I had to peel off my ear skin to hide the dark elf marks. Then when I turned ten, I peeled my fingertips, and I was supposed to cut my arm skin off when I was thirteen but couldn't do it, so I've hidden it my entire life. And just now, one of those flying creatures tore the clothes hiding the marks, and now I am telling this to you!"

"F-flying trotters!" The light elf exclaimed, "those c-c-creatures are flying trotters!"

"Oh, and I also forgot to mention that the witch cast a curse on my bloodline," Reyna added.

"She casted a what on your what?" I mumbled.

"A curse on my bloodline," she repeated, "I still don't know what it is—or what it does—but when it starts to take effect, it won't be pretty."

"So then who's Renna?" I asked again.

"A witch that can do many things. She lives in a swamp far away from here and is evil incarnate, so make sure you never encounter her."

"I... I am sorry to interrupt, b-b-but why are you here, and h-how did you cross the border?" The light elf asked.

"Do you remember the Shadow War?" I began to explain.

"Y-y-yes."

"Basically, the shadows escaped and are coming to destroy this kingdom," Reyna said before I could.

"S-so it wasn't a j-j-joke!" The elf breathed heavily, "you need t-to warn the-the Queen!"

"That's what we're trying to do. And you are going to help us," I said, tilting my head.

"Y-yes!" The elf went up to one of his drawers and took out a dusty piece of paper, "here you huh-have a map! Yuh-you can see the t-t-tall building just to the left of the Quee-Queen's castle. You need to go b-behind it, and there will be a hole that will lead you to the castle's catacombs."

"Can't we just get in through the main gate?" Reyna asked, "It'll be quicker."

"It's heavily guarded, bu-but it's your choice," the elf gulped, "I-I-I don't really recommend it, b-but if you'd like..."

"Where do you want to go, Krell?" Reyna asked, "It's your choice."

Part of me wanted to go through the secret path, while another part wanted to go through the main gate. I couldn't decide, so I just stood there for a few seconds.

"Secret path," I finally said, "It'll be stealthier and more effective."

"Coward," Reyna laughed, "c'mon, let's go."

And there we were, walking along the back of the building that supposedly had a hole behind it. That's obviously assuming the elf hadn't lied to us and it was actually a heavily guarded place, which I hoped wasn't the case. When we finally reached the building and jumped the backyard fence, there was a single guard watching over the catacombs' entrance.

"Let me handle this," Reyna said, reaching for her two daggers.

"Wait!" I grabbed her arm and pulled her closer, "can you stop killing for a second?"

"What?"

"I said, *can you stop killing for a second?*" I slowly repeated.

"Oh, I heard you. I was just making sure you actually said what I heard."

"Look, it's not that I want to stop your *elf traditions* or anything, but I feel like it's not necessary to kill every single person you see!" I argued, "I mean, he has a life and is just doing his job."

"Are you really going to do this right now?"

"Yes! Be merciful for once!"

"Who's there?" The guard heard my voice and approached, "you mischievous little thieves!"

He sprinted at us, raising his spear over our heads and attempting to stab us. Reyna blocked the attack, pushed the guard away, jumped over him, and tried to stab her daggers into his chest. But the guard roared and launched her to the other side of the yard, just beside the hole. She was getting punched and thrown around, and although I was willing to help, I couldn't find the courage to do so. Then she was hurled towards the hole that led to the dungeons, and before she fell in, she called out my name.

"Krell!" She yelled in agony, "help!"

I hesitated at first, but seeing Reyna in danger triggered something within me. I ran to the edge of the hole and tackled the guard inside, which unfortunately meant I fell in too. So then the three of us plunged straight into the kingdom's catacombs.

Chapter 8

The hole was exceedingly deep, and the longer I fell, the slimier my chances of survival became. However, I eventually reached the bottom and landed on top of the guard, who cushioned my fall.

"Ouch," Reyna rolled to the side before the guard collapsed over her.

"Is he…?" I asked, somewhat relieved that he was no longer alive, but also shocked because I was responsible for his death.

"I think—" Reyna started, but the injured elf grabbed my arm and spoke in a very low tone.

"You don't know what you've gotten yourself into…" He coughed blood, "these catacombs hold the most dang—"

Before the guard could finish speaking, Reyna slashed her dagger at his arm, severing his hand. The elf screeched in fear and bled out moments later.

"What did you do!" I yelled, noticing that the man's hand was still gripping my arm even despite it being detached.

"He really needed to die."

"But he was trying to tell us something!" I said

"Probably just another trap," Reyna rolled her eyes, "you really need to stop trusting every single person you meet."

"It wasn't a trap! He was saying something about these catacombs! He said they were dangerous!"

"What did you expect?" Reyna laughed, "for this place to be harmless? Now c'mon, the castle's entrance should be somewhere around here."

"But, Reyna," I called, trying to get her attention, but she was already walking away, leaving me alone in the darkness of the catacombs, "Reyna, wait!"

She didn't listen and kept running through the tight, gloomy stone hallway. I rushed after her, but was surprised once I noticed the many skeletons on the walls, some creepier than others. One of them had a hole in their skull, while another had a crushed neck as if it died by strangulation. Others had their bones clustered together by thick vines similar to the ones surrounding the Nature Kingdom. The last skeleton I saw—and definitely the weirdest—had no arms and a split skull with a vine piercing it. There were even beautiful flowers blooming at one end of the vine.

"What caused all this?" I asked, examining the skeletons, "I've never seen anything like it."

"Me neither," Reyna replied, equally confused, "and the only reasonable explanation is that the Queen of the Nature Kingdom is the one responsible. I thought she was peaceful, but apparently she's more brutal than the elves."

Then a skeleton fell out of the wall just as I was walking beside it. Terrified, I fell to the ground and started screaming.

"Get it out! Get it out!" I cried for help, but Reyna unemotionally pushed it away.

"It's just a skeleton; don't be so dramatic."

"It could come to life, *ya know*?"

"Dead things cannot come to life, *ya know,*" she said, clearly mocking me.

"Can we just get out of this place?" I said, but something happened afterwards.

The catacombs went dark. I stopped walking through the eerie corridor and stood motionless, wondering if Reyna had any idea how to light up the place.

"What happened?" My voice shook as I asked.

"The catacomb entrance has been shut," Reyna gulped, trying not to panic, "grab my hand."

"There, I grabbed it!" I held her hand tight, "why is it so cold though?"

"Krell..." Reyna started saying, "that isn't my hand."

Before I could process her words, she grabbed something from her pouch and cracked it open. It was a light orb that illuminated its surroundings when shattered. I glanced down and realized what I had been holding the entire time: the hand of a skeleton. And the skeleton was somehow moving.

"Is it alive?" Reyna whispered,

The skeleton tilted its head and extended its arms to Reyna, grabbing her face and opening its mouth. The vine impaling its throat started moving and somehow wrapped itself around her neck. I immediately recalled my sword and slashed the vine, freeing her from the skeleton's grasp.

"You said these skeletons wouldn't come to life!" I yelled.

"I haven't visited the kingdom in years; I don't know what to expect!" She screamed back.

Then all of the other skeletons began tearing themselves from the stone walls, moving their limbs, and slowly limping towards us with various weapons made of thick vines.

"Run," Reyna mumbled, "run!"

We tried to do that, but there were even more skeletons in front of us, swarming the entire corridor. We had no other choice but to ram through them and hope nothing would happen.

"We need to get out of here!" I yelled, chopping the skeletons.

There was no sign of an exit, but we were relieved once we saw a bright blue light at the end of the hall. It wasn't a way out—although it seemed to be some sort of door—but rather a short sentence.

"What is this?" I panted, examining the words as Reyna shot the skeletons.

What dies soon after it is born, but continues living for eternity?

"What is this!" I repeated, not finding any sense in the sentence.

"What does it say?" Reyna looked at me briefly and continued shooting the skeletons.

"It dies soon after it is born, but continues living for eternity?" I gulped, "what does it even mean?"

"It's a riddle!"

"A riddle?"

"Yes, a riddle!"

"What does it mean?"

"I don't know! Figure it out!"

"Alright..." I took a deep breath.

I blankly stared at the sentence, but it didn't even look like a phrase anymore—just a small cluster of random words. When I needed clarity the most, my mind was blocked.

"*Skeletons*!" Reyna yelled, "try *skeletons*."

"*Skeletons*!" I yelled to the wall, but the sign turned red, indicating it was incorrect, "it didn't work!"

"*Kings and Queens*!" Reyna tried again, "try that!"

"*Kings and Queens*!" I said to the wall, but the sentence turned red again, "nothing is working!"

Then something came to mind.

"What lives forever, but dies as soon as it's born..." I repeated one last time, "*the present.* The answer is *THE PRESENT*!"

The glowing sentence turned green, and the door slowly began opening. The answer to the riddle wasn't hard to figure out, but I still screamed in excitement once I guessed it right.

"Run!" Reyna dashed to the door, but just as she entered, one of the skeletons grabbed her leg and threw her to the ground, "Krell! Help!"

I turned back and used my sword to cut its arm open. Before the skeleton could enter the castle, Reyna kicked it away, and I slammed the door shut. We both fell back and lay on the floor, panting, but as soon as we looked at each other, we started laughing.

"We did it," I coughed.

"Oh, that was worse than hell."

I kept giggling, looking at her and wondering what to do next, but she got back on her feet and said we didn't have any time to waste.

"What's the plan?" I followed her up some stairs, "we just head up to the Queen and tell her: *hey! The shadows escaped! Come and help us on our journey to save the lands!*"

"I mean, if she's peaceful, sure," Reyna sighed, "but judging by the corpses in the catacombs, it might be a lot more difficult than that."

"I just hope she believes us. I mean—"

"Sh!" Reyna covered my mouth, "this is where most of the guards are located. From now on, every corner of this castle will be filled with them, deadlier than the one we fought outside."

"Are you saying all of this to intimidate me, or...?"

"I'm telling you this as a warning."

She peeked around the corner and walked into the hallway, but surprisingly, there were no guards around. She cautiously made her way to the main staircase, and although we had already breached the castle's walls, the place seemed deserted.

"Didn't you say every corner of this castle would have dozens of guards?" I asked, stealthily walking through the hall.

"Hm..." Reyna whispered, "last time I came here, the place was swarmed with them."

"When was the last time?"

"A few years ago, before the Trotter War."

"Different times," I said, "maybe the Queen lowered the security."

"Maybe," Reyna skeptically said.

We both walked up the stairs, waiting for a light elf to appear out of nowhere and stab us with his spear. Weirdly enough, nothing happened—it was as if the place was abandoned. As we reached the top of the stairs and arrived at the second floor of the palace, Reyna pulled out her daggers and stared at the excessively long hallway in front of us. Just as we thought we were finally safe, the sound of cracking wooden planks was heard nearby.

"Don't make a sound," Reyna whispered, leaning against the wall and standing still.

The footsteps crept closer, and it was clear someone was nearing the corner at the end of the hallway. But as I thought about it, the footsteps were too loud, and the hall was too long, so it didn't make sense.

"They're not coming from this corridor," I realized when a hand tore through the wall we were leaning against and pulled Reyna back.

"Get off me!" Reyna kicked the creature holding her.

It was a light elf guard, similar to the one we fought outside the catacombs, but this one seemed stronger as he could reach his hand through a brick wall.

"Let her go!" I didn't hesitate and jumped onto the elf's back, stabbing him.

For a second I thought I had killed him, but I was proven wrong once he slammed his elbow into my nose and sent me flying across the corridor. The big elf then charged his giant horns at my chest, but I dodged, and he got stuck on the wall instead. When I stood up, I realized the elf couldn't get his horns out of the wall, so he grabbed his spear and cut them both off, leaving his weapon behind.

"What is he doing?" I asked, stepping back.

"Doing anything he can to kill us."

The elf kept his broken horn and slammed it at Reyna's arm, but she continued defending herself. I intervened by slashing my sword at him, but the guard tore the weapon out of my hands and stabbed the horn into my stomach, leaving me defenseless on the floor.

"Hey, bastard!" Reyna yelled, distracting him.

That gave me enough time to rip the horn out of my skin and stab the elf's leg with it, knocking him down. Before I could do anything else, Reyna jumped over him and slashed his throat without hesitation.

"You killed him?" I asked, cleaning the blood from my clothes.

"Duh," she replied sarcastically, noticing the strange look on my face, "what's wrong?"

"I thought you wouldn't kill anymore."

"Oh, don't start with that!" Reyna rolled her eyes, "I did what I had to do! If I hadn't slashed that elf's throat, we would both be dead!"

"There are other ways of solving problems than just killing people!"

"I am not going to change my elf traditions just because you tell me to!"

"And I am not going to endure this entire journey watching you slaughter every living being you see!"

"Look, let's just find the Queen before anything else happens," Reyna sighed and tried walking away.

"Oh, don't change the subject!"

"I'm not doing that!"

"Yes you are!"

"I will go find the Queen on my own! You can stay here if you'd like."

She marched away, leaving me standing awkwardly in the hall with a dead elf beside me. I was about to follow her, but knew it would be better if I searched for the Queen myself. So, I turned back to the staircase and made my way to the castle's third floor in search of the master bedroom.

"*Hi! I'm the Prince, and I am here to warn you about...*" I practiced what I'd say once I found the Nature Queen, "no. *Nature Queen, the kingdoms are in great danger, and you are the only way we can save them!* Meh. *Nature Queen! The shadows have escaped, and we need the help of all the kingdoms to save the lands!* That will probably get her attention."

After practicing, I reached the third floor of the palace, but it was almost impossible to guess where the master bedroom was, especially with dozens of doors around the hall.

"Oh, you've got to be kidding me," I sighed, walking to the first door to my right.

The room was full of weapons—mostly spears and daggers—but there were some display swords made out of thick vines. The second room had hundreds of armors—from silver helms to golden chest plates that seemed to be made for the Queen herself. The third chamber was the oddest as it didn't have any windows, was pitch black, and all I could see were some chains on the edges of the room, like some sort of lift. Then I heard a growl at the back of the chamber and saw a pair of eyes glowing with scarlet light. I didn't know what it was, but my first instinct was to close the door as quickly as I could and run to the last door in the hallway. I hadn't realized it before, but vines came out of the crack below the door.

"Bingo!"

I slowly opened the door and peeked through the small crack, noticing the giant bed, emerald-painted walls, and portraits with vines growing around them. There were two stands beside the bed, one holding many books, and the other full of locked drawers. Glancing carefully, there was no sign of the Queen. It seemed she wasn't in the castle at the time, so I entered the bedroom and began examining everything inside. The books in the stand were mostly boring, discussing themes of despair, loss, love, and grief. But one caught my attention: an autobiography of one of the most famous elves in the kingdom. A small portrait of him was on the back of the book, and it didn't take long for me to realize it was the elf we had fought in the hallway—the one Reyna murdered.

"Oh..." I clutched my eyebrows in anger.

I read the paragraph in the back of the book and learned that the elf was called Virnus. He was peaceful, but when anyone tried to mess with the kingdom's dynasty, he would do anything to defend his people. He helped rebuild the kingdom after the

Trotter War, and was a symbol of glory for the light elves. Above the paragraph, there was a sketch of the elf standing beside his wife and two children.

"Why did Reyna...?" I asked myself when a hand grabbed my head and pulled me back.

I thought it was Reyna for a second, but when the hand pulled away from my face, I realized it was the Nature Queen: Ivy. She was just like described in the books I read—tanned skin, blood-red hair, green eyes, and a face that always seemed furious. She wore a dress made of plants and vines that reached her knees, and her arms were covered in some sort of green dust that colored her skin. The green color appeared to be spreading to other parts of her body, especially her neck, which was tinted an emerald hue. She glanced at me briefly before speaking in her low-pitched, hypnotizing voice.

"The Prince himself," she roared, "you... You!"

She grabbed my neck and tossed me to the floor, pressing her hand against my skull as the wooden planks below me creaked, and I screamed in fear.

"You thought your father could send you to assassinate me without there being any consequences?" The Queen breathed heavily, "well, these are the consequences! I am going to skin you alive and send the remains of your body to the Main Kingdom so your father realizes what loss actually feels like!"

"I'm... not here to... fight..." The air began fading away.

"That's what they all say," my skull cracked as she spoke.

Then the floor cracked open, and I fell through it, crashing through several floors before collapsing in the castle's basement. I hit my head on the stone ground and caught one final glimpse of the Nature Queen staring at me from above before I lost consciousness.

Chapter 9

I woke up where I had landed, my forehead bleeding and my arms bruised and scratched. Reyna was kneeling by my side, trying to wake me by snapping her fingers and shaking my shoulders.

"Wake up!" She snapped one last time before I regained consciousness.

"Where are we?" I asked, but she ignored my question.

"Follow me!" Reyna stood up and ran across the dark cavern we were in.

"What's going on?" I followed steadily, covering my bloody forehead.

"Quickly!" She yelled.

"Reyna?"

"Follow me!"

"I'm asking you a question!"

"We're almost there!"

"Reyna!"

"We're here!" She led me into an underground arena with four pillars supporting the roof, and a small opening in the stone ceiling, providing dim illumination. I looked around in confusion, glancing back at Reyna after a few seconds.

"What is this?" I asked.

Reyna giggled and walked behind one of the pillars. Before I could say anything, someone else emerged from the other side—a man whom I immediately recognized: my father. He was wearing the same robe as when I last saw him, with his golden crown placed over his carbon-colored hair. The pearls and emeralds shone so brightly that I had to squint my eyes just to observe him.

"Son, your mission was unsuccessful. You are a disgrace to my family. Everyone hates you. You're the reason your mother died. You are a disappointment—a mistake!"

"What?" I furrowed my brows.

"Yes!" My father walked behind the next pillar, and another person emerged from the other side: my mother.

"Son," my mother said, smiling.

"Mom?"

"I wanted you to die that day with me," my mother continued smiling, but a single tear rolled down her cheek.

"Huh?" I kept my teeth clenched, not because I was sad, but because I knew someone was creating the illusion.

"All your father said is true. I hate you, and I'm furious that I had to spend the last few months of my life by your side. You are the reason I'm dead! But to be honest, I'm glad I am not alive any longer—I don't have to look at your disgusting face ever again," she sobbed.

"This isn't real... This isn't real..." I whispered to myself.

"Yes, it is," she said, walking behind the next pillar as a new and unexpected person came out the other end.

"Oh, I should've killed you that night," Osrov—the Shadow King and explorer who first discovered the Khan—began speaking, "I should've killed your whole family that night!"

Then he crossed the final pillar. I clenched my fist and gulped, wondering what other person might appear. But when I saw a teenager in a blue coat approaching, I gasped, realizing it was me.

"We are a disgrace," he said, speaking with my exact tone and voice, "we should've died that night alongside our mother and father. That would've made the lands better! Maybe if we had died that day, the war would never have arrived, and the serpent would've never overtaken the lion."

"You are not real!" I pressed my hands against my ears, shut my eyes closed, and screamed.

I built the courage to open my eyes and recall my sword, ready to face whatever stood in front of me. But just as I raised the weapon over my head, I realized that an unknown person had taken his place. He had blonde curly hair, a unique set of white clothes, and violet eyes that stared at me menacingly.

"Wasn't that great?" The man chuckled, glancing at the walls of the arena.

I looked around, noticing the laughing crowd glaring down at me from bleachers at the top of the grotto. I gulped and tried pulling myself together after all the trippy illusions I had experienced.

"And that was just a warm-up for this evening's show!" The man said, "bring out the beast!"

The sound of metal chains echoed from above, followed by gasps and screams of excitement from the light elves on the bleachers. I hesitantly looked up and noticed a descending lift with a cage on top, holding a magical creature with horns that blew smoke, and a body covered in scales and lava.

"I'm going to fight that?" I refused.

"What? You're not killing that... beast?" The man chuckled along with the audience.

"I won't."

"Well, then I guess this fight won't last long," he smiled, standing on a platform that raised him to the crowd, "good luck."

The cage opened and the crowd cheered, ready for a spectacle they probably paid for. Although the creature seemed dangerous, he didn't move once given the chance. He stood weakly and depressed, not wanting to fight me.

"Today we have a creature named nympho. These monsters inhabit the swamp of the lands and are so rare that this is the first time we've ever captured one. It's fair to say that this fight will be unique and epic!" The man explained as the crowd cheered, "and on the other side we have the sixteen-year-old Prince. It's pretty obvious who'll win this fight!"

The creature stood motionless, everyone waiting for it to act.

"Guess we need some motivation, huh?" The man said, raising his hand towards the creature and using his powers to electrify it.

The nympho became enraged and charged at me as I was the only person within his reach. He used his horns to send me flying across the arena, then opened his mouth to spit lava at me, but I evaded by rolling to the side.

"This fight is getting interesting, am I right?" The host of the clash laughed.

"I don't want to fight you!" I yelled at the creature, hoping he understood my words.

"I don't have another choice!" The creature surprisingly spoke.

He weakly limped in my direction and slammed his arm on my stomach, but before I was launched away, I stabbed my sword into the ground and balanced myself. The creature hesitated before kicking my face and ripping the weapon from the ground. He walked over to me and took a brief glance at the chanting crowd watching from above.

"I am sorry," the creature raised the weapon over my chest, but I immediately stole the sword from his hands by recalling it and slashing at his feet.

"Finish him! Finish him!" The crowd kept chanting as the nympho crawled back and looked at me with fear.

"I'm not going to kill him!" I screamed, "I won't kill an innocent creature for your pleasure!"

"What a boring contestant!" The man laughed.

"I need to warn you about something!" I said to the audience sitting atop the arena, "the shadows are coming!"

"Shadows?" The man looked into the crowd and chuckled, "you mean the ones that are locked far away from here?"

"They have escaped and will come to destroy this kingdom! That's why I'm here to warn you!"

"You must be crazy, boy!"

"You have to trust me, ple—"

That was when an explosion erupted beside me. I flinched and pulled back, noticing a slim figure with horns standing within the smoke: Reyna.

"Krell!" She sighed with relief.

"I won't let you escape!" With a flick of his finger, the man electrocuted me.

"Hey, shifter!" Reyna shot an arrow at his chest, killing him instantly and freeing me from the electric torture, "it was a shapeshifter! It can turn into your worst fears!"

It all made sense. The man was transforming into Reyna, my parents, the Shadow King, and even myself just to scare me off. For the first time since I met her, I was glad Reyna killed that bastard.

"Krell, come on!" Reyna grabbed my hand and pulled me out of the arena.

We made it outside, where we were greeted by dozens of light elf guards pointing their spears at us. They creeped closer, ready to kill.

"Leave them to me," a distant voice was heard.

The guards stepped back as the ground shook and eventually cracked open. The Nature Queen emerged from below, wearing a long dress made out of leaves and fisting a sword created with vines and thorns. What stood out for me was the pair of large, green wings coming out from her back, covered in bugs and butterflies.

"I gave you a warning, Prince," she said, "you didn't heed it and now you will get killed by me: Ivy, the Nature Queen."

She thrust her sword at us, leaping with the help of her wings and smashing the ground, hurling Reyna to a nearby cabin, where she hit her head. Ivy glanced at her and then smirked at me, ready to take advantage of my vulnerability. She flew in my direction, pushing me to the ground and standing over me.

"This is your end, Prince," she panted.

"The shadows are coming! They will destroy this kingdom and all the others! You need to help me stop them, please!" I cried.

"Lies, lies, and more lies!" The Nature Queen tried stabbing my arm, but Reyna tackled her before she could.

"Krell isn't lying! The shadows have escaped!" She tried to convince her.

The Queen growled and flapped her wings at Reyna, stunning her before grabbing her neck and tossing her away.

"It's just you and me now, Prince," she smiled as I hid behind a shack.

"How am I going to do this?" I whispered to myself, "she is a literal Queen, and I'm just a useless kid!"

"You can run, but you can't hide!" The Queen screamed.

I built the courage to stealthily approach her while she searched for me elsewhere. She didn't notice me, so I recalled my sword and slashed one of her wings off. The Nature Queen cried out in pain, and caught me before I could escape.

"What have you done!" She exclaimed, strangling my neck, "my wings! My flowers!"

I thought she'd choke me to death, but instead, she raised her hand and made the ground rumble again. Vines emerged from the ground, entangling around Reyna's unconscious body and dragging her closer.

"You're gonna tell me who sent you here, or I'll kill her," the Nature Queen closed her fist and the vines tightened around Reyna's body.

"I already told you! I came here to warn your kingdom about the shadows!"

"Lies!" She tightened the vines.

"I am telling the truth!"

"With each lie you tell, I press harder!"

"It's not a lie!"

"Lie!"

"I am telling the truth, I swear!"

"Lies, lies, and lies!"

Reyna's face began turning purple.

"Stop it!" I felt something inside me—something burning.

"I am not stopping until you tell me!"

"I said *stop*!" I screamed with a deep voice and nightly eyeballs.

I felt anger—rage—as if all I wanted to do at that moment was to kill. It wasn't me—it was someone different. I couldn't even understand the feeling, but it burned through my veins, controlling me and making me do things I didn't want to. Then something exploded inside of me—literally. My body emitted some black smoke that detonated as soon as I screamed, launching the Nature Queen away and freeing Reyna and I from her deadly vines. I passed out for a few seconds, but when I opened my eyes, the first thing I saw was the Queen lying on the ground, unaware of what had happened.

"What's going on?" She panted, looking at me in utter confusion, "might as well just finish me off and complete your mission, am I right?"

"No," I offered my hand to help her get up from the ground, "I will tell you one last time: we aren't here to kill you."

"The shadows are locked up far away from here. There is no way they could ever—"

A loud thud echoed through the kingdom, shaking the castle's walls as if a giant had collapsed over the village. We both gasped and stared into the distance, noticing that a key monument from the kingdom was no longer there. The thick vines surrounding the Nature Kingdom turned to ashes after a dark force ripped them apart and burned them to the ground.

"What happened?" The Queen muttered, "did you do this?"

"It's..." I took a deep breath before speaking, "*the shadows.*"

They had arrived. In the blink of an eye, the obscure creatures sprinted through the streets of the kingdom, tearing apart houses and transforming the light elves into shadows. The Nature Queen and I watched it all from atop a hill, knowing the creatures would eventually reach us.

"W-what?" The Queen asked, "the shadows escaped?"

"Yes! For the thousandth time!"

"Everyone run! H-help each other..." Although she knew she couldn't do anything, Ivy kept trying.

Then the terrifying sound of slowly approaching footsteps was heard, accompanied by a muttering voice. As we glanced into the sky, we observed the Shadow King—Osrov—descending on a staircase made from his dark magic.

"Osrov," the Nature Queen gulped, aware of the threat he posed.

"Hi, my dearest Queen," Osrov reached the ground.

His voice was deep and stuttered, speaking slowly and confidently. His appearance was distinct from all the other shadows running around the village. His face was recognizable, with his mouth, nose, and dilated pupils visible, along with his dark purple eyes and corrupted skin. He wore a black hood that partially covered his eyes, a baggy dark cape, and simple pants that seemed to be made out of metal.

"Why are you here?" Ivy asked Osrov.

"Oh, Ivy, after all that time I was locked up, I needed a second chance to heal the lands. What better way to do so than taking over your kingdom?" Osrov smiled, revealing his yellow teeth, "oh, and the Prince, how could I ever forget about the Prince? I should've made you join your mother that night."

I simply looked at him, trying not to show any expression.

The Queen grunted and raised her hand at Osrov. Vines cracked the ground in an attempt to entangle the Shadow King, but he grabbed them with his bare hands and turned them to dust.

"You're gonna need to try harder," Osrov grinned.

Just as he said that, Reyna appeared from above and jumped to Osrov with her daggers in hand. She tried stabbing his chest, but he dodged and bumped his head against hers, tossing her away.

"He's too strong," Ivy shook her head, grabbing my hand and trying to run away.

As we were about to escape the Shadow King's reach, something fell from the sky and onto the stone street in front of us, blocking our path. They were two shadows with long hair and wide white eyes. Their teeth were sharp like knives, with long tongues resting on their chins, and scrawny legs that trembled with each step they took.

"Look who we have here," one of them laughed, "Prince Krell. How's your mommy?"

"Sister!" The other one sarcastically yelled, revealing that the two shadows were siblings, "don't make family jokes around Reyna; she could get really, really... sad."

"I'm going to kill you," Reyna said through clenched teeth as I stood in shock, not knowing what to do or say.

"Oh, I am going to murder you and make you join your family in hell," one of the sisters approached her.

"And so with you Krell," the other followed.

"Enough with both of you!" Osrov screamed, "you know the agreement!"

"Yes, my King," they both said sarcastically, giggling afterwards.

"How did you escape?" I asked Osrov with a low, stuttering voice.

"That is something we cannot tell you, young man," Osrov took a step in my direction, "but you will find out soon enough."

In an attempt to trap the Shadow King, Ivy made the ground rumble, controlling vines to catch Osrov's legs. However, he used his uncanny magic to sink them back into the street.

"You can't stop me. None of you can."

"I know... but *he* can," the Queen smirked and placed two fingers on her lips, whistling in a strange tone.

"What are you doing?" I whispered, just as confused as Osrov and the sisters.

When I least expected it, a blaring sound erupted from the castle behind me, and I could've never guessed what was about to happen. A giant serpent destroyed the roof of the castle, soaring into the sky and skidding its tail as it made its way towards us. Osrov tried using his dark powers to stop the levitating creature, but it was massive, so he had no other choice but to back away.

"Hop on!" The Nature Queen yelled as the serpent reached us.

I hopped on alongside Reyna and Ivy, who commanded the snake to flee the crumbling kingdom. Looking back as we started ascending, I caught a glimpse of the Shadow King's hauntingly deadly stare.

"Wait!" I yelled, "what about the light elf?"

"Krell, you aren't serious, right?" Reyna sighed.

"What light elf?" Ivy glanced at us in confusion.

"A stuttering light elf Reyna and I met earlier," I explained, "we need to go find him."

"We have no time!" Reyna argued.

"She's right," Ivy agreed, "if you go down there again, you won't survive."

"But..."

"No excuses; we have to leave!" Ivy guided the flying serpent.

Even though we were hovering hundreds of feet over the Nature Kingdom, I could still hear the screams of light elves being transformed into shadows. The place darkened with each passing second, corrupting the kingdom Ivy had spent years rebuilding.

"You are going to tell me what's happening right now!" Ivy demanded as vines emerged from the serpent's back and restrained us, "how did they escape!"

"We can explain if you let us go," I pleaded.

"I won't let either of you go until you tell me what's going on!" She cried.

"Alright..." I gasped for air.

"The shadows escaped!" Reyna explained before I could, "I don't know how they did it, but they are using their darkness to corrupt anyone they see! They have taken my tribe along with many others that inhabit the outsides. It seems they've started doing the same with the kingdoms."

"No! The King from the Main Kingdom said they would never escape!" Ivy freed us both.

"That's what I thought," I sighed.

"Look, we need your help to stop the shadows. We need the help of all the other kingdoms so we can come together once again and stop them from taking the lands for themselves," Reyna tried shaking the Nature Queen's hand, "are you with us?"

She was about to accept the offering when a strange creature grabbed Reyna's foot and dragged her off the flying serpent. Luckily, she gripped the serpent's scales before she fell.

"Krell! My bow!" She screamed, trying to kick the mysterious creature pulling her leg.

I dashed to her bow, which was lying on the serpent's back. I had never used one of those before, but I managed to place an arrow on the bowstring and aim directly at the creature, which I soon realized was a shadow. I had never examined one closely, but it looked exactly like a person, except its figure was darkened, and the only visible traits were large eyes and sharp teeth. Before I knew it, the bow I held darkened, and the arrow seemed to absorb some sort of mystical energy. I let go of the string and managed to hit the shadow in the head. Although I heard the shadows were undefeatable, the creature became ashes immediately after being struck. I didn't pay much attention to it and simply helped Reyna by pulling her back up.

"I need to check if there are more shadows!" Ivy rushed to the serpent's head before noticing what I had done.

"Cool, huh?" I smirked at Reyna, but her expression remained unchanged, "I just figured out I could do it! It's so weird, but it looks like I can kill shadows with it."

"Krell," Reyna murmured.

"When I was with the Queen and you were being..." I continued.

"Krell," Reyna raised her voice.

"And then now what I did with your bow..." I kept going.

"Krell!" She finally shouted.

"What?" I kept smiling.

"Since when have you—?"

"Like, ten minutes ago with the Queen. Why?"

"It's dark magic," she looked deep into my eyes.

"What do you mean?" I laughed nervously.

"That sort of magic can only be used by the shadows, especially the ones who've mastered it."

"Are you saying that—?"

"You have dark magic inside you."

PART IV
TROTTER MOUNTAIN

Chapter 10

"I don't know what you're thinking, but I'm not a shadow!" I yelled back at Reyna.

"I'm not saying you're a shadow," she sighed.

"Well, it sure looks like it!"

"I'm just saying you have dark magic inside of you!"

"Isn't that the same thing?"

"Maybe... maybe your parents aren't really your parents," Reyna said, "or at least your father."

"So you're saying my dad isn't my real dad?" I rolled my eyes.

"Well, he has dark skin, and you—"

"Are you even listening to yourself?" I raised my voice, "if I were adopted, or had another father, I would've figured it out by now!"

"Well, that darkness couldn't have come out of nowhere!"

We both stood in silence, each expecting the other to apologize, but Ivy interrupted before the argument could go any further.

"Hey, do you wanna stop yelling and tell me where we're heading next?" She petted the flying snake's giant head, "the serpent is moving in circles waiting for you."

"Trotter Mountain!" Reyna and I said simultaneously, then looked at each other and rolled our eyes.

"Trotter Mountain? Like, where the Frost Kingdom is located?" The Queen of the Nature Kingdom asked, "oh, I'm not going there."

"Why?" I tilted my head.

"The Frost Queen and I aren't really the best of friends," she reluctantly explained, "she's the one who started the Trotter War in the first place, and the reason my mother's dead. I don't want to see her face ever again."

"I thought your mother died during the Shadow War," Reyna glanced at her in confusion, "or, well, the King murdered her."

"Oh, that was my grandmother," Ivy replied.

"What?" Reyna and I exclaimed at the same time, "stop!"

"Yeah, my grandmother—Ivy—was murdered by the King of the Main Kingdom, leaving Ivy II as the new Queen. She was killed a few years ago during the Trotter War, which meant that I had to become the new Queen of the Nature Kingdom. And here I am, Ivy III!" She explained.

"Why are you all called Ivy?" Reyna asked.

"I didn't even know the first Ivy was dead," I added.

"Yeah, people always get confused—they think I'm fifty years old!" She laughed and then looked at our uncomfortable faces, "I'm eighteen years old. Did you really think I was fifty?"

"I mean... you look older," Reyna murmured.

"Oh, shut up!" She turned around, hiding her chuckle and tapping the serpent's back, *"siclogatl, da frot qeem, arre! Arre!"*

"How much until we get there?" I asked.

"Three hours," she said, "four at most."

I laid on the back of the serpent as Reyna did the same at a distance, clearly infuriated. I took a deep breath and looked at the sky, realizing it was my first time flying, and it was exactly how I imagined it. As I leaned to the edge of the serpent and took a peek down, I noticed the lake below me, with animals and creatures drinking water from it. To the left of that lake, I caught a small glimpse of the Main Kingdom's steel wall. It was impressive how a few hours before that moment, I was laying on my bed, hoping to get out of the Main Kingdom and dreaming fantasies of the outsides. It had all happened so slowly that it seemed like I had already spent several weeks on the journey when, in reality, not a single day had passed. I had visited an elf camp, a lake, the Nature Kingdom, an arena, and I was hovering the outsides on a giant serpent. If someone would've told me that the day before, I would've laughed in their face.

"So, Prince," Ivy approached after I spent more than an hour admiring the view, "why are you here?"

"Huh?" I understood her question; I just didn't know what to say.

"Why are you here?" She repeated slowly.

"What do you mean?"

"Do you want me to explain it with apples and pears?" She laughed, "what brought you here? Why are you here with me? Why are you saving the lands from the shadows?"

"I've never thought about it."

"Are you doing this because you care about the lands, or just to get recognition? Are you doing this to stand up against your father, or to reunite the kingdoms once again?" She asked.

"I guess I just want my father to know I'm not worthless," I said, reminiscing all the moments of shame, "and obviously to help the lands and stop the shadows from destroying them."

"There's good in you, Krell. I can sense it," she smiled, "unlike your father, of course."

"We're very different," I forced a chuckle.

"And what about you, dark elf?" Ivy asked.

"Oh, me?" She reacted.

"Yes, you," Ivy squinted her eyes, "your name was *Reyna*, am I right?"

"Yes. And all I want to do is avenge my family," she unemotionally said, "assassinate the shadows who transformed them."

"Don't worry, we will do so," Ivy comforted her.

Reyna and I looked at each other, waiting for an apology, but neither of us said anything, so we both looked away.

"What is happening between you two?" Ivy asked.

"Nothing!" We yelled at the same time.

"Alright, no need to get mad."

When everything seemed calm and no one expected it, the serpent violently shook, screeching and tossing its tail around like a rope. I almost fell off the edge but luckily held onto the creature's scales before being launched away.

"What's happening?" Reyna panted.

"I don't know!" Ivy rushed to the serpent's head and spoke to it, "*Sersh, le va ets hapineng! Jun huyt! Levi ti moi!*"

The serpent proceeded to scream and stopped flapping its tail, plummeting to the ground with us on top of it.

"What is happening!" I yelled as the serpent dropped.

"Someone shot it!" Ivy panicked.

"What are we gonna do?" Reyna held herself with the creature's skin.

Ivy steadily approached us, screeching as she raised a hand and summoned a vine that wrapped around our bodies, pulling us together. After a few seconds, the vines formed a massive ball that protected us, and although we were still plunging down, I was certain we'd survive once we reached the ground.

"It hurts!" Ivy panted, holding the liana together.

Then the ball bounced and finally stood still after a couple of seconds, signaling our safe landing. In the blink of an eye, the vines became ashes, exposing us to the men who had shot the serpent down: my father's guards. The smiles on their faces clearly showed they had been looking for me for a long time.

"Did you bring them here?" The Nature Queen stood up and asked me.

"They hate me as much as they hate you," I sighed, recalling my sword and stepping back, "they've been hunting us for a while now."

"We've given you enough chances, Prince Krell," one of the guards said, " we won't show mercy any longer."

"Neither will we," Reyna prepared her daggers.

"We will kill the Nature Queen just like we killed her grandmother," one of the guards whispered to another as Ivy tilted her head, "Did you hear us, or do we have to repeat it? We will kill you just like your grandmother!"

"You shouldn't have said that," Ivy's eyes blazed.

If the guard had known what she was capable of, he would've never spoken in the first place. Vines strapped his legs and pulled him to the ground. They soon began climbing his body, circling his waist and pressing against his chest.

"Help..." The guard cried, but his companions stood back, knowing they couldn't aid him.

When Ivy closed her fist, the vines crushed the man's body, cracking his bones and snapping his neck.

"Witchcraft!" The guards muttered to each other.

"Oh, and that's gonna happen to all of you," Ivy ragefully smirked.

Reyna took those words as a call to murder the guards, so she leaped to one of them and slashed her dagger into his eye. She kicked the injured man to the ground, and Ivy summoned a couple of vines to grab his defenseless body and sink him underneath. While all that was happening, I hid behind a tree, knowing I wasn't going to harm anyone. I didn't see the guard sneaking up behind me at that moment, and when I least expected it, he dragged me into the brawl. Instead of a spear, he fisted a sword—one from the Royal Museum of the Main Kingdom. He either stole it, or had permission from the King to borrow it, indicating he was strong enough to wield it. He attempted to stab my chest, but I moved aside and recalled my weapon for a fight I didn't seek.

"The King himself gave me permission to use this sword," he said, "for the sole purpose of killing you."

"What a lame purpose," I gulped, blocking his attack with my sword.

"You're actually a good fighter," he wiped his runny nose, "I thought all you did was hide from guards and jump across roofs."

"Then you've underestimated me!" I swung the sword at his chest armor, breaking it.

"Why are you doing this?" The guard coughed, "everyone in the lands would like to be a Prince! Everyone wants to be part of the royal family and become the next King of the Main Kingdom! Why won't you accept your place?"

"Being a Prince is the worst thing you could ever imagine!" I accidentally struck his face and lacerated his eye, "I'm sorry! I didn't mean to—"

"Ah!" He thrusted his sword at my stomach as soon as I approached him.

I ran away, but his attacks were hard to evade, especially when he wouldn't stop chasing me. When I felt the cold touch of a steel sword against my back, I ran around a nearby tree and caught the man off guard by smashing the hilt of my sword against his nose, rendering him unconscious.

"Phew," I panted, wiping the sweat from my forehead and watching Reyna and Ivy dispatch the remaining guards.

It was odd how I tried my best not to kill anyone while they slaughtered anyone standing in their paths. Reyna sliced the guards up with her daggers, and Ivy used her mighty abilities to crush them. It became even bloodier when they worked together—Ivy tied them to the ground and Reyna stabbed them to death while they helplessly screamed.

While I was observing, a guard tackled me and tried using a tiny knife to finish me off, but Ivy quickly noticed and sent him flying across the forest with her vines. Of course, Reyna had to ensure he had truly died, so she pierced his throat with her dagger once he flew over her head.

"I forgot you were even here," Reyna cracked her neck.

"You were standing very quietly back there," Ivy coughed.

"Why weren't you doing anything?" Reyna asked.

"Because you're killing them all, and that's something I cannot follow!" I yelled, trying not to seem angry, "I won't kill people who have families and lives!"

"It's either *kill or get killed*!" Reyna repeated the same phrase she had said before, "and you can only choose one."

"Look, Krell," Ivy sighed, "I know you don't want to kill, but it's the only way to survive in these lands."

"I won't kill, no matter what."

"Help," someone coughed from far away.

It was a guard—the one whose eye I accidentally cut and eventually knocked out. He was weakly crawling towards us, covered in blood. Reyna approached him and lowered her daggers to his neck, glancing at me momentarily.

"Reyna, stop," I said in a low tone.

"Please, I won't say anything... just don't kill me," the guard coughed blood.

"No loose ends," Reyna ran the dagger across the man's throat.

It was obvious she did that just to irritate me. She was waiting for me to apologize for what happened earlier, so she killed all those guards in an attempt to provoke me further. I didn't like the way she was acting.

"Why are you doing this?" I whispered, ensuring Ivy wouldn't hear my words.

"Doing what exactly?" She acted confused.

"You know exactly what I mean," I said, "look, I'm sorry about what I said before. I was confused, but that doesn't justify what you just did."

"What, that I killed the guy who was trying to kill us?" She chuckled, "what else did you expect me to do?"

"He was begging for his life, Reyna!" I raised my voice, "I'm sorry, but there are other ways to stop these guards than killing them in cold blood."

"Look, I have my ways and you have yours—I have already told you that many times! It's not my fault you don't understand."

"Just try to think before you act," I said at last.

"I'll try, but please stop reminding me not to kill every time we have an encounter."

"Hey!" Ivy interrupted, "I was going to tell you to hurry up, but it looks like you're having a serious... *talk*."

"It's fine," I sighed.

"Yeah, it's fine," Reyna said, looking at me before walking away.

"Krell," Ivy whispered when Reyna wasn't looking, "are you and her together?"

"Wow! That was too quick and direct," I nervously laughed.

"Are you?"

"No! We just met a few hours ago."

"Alright, I was just making sure..." She hesitated, "I was just confirming that those little talks you have aren't like... well, that you aren't in a relationship... Oh, you know exactly what I mean."

I awkwardly walked away moments later, oddly staring at Ivy, who was still processing what she had just said. I was searching for Reyna—wondering if she knew the path to Trotter Mountain—but I couldn't find her anywhere. As I called her name, I heard the sound of galloping nearby, and when I turned around, I noticed Reyna was riding a horse.

"Look what I just found," she smiled, using a leash to control the horse's movement.

"Where'd you get that?" I examined the beautiful maroon mount.

"The guards couldn't have arrived here by foot," Reyna explained, "they used these horses."

"*These*?" I repeated.

"Oh, they've got many more," she said, but was distracted by something behind me, "what the hell is going on with Ivy?"

She was kneeling on the grass, leaning her head on the flying serpent that had been shot to the ground by the guards. She seemed to be praying—honoring its death.

"*Iny la kihkn ui tyuh khy,*" she said in an unknown language, *"yhu olh ilj olivt killa, la Ivy de le matin, mai onst la vill."*

"Ivy, are you alright?" I approached.

"*Sersh*," she wiped her nose.

"I'm sorry?"

"*Sersh*," she repeated, "his name was *Sersh*. He was one of the greatest creatures in my kingdom, not only for his looks and strength, but because of his heart, his mind, and his soul. He was a pure one."

"Why were you praying?" Reyna asked.

"Being the Queen of the living means I can grant life, but it also means that I can take it away," she sobbed, "he barely survived the attack, but he was in pain—someone had to end it."

"I'm sure it was a great creature," I comforted her, "I mean, it helped us escape the shadows."

"*He* was also the only one who survived the attack," Ivy snorted, "the last one left."

After wiping her tears, she touched the ground and commanded the grass to pull Sersh underground. Once he was buried, Ivy sat down and offered one last prayer.

"*La va perdone, Sersh. Thathu enug de un enterro yer we coug gull ou*," Ivy kissed the ground and stood up, glancing at the horses, "where did you find them?"

"The guards," Reyna said, "guess they won't be needing them anymore, so we might as well take them to the Frost Kingdom."

"Great idea," Ivy said, "if those horses are in good condition, we should arrive at Trotter Mountain in less than two hours."

"Faster than the shadows?" I asked.

"Probably," Ivy guessed, "but we can't waste any more time."

"Then let's get moving," Reyna guided us to the other horses.

There were three more, all tied to a nearby tree. One was white with black spots across its body, the second one was brown with dark fur on the back of its head, and the other had shiny silver armor strapped around its chest and paws.

"I want the one with the armor," Ivy immediately said.

"Really?" I pouted

"What?" She chuckled, "I picked him first."

"Just grab one," Reyna sighed.

I chose the brown one as it was the most eager to ride, but as soon as I untied it from the tree, it galloped away and pushed me to the ground, staining my clothes with mud.

"Really?" I spat dirt as Reyna laughed loudly, wanting me to notice her, "it's not funny."

"Yes it is," Reyna couldn't stop laughing, "oh, your face is full of mud now!"

"And also your mouth," Ivy tried to laugh, but it was hard to do so because of Sersh's death.

"You are very different," I said to her.

"What?" She stopped chuckling.

"I mean, an hour ago you were trying to murder us, and now you're... you're our friend."

"I trust people very quickly, which has led to being backstabbed several times," Ivy explained in a depressing tone, "oh, and I'm not your friend."

"That's exactly what Reyna said before we became friends."

"We're not friends," Reyna was quick to reply.

"Oh," I laughed nervously, "anyway, I guess we need to go now."

"That's what we've been trying to tell you this whole time!" Reyna rolled her eyes, "now grab the horse and come on."

I untied the black horse and sat on its back. The mount shook its head and galloped alongside the other horses. The path to Trotter Mountain was going to be hard as the giant serpent had barely gotten us halfway there. It was going to be a long journey, and it was going to feel even longer with the lands' fate in our hands.

CHAPTER II

While Reyna, Ivy, and I galloped towards Trotter Mountain, my father was desperate. Ever since I escaped his kingdom, he had been looking for me relentlessly, which might've seemed normal because I was his son, but judging by how he treated me, he was likely only sending guards to kill me. He didn't care about what I was getting myself into, or the shadows escaping his *impenetrable prison*—he didn't even care about me! All he wanted was for me to pay for my actions, and he was doing everything he could to achieve that objective. He was sending dozens of guards to hunt me down, or hiring bounty hunters to kill me, but I wouldn't let them achieve his goal.

> Letter by: King Henrius Kovner III
> WANTED
> KRELL KOVNER
> REWARD: $ 1,920,000
>
> DEAD OR ALIVE
> Any clues on Krell Kovner's location should be reported to the castle.

My father made the poster himself, nailing it on the doorstep of every house in the kingdom. Every villager read the letter and was advised of my escape, including bounty hunters who were permitted by my father to leave the kingdom to murder me, or—in the worst of cases—drag me back into the Main Kingdom.

"Sir!" One of the guards burst into my father's room as he sipped a glass of wine.

"If you enter my room like that again, you'll be sent to the dungeons!" My father yelled.

"Yes sir. S-sorry sir, but this is important!"

"What is it?"

"We have news about your son."

"Don't call him my son! He's lost that privilege already."

"Y-yes! As I was saying, the troops found your son. He is traveling the outsides with the female elf and the Queen," he reported.

"What Queen?"

"The *nature* one."

"They convinced her too? I'm not surprised," he said, clearly angered, "where is Krell?"

"Th-that's the thing sir—they killed all the guards you sent," he said slowly, "the only survivor reported they were too powerful. We need more troops, sir!"

The King threw the glass of wine to the floor and screamed as the guard closed his eyes and covered his ears.

"You are going to find Krell, and you'll murder him, understood? I don't care how many men I lose, but I will have him screaming in agony on the ground as I watch him suffer!" The King screamed, "if the Nature Queen is with him, they must be heading to the Frost Kingdom. Send all the men we have, and if you don't capture them by then, I'll have you killed by dawn."

"Yes sir!" The guard sprinted out of the room.

My father took a deep breath and then screamed at the top of his lungs, ensuring the entire kingdom listened.

*****

"What do you think will happen?" I asked as our horses traversed a muddy rainforest.

We had been galloping for more than an hour, and the horses were already getting tired. The worst part was that we were nowhere near the Frost Kingdom, and although the temperature had dropped a bit, there was no sign of snow or fog.

"What do you mean?" Reyna asked.

If I was being honest, I didn't like her attitude at that moment. She was distant, mad, and sometimes even annoying. I thought she was acting that way because of the argument we had a couple of hours before, but it wasn't that big of a deal.

"You know, the shadows," I clarified.

"They're either going to destroy the lands, or we are somehow going to convince every King and Queen to join our cause and save the lands," Reyna said, "which is very unlikely."

"Judging by Reva's attitude, I doubt we'll be able to convince her," Ivy laughed, "she is a psychotic machine who only cares about power."

"Who is Reva again?" I asked.

"The Frost Queen, duh," Reyna rolled her eyes for the thousandth time.

"Sorry, I didn't know."

"How do you not know who she is if we are literally about to infiltrate her kingdom?"

"Can you stop arguing?" Ivy interrupted us.

"What do you know about Reva?" I asked her.

"She's just a privileged, impolite, greedy son of—" She started saying.

"What do you mean by greedy?" Reyna interrupted her.

"She always gets what she wants no matter what. She doesn't care about anything around her as long as it benefits her. That's why she lied to the Trotter God and sent the trotters to kill my mother."

"I'm sorr—" I began.

"If you didn't take part in it, then you have no reason to apologize," Ivy said, "it was something my mother told me when I was a child."

"Hey!" Reyna yelled out of nowhere, "look!"

I hadn't been paying attention to the path ahead, so when I noticed the white particles dropping from the sky, I was pleasantly surprised. I saw the same dust-like substance covering the ground and realized it was snow. I had never seen it before, and although it had been described to me, I never imagined it would be so beautiful.

"We must be getting closer to Trotter Mountain," Ivy said, "from now on, we'll find creatures that never leave the snowy terrains, so be careful."

Right after Ivy said that, I felt something cold grab my leg as if the snow itself was gripping my body. I glanced down and noticed a lifeless gray hand emerging from the snow. I screamed, but the limb dragged me off the horse and tossed me to the ground. Reyna and Ivy noticed my struggle and jumped off their mounts in an attempt to free me, but more hands climbed out of the ground and began burying me alive. Reyna grabbed my arms and used all her might to try to pull me out, but it was impossible—the hands were too strong.

"You're going to rip my legs off!" I yelled in pain.

"I have an idea!" Ivy started to dig in the snow.

"Use your vines!" Reyna commanded.

"I can't do so in low temperatures!"

Ivy pushed the snow aside in search of the murderous hands, but one of them jumped out of the ground and grabbed her face, pulling her down. Reyna gasped and turned her attention to Ivy, who had lost her ability to breathe. As soon as she stood up to help her, another hand caught Reyna off guard and began dragging her underground. It looked like we were going to die at that point—Ivy couldn't breathe, one of the hands had Reyna's mouth and nose covered, and I was about to be buried alive.

Chapter 12

Watching Ivy and Reyna struggle to breathe as some hands pulled them underground in an attempt to kill them was far from reassuring. I thought it was the end until I heard a deep, loud voice.

"Look who we have here, brother," I heard in the distance.

There were two big guys with filthy red beards and leather clothes. Both of them held a deadly hatchet, which they wielded proudly and confidently. From their relieved grins, I knew they had been looking for us.

"Help me and my friends!" I yelled, about to be dragged underground.

"Should we help him, Andez?" One of them asked the other.

"You tell me, Ginock," he replied, "the bounty said he was to be captured dead or alive!"

"But if the hands suck him into the snow, we won't be able to capture him!" Andez told his brother.

"Alright!"

One of the brothers chopped the hands with his hatchet and pulled me out of the snow. I was safe, but Ivy and Reyna were still in danger.

"You have to help them! They are running out of air!"

"We came here for you!" Andez grabbed my arm and said, "we don't care about them!"

"Why are you here?" I asked.

"There is a bounty—your daddy placed it!" Ginock laughed.

"Almost two million vanes!"

"You can get more than that!" I yelled desperately.

"How is that?"

"That girl right there is the deadliest elf in the lands, and that one there is Ivy, the Nature Queen!" I panted, "imagine how much you will get if you turn them in! Ten million vanes! Fifteen!"

"Should we?" One of them asked.

"Ah, let's just do it!" The other pulled Ivy and Reyna out of the snow as they both panted in fear.

"Krell! How did you pull us out?" Ivy asked, then opened her eyes and saw the axe-wielding brothers.

"I guess they won't care if we bring them dead, huh?" They both laughed in the same stupid tone.

Luckily, I was lying behind the brothers and managed to recall my sword and stab one's leg, pushing him to the ground afterwards. Reyna grabbed her daggers and leaped at the other brother, slashing his chest and assassinating him.

"Andez!" The remaining brother screamed in shock.

He attempted to flee, but the hands emerged from the snow, grabbed his legs, and buried him alive. The only trace left of him was his hatchet, which remained intact upon the snow.

"We need to get out of here! The hands will return!" I stood up, panting.

"Those things don't kill frequently," Ivy said, "don't think they'll wanna bury any more of us."

"Then we must get out of here before they come out again," I panicked.

"Wait one second," Ivy picked up the hatchet of the deceased bounty hunter, "although those guys were complete assholes, they still had these pretty neat axes. They must be worth more than five hundred thousand vanes!"

"Why would you even need weapons? Can you use your plants?" Reyna asked.

"Vines, not plants. And remember, my powers don't work in snowy terrains," Ivy explained, "guess this'll be the way to defend myself meanwhile."

"Great, but we need to get out of here," I recalled my sword and climbed onto the horse, ready to ride to Trotter Mountain.

"Chill out," Reyna said in the same annoying, low-pitched tone, "Ivy already said they won't be coming back—stop being so paranoid."

"I'm just being careful," I replied, "unlike others that don't care about consequences."

"Just stop it!" Ivy yelled, "you're like an old married couple."

"We're not mad at each other! But an elf and a Prince can't get along," Reyna said, mounting her horse, "isn't it obvious?"

"In these lands, everything is possible," I said.

"You know what? Let's just go," Reyna galloped away without a warning.

Ivy and I remained silent, simply following her, hoping she knew the way to the mountain. Most of our journey was quiet—no one spoke—we just galloped our horses toward our destination. Strangely, no other monster appeared, and since I didn't see any trotters around, I began to doubt if we were even on the right path. Nevertheless, Ivy kept insisting that we were getting closer and that it was only a matter of time before we reached the infamous Trotter Mountain. Just as I was about to complain again, we saw a giant foggy silhouette in the distance.

"Is that it?" I asked Ivy, with Reyna still ahead of us.

"Definitely," she sighed, "I could recognize that mountain anywhere."

We continued riding toward Trotter Mountain as the shadow merged into an actual structure. It was so colossal that we couldn't even see its peak hiding above the clouds. It took us a few minutes to reach the icy entrance of the mountain, and when we did, Reyna sighed, jumping off her horse.

"Are we going to head inside, or are you just going to stare at it?" Reyna rudely complained.

"Calm down," Ivy said, "if we're not prepared, we could get jumped by hundreds of trotters."

"What if they're not here?" I asked, "there aren't any outside the mountain."

"They could be anywhere," Ivy wiped the snow from her hair.

"Then let's be careful," Reyna replied.

Ivy and I dismounted and released our mounts into the wild, knowing that after leaving the Frost Kingdom, we likely wouldn't need them again.

"Where is the entrance?" I asked as Ivy examined the mountain.

"If I'm not wrong, it should be right over..." Ivy gently touched the walls of the mountain, searching for a secret passage, "here!"

The ground shook as the mountain spat chunks of ice from its crust as if it were melting. Then a gate was revealed beneath the ice—a very large one indeed. But when a chunk of the mountain split open, an avalanche rushed down its peak and toward us.

"Run, run, run!" I screamed, sprinting inside with Ivy and Reyna by my side.

By the time the avalanche reached the ground, we were already inside the mountain. I was relieved that we had survived the disaster, but once I realized the snow was blocking the entrance and we were trapped inside the mountain, the panic returned.

"What did you do, Ivy?" Reyna stormed after her, "now we have no way out!"

"If I hadn't done that, we wouldn't even be alive in the first place!" She yelled back.

"How did you know it was a way in?" I interrupted their argument.

Ivy sighed: "Reva and I were good friends a long time ago. She was a few years older than me, and we used to hang out all the time. But then she became Queen at a very young age and has been unbearable ever since. She does everything to satisfy herself and doesn't care about others. Then she stole a precious artifact from the Trotter God and blamed it on my mother, starting the Trotter War."

"That's sad..." I began, "but that didn't really answer my question."

"Oh, right!" Ivy said, "a weird mechanism, I don't know."

"Could you stop explaining everything to Krell and instead tell us where to go?" Reyna rolled her eyes, "do you even know how to enter the kingdom?"

"I partially remember," she muttered, "follow me."

I was truly surprised by how bright the inside of the mountain was, especially because of the clear blue ice that illuminated the whole place. The snow was perfectly intact and there was no dripping water on the stalactites on the roof, which meant that the ice wasn't melting anytime soon.

"It's freezing over here," I hugged myself, trembling.

"It's your first time in the snow—it makes sense why you'd be cold," Ivy reassured me, but Reyna wasn't so polite.

"How could you even be cold, though?" She laughed, "I haven't been in the snow for many years, and I'm perfectly fine."

"I guess I'm not used to cold temperatures," I tried to avoid an argument.

"Here!" Ivy's voice echoed through the frozen walls.

I approached her, noticing the ample piece of wood with hanging chains at her side. It looked exactly like the lift at the Nature Kingdom, but it was ten times bigger and could actually hold more than one person.

"Are we really gonna use *this* to go up?" Reyna sighed annoyingly.

"Yes. Or did you think we were gonna climb our way up?" Ivy asked.

"Honestly, yeah."

"You thought I climbed Trotter Mountain each time I visited Reva?" She laughed, "if that was the case, I would've stopped being her friend the day I met her."

"Come on!" I interrupted, "the shadows are probably heading here already. We need to move."

Ivy walked to the other side of the lift and pulled a lever, setting it in motion upwards toward the mountain's summit, where we'd hopefully find an entrance to the Frost Kingdom. As the chains began raising us, a loud and mysterious horn blared from afar.

"Aren't there hundreds of dragons and trotters guarding this place?" Reyna ignored the sound, keeping her eyes peeled for any creature.

"There were some a few years ago," Ivy explained, "I'm pretty sure they built this lift to avoid the dragons stalking the mountain. But you should be aware of humans and bounty hunters—I've found an unbelievable amount of them surrounding these walls."

Just as Ivy said that, a strange artifact landed on the lift. It had an emerald hue, blinking repeatedly and making a ticking noise, like some sort of countdown.

"Is that a...?" Reyna murmured.

"Tabron!" Ivy screamed.

The small artifact exploded, covering the place with thick smoke that blinded the three of us. Our ears began ringing, and when I thought the smoke would fade away, it kept growing thicker.

"Here they are!" I heard from far away.

Jumping into the lift was a muscular man with a cape and chunky armor that shone through the blinding smoke. He took a few steps through the mist and lowered his hood, revealing a face I recognized: a bounty hunter from the Main Kingdom.

"Been a long, long time since I've ever seen someone like you, boy," the man laughed, showing his dirty green teeth.

"Get away from him!" Reyna cluelessly ran through the smoke, trying to find the man, but he grabbed her first and threw her aside.

"You know how much they pay for this job?" The man laughed, "almost two million vanes!"

"Can I turn myself in then?" I joked, trying to lighten the otherwise frightening situation.

"You're tough, eh?" He spat, "looks like this fight won't be as easy as I thought."

"Hey!" Ivy yelled, "over here!"

She tried summoning vines to catch the bounty hunter, but forgot that in snowy terrains she couldn't do so. The man directed his attention to her, but I took advantage of the distraction and tackled him to the ground, attempting to strangle him with my bare hands. Of course, I didn't match his strength, so he slapped my face and hurled me to the other side of the lift.

"The hatchet!" Ivy remembered, reaching for the holder on her back.

"Reyna," I weakly called her name, but she seemed to be lying unconscious.

"Reyna ain't helping you," the man placed his leg on my neck and stomped.

The air faded away—all I could do was stare at the bounty hunter's face before he crushed my neck. I gasped in despair when the man's face was slashed open, freeing me from his grasp. Ivy stood behind him, blood staining her beautiful green dress and blending with her scarlet hair.

"Ivy?" I panted, wiping the blood, "God, what did you do!"

"What had to be done," she muttered.

"Holy!" Reyna exclaimed, holding her aching head, "who did this?"

Ivy simply raised her hand.

"Why are you even asking if you know I wouldn't kill a soul?" I tried to chuckle but felt a touch on my leg.

It was the dead man, laughing.

"You thought it'd be so easy?" The bounty hunter's face returned to normal as if it had never been split in half.

"What?" I stuttered.

"W-w-what?" The man mocked me, "regeneration magic. Not like you've ever heard of it."

Reyna tossed a dagger at the man, aiming for his eye, but as soon as it touched his skin, it ricocheted back.

"You can do anything you want, and it still won't hurt me!"

Reyna pulled out her bow and shot the man several times, but only a few arrows penetrated his skin. Although it seemed like the man would resist each hit, the more she shot him, the weaker he became.

"It's working! Keep doing that!" Ivy yelled as Reyna continued firing.

The man's patience was waning, eventually exploding with rage and charging at Reyna. Before he could reach her, I leaped and stabbed his arm with my sword. He regenerated almost immediately, but the punctures still weakened him somehow.

"Throw him off the lift!" Reyna commanded.

"Throw him, Krell!" Ivy repeated.

I wanted to do so but simply couldn't. The bounty hunter was kneeling on my feet at the edge of the lift, and although I knew that once he reached the ground, he'd regenerate, it felt wrong.

"What are you doing?" Reyna cried.

The man laughed malevolently, and while I was lost in my thoughts, he stood up and pushed me off the lift.

"Krell!" Reyna screamed.

"There is not a single bounty I haven't completed. You will not be the exception!" The man said, "I am the unstoppable rage monster—I am the—"

While the man was unaware, Ivy dashed at him and struck her hatchet into his chest, pressing harder until the bounty hunter fell off the lift. At last, we'd gotten rid of him.

"Krell," Reyna ignored the successful defeat and ran to the edge of the lift, "please, no!"

"Reyna?" I was standing behind her the whole time.

"Krell!" Reyna gasped and hugged me tight, "I thought you died! How did you...?"

"I held myself with the lift's edge and pulled back up," I blinked repeatedly, overwhelmed, "it's alright, Reyna."

"I'm so sorry," she couldn't stop holding me.

"Sorry for what?" I asked.

"For being a total asshole these past few hours. Ever since we argued, we've been on different paths, and we won't be able to achieve our goal if we remain like that," Reyna paused for a moment before continuing, "do you forgive me, Krell?"

"Yes," I replied immediately, "don't worry about it."

She then held me tighter, crying on my shoulder as I embraced her back.

"Was I supposed to stay quiet the whole time, or was I supposed to add something and hug you back?" Ivy laughed awkwardly until we opened our arms to her, "oh, I've known you for a couple of hours and we're already doing this crap."

"When I first met you, I thought it would be impossible to get along, but now we are this... *team*, I guess," I said.

"And this *team* is going to get bigger as we recruit more allies," Reyna stated, pulling apart.

I never really knew how lifts worked, but when it came to an abrupt stop while we were still more than twenty feet from the summit, I knew something was wrong.

"It's stuck," Ivy sighed, "how will we get up there?"

"I have an idea!" I smiled, reaching into my pouch and grabbing something, "the grapple hook!"

"I completely forgot we had that thing," Reyna said, shooting a grapple arrow to the top of the lift and hooking it on the rocky ground.

"Why didn't you use them before?" Ivy asked with a relieved laugh.

"The last time I found it useful was before entering your kingdom, Ivy," I recalled, "after that, I forgot it even existed."

"You shouldn't," Ivy said, "that thing can be a life saver, let me tell you."

Reyna ignored her and began climbing the rope the grapple arrow had left behind, pulling herself to the mountain's peak.

"You can go first if you'd like," I told Ivy after hurling the grapple hook to the top of the wall.

"Don't worry about it," Ivy calmly replied, "go first and toss me the rope once you get to the top."

"What's taking you so long!" Reyna cried from above.

"Coming!" I yelled back, steadily wrapping my body around the rope.

As I made my way up, I noticed the ice stalactites on the walls and the clear blue snow covering the gray rocks. Although it was slippery, I still managed to place my feet and boost myself up to the summit. When I finally reached the top, Reyna grabbed my hand and pulled me up.

"Ivy, start climbing!" Reyna didn't seem to want to waste any more time.

But something went terribly wrong.

As Ivy reached the rope, the lift shook as if it were about to plummet to the ground. Indeed, the lift dropped to the bottom of the mountain, scraping snow off the rocks and making an awful screech. Ivy was trapped, about to fall to her death on a rope that could tear at any second.

"Hold on Ivy!" I watched her from above.

"H-help!" She tried whispering but accidentally screamed.

"Don't look down!" Reyna tried comforting her, "try climbing up!"

"O-okay!" She panted in fear.

She placed her right hand a few inches above her left, sliding her legs and trying to get closer to the top. She repeated those movements a few more times until she got exhausted.

"I can't!" She cried.

"You need to do it, Ivy!" I encouraged her.

"Keep on going! You're only a few feet away!" Reyna added.

It was definitely more than a few feet.

She kept skidding her way up, slowly and carefully. She was about to reach us, so I stuck my head out into the endless void and lowered my arm, wondering if Ivy could reach me.

"Hold my hand," I noticed the terrified look on her face.

She tried but was petrified. It never crossed my mind that a Queen could be scared of heights.

"Just reach out!" I cried.

She separated her right hand from the rope—the only thing keeping her alive—but before our fingers touched, she slipped down the rope and fell into the void with the grapple hook in her hands.

"Ivy!" Reyna and I screamed simultaneously, glancing down, knowing no human could survive that fall.

"I'm here!" A trembling voice echoed through the moist rocks.

"Ivy?" I gulped, wondering if it was actually her.

"Y-yes!" Her voice broke, "I managed to hook t-the thing to one of the rocks."

"The grapple hook?" I asked.

"Yes, that thing! I hooked it with one of the rocks!"

"Can you climb up here?" Reyna asked

"I-I can't!" Ivy cried, "my hands—they're bleeding! I can barely feel my fingers."

"Can you find another way up?" I asked.

"I'm close to the ground—I think I can drop down and search," she said.

"Do that! We'll be waiting for you!" Reyna yelled.

And then we stopped hearing Ivy's voice.

"What do we do?" I asked Reyna.

"Move forward," she hesitantly nodded, "maybe we can find a way to enter the kingdom."

"Alright," I nervously agreed.

"Follow me."

Reyna stood up and paced through the icy walls of Trotter Mountain, which were similar to those on the foothills. The path ahead wasn't long, and within a couple of minutes, we were standing in front of a colossal wooden door. I didn't want to jump to conclusions, but it seemed like the entrance to the Frost Kingdom.

"This should be it," I gulped.

"I didn't think it would be so easy," Reyna clicked her tongue against the roof of her mouth.

"So the whole lift incident wasn't enough for you?" I teased her.

"Nothing will ever be enough for me," she replied menacingly, then laughed.

"Are you ready to open the door?" I asked, shaking my hands and jumping up and down.

"At three," Reyna placed her hands on the door and took a deep breath, "one... two... three!"

We both pushed the door with all our strength, struggling to flip it open. Not in a million years would I have guessed what we'd encounter behind that gate—although it might've seemed obvious to some.

"Is that...?" I mumbled, looking at the giant figure standing in front of me.

"The Trotter God," Reyna gulped as we both glanced at the massive stone throne and the God's menacing stare, looking directly into our soul.

PART V
SUB-ZERO

Chapter 13

The Trotter God was larger than I expected. It resembled the trotter king I had encountered earlier, but with some slight differences. The creature had rock-hard skin with blue and red horns atop its circular head, gleaming with lava and ice on each side. Runes were carved on the God's head, and although I wanted to read them, I couldn't understand a single symbol. I was already unnerved, but when I noticed the large weapon the Trotter God held, I audibly gasped. It was a massive boulder that looked like it was pulled straight from the God's skin.

"We should wait for Ivy," I suggested, wanting to turn around and leave.

"No!" Reyna replied angrily, "he, or... *it* will recognize her! Maybe we can tell him what is happening, and he... *it* will help us!"

"Wouldst thou dare to challenge me?" The Trotter God whispered, yet its voice still managed to rumble the room.

"We aren't here to fight," Reyna gulped, staring at the God in awe, "we're here to warn you of a great danger."

"The shadows," the Trotter God took the words out of our mouths.

"How do you know?" I asked, taking a step forward.

"The trotter kings dost whisper all to mine ears," it explained, "I know thou art embarked upon thy humble quest to gather the kingdoms. Thou art accompanied by Ivy, am I not correct?"

"I—"

"We killed her!" Reyna said before I could, "she was slowing us down, and we had to do so."

"Yes!" I lied, "we threw her off the mountain!"

"Courageous," it smiled at us. I never thought something so monstrous could act and speak like an actual living thing.

"So, will you let us in?" Reyna asked.

"Perhaps," it growled.

"What do you mean by *perhaps*?" I nervously said.

"I must first confer with the Queen," it declared, "for her kingdom, her decrees."

"No!" I yelled relentlessly, "I mean... *no*."

"Why not, noble Prince?"

"Because..." I tried to find something to say.

I discreetly glanced at Reyna, who had her hands wrapped around her bow, placing an arrow on the string behind her back, hoping the God wouldn't notice her.

"Dost thou believe I am blind to thy presence?" The Trotter God grinned, "I grant thee but thirty seconds to flee and seek thy refuge."

"Then we'll have to wait thirty seconds," Reyna gulped, aware of the risk she was taking.

"What are you doing?" I whispered.

"I don't even know," she mumbled back with stress.

"Thou knowest not the peril into which thou dost venture," The Trotter God warned.

"Maybe we do, maybe we don't," Reyna breathed heavily.

The Trotter God's patience ceased. It rose from its stone throne and placed the boulder over its shoulder, growling as it stared at our frightened bodies. The God's body changed color to an aquamarine hue—the traces of fire leaving its body. I recalled my weapon and held it in front of me, trying to intimidate the creature, but it clearly didn't work. That was when Reyna let out an awful scream and shot an arrow at the trotter's head.

"Thou hast wrought a grievous error," the Trotter God grunted.

"Krell," Reyna said nervously, "run over to him and climb him!"

"What?" I had to make sure I heard right.

"Climb him—or *it*—I don't know!"

"How am I even supposed to—?"

"Take my grapple hook!" Reyna tossed me the metal claw attached to a rope, "I will distract it, go!"

"But—"

"No *buts*, just go!"

I didn't take a moment to think about what I was doing; I just started sprinting towards the beast, trying to figure out how I was going to climb it. Reyna was still firing arrows at its head, but they didn't seem to be doing any damage. At least it was creating a small distraction as I stealthily approached the God's back.

"For thou hadn't the chance to flee, yet now thou shall taste the bitter fruit of consequence," the Trotter God growled.

The Trotter God screamed at the top of its lungs and slammed its weapon to the ground so hard that I fell to my knees. I thought I could simply get up and keep running towards the trotter, but small shards flew at my body, impaling my arms and legs. Each time he used his weapon, ice shards emerged from the ground and were hurled across the arena. I stood up in pain and limped determinedly.

"Oh, damn it!" I laid down after a few seconds of walking and tried to remove the shards from my legs.

I pulled the shard from my right leg first, but as my nails dug into my skin, the Trotter God slammed its weapon to the ground again. I was lucky to stay still and remove the sharp object from my leg. Ignoring the pain, I stood up and continued running. When I was at a certain distance, I threw my grapple hook and anchored it on the Trotter God's skin, climbing as fast as I could afterwards by placing my feet on its rock-hard skin and moving upwards. Before I could reach the waist of the Trotter God, something hugged my body tightly. It grabbed me and pulled me upwards, and as I glanced below, I noticed the trotter's colossal hand.

"Krell!" Reyna shot arrows at the hand, but they didn't seem to work.

"For I am ever watchful, like the trotters that gaze upon the lands!" He pressed harder on my skin.

"Krell, hang on!" Reyna didn't know what to do.

"Hey, bastard!" I heard a screeching scream from below with a rageful yet trusting tone.

As the Trotter God and I glanced below, we watched Ivy slowly walk into the arena with the same menacing look she had when I first met her. Her hands were covered in blood, matching the color of her messy, granite-entangled hair. She kept pacing towards the Trotter God, unworried, with her hands raised in the air.

"Ivy, the Queen of nature," the Trotter God chuckled with a growl, "dost thou intend to call forth thy vines?"

"Of course," she smirked.

Vines tore the ground and grabbed the trotter's feet, pulling it down to its knees. The hand released me after the Trotter God's hands were pulled and attached to the mountain's walls. I plummeted down, but before I hit the ground, liana held my body and cushioned my fall.

"How did you even…?" I asked with confusion.

"The blood in my hands," she explained, "it brought heat to my body, which allowed me to summon the plants frozen deep within the mountain's crust."

"Clever," Reyna smiled, "but we need to end this quickly, or your powers will start fading away!"

The Trotter God's head was pulled to the ground and wrapped in vines, giving me the chance to land a couple of hits before it regained consciousness. Blood gushed from its skull, and just as I was about to deliver a final strike, the colossal hand ripped the sword from my grasp and tossed it aside.

"Krell!" Reyna yelled, "Ivy cannot use vines anymore!"

"Find something to kill him!" Ivy suggested.

I hesitantly dug my nails into the wound in my leg, clenching my teeth as I pulled out the ice shard that had impaled me earlier. I raised it over the head of the trapped trotter and stabbed its skull, feeling both guilt and satisfaction.

The Trotter God grunted in pain, probably weakened—I hoped not dead. It tore the vines apart and slammed its fist to the ground, somehow cracking it open. The arena collapsed and we all began falling into what looked like an endless void, but was just an entrance to the Frost Kingdom lying below us.

I remembered the ball made of vines that Ivy once used when we fell off the flying serpent, but her powers had ceased working after the blood on her hands dried. I glanced at the falling Trotter God by my side and then collapsed into freezing water, sinking several feet before diving back up.

After reaching the surface, I took a deep breath and held myself with the unconscious Trotter God floating beside me. Ivy and Reyna surfaced after a couple of seconds, but I was too captivated by the view of the kingdom standing in front of me.

"We need to get out of here," Reyna said before I could examine the kingdom further.

We began swimming to shore, but people seemed to be surrounding the stone path outside the lake we were in. Light elves in rural clothing and silver armors yelled at us, but we were too far to interpret their words. As soon as we reached land and climbed into the village, we started hearing the whispers and murmurs.

"They killed the Trotter God, goodness!" One said.

"Is that the Nature Queen, an elf, and a *human*?" Another one asked.

"That is no human! That's the Prince from the Main Kingdom—the son of the King!" Someone replied.

"Disgusting rat! Return to your kingdom!"

"Those are deadly elves! I am leaving!"

"Curse you!"

"You killed him!"

"Someone call Kyra!"

"Kill them! Kill them! Kill them!" They all changed in unison.

That's when I felt a dry hit on the back of my head, and after that, I didn't remember a single thing that happened.

Chapter 14

"Wake up," I heard someone call out to me.

I slowly opened my eyes, trying to figure out what was in front of me. It took me a while to notice my mother lying on the floor, glaring deep into my eyes. She was wearing the same black dress that she wore to festivals and important events—the one featured in every portrait of her throughout the kingdom. Seeing her face, I could already guess her entire personality—her kindness. Once I wrapped my head around what was happening, I realized I was dreaming.

"Mom," I smiled, knowing it wasn't real, but still trying to enjoy the brief moment.

"Krell," she stood up alongside me.

"I miss you," I cried on her shoulder.

"I do too," she embraced me, "I am so proud of you. I am so proud of what you've accomplished."

"I miss you so much," I repeated, "I wish you were here with me."

"You have spent your entire life without me, Krell," she said, "you have grown independent, and you have a great responsibility which you need to accomplish—I know you will."

Then her body became yellow particles as if she was slowly fading away. I knew she was about to disappear and my dream was about to end, but I wasn't ready to let her go.

"I love you, mom," I said, hugging her tighter.

"I love you too," she replied, placing her hand on my forehead and smiling, "but you need to wake up."

She gently pushed my head back, yet it was somehow strong enough to throw me to the floor. Before I could realize it, I was already sinking into the darkness.

I woke up with a sudden gasp, breathing heavily as I noticed the smoke coming out of my mouth each time I exhaled. I was inside the Frost Kingdom, lying on a cold floor made of ice—I remembered everything.

My surroundings were unique. I was trapped inside a prison, but instead of metal bars like the ones in the Main Kingdom—the cell had ice spikes and poles stacked, leaving behind tiny holes that granted me diminished visibility. I searched for my sword—I even tried recalling it—but it wouldn't come back despite my best efforts.

"You finally wake up," someone said in the room next to mine.

"Ivy?" I realized who it was, "where are we?"

"Reva's dungeons," Ivy explained, "or, well, the Frost Queen's dungeons."

"Where is Reyna?" I glanced at the empty cell to my right.

"Reva must've taken her elsewhere," Ivy sighed, "we just need to wait for her to show up so we can persuade her, which won't be easy."

"Persuade me of what, exactly?" Someone walked through the corridor outside our cells.

It was a woman, whom I guessed was Reva. She wore a blue dress made of animal fur with tiny ice shards on the top and bottom. Her skin was white as snow, just like her hair, which barely reached her neck. Her eyes were a pristine shade of blue, and she surprisingly didn't have any special shoes or coat to protect her from the cold.

"Reva," Ivy murmured.

"Ivy!" She laughed with excitement, "how long has it been?"

"Don't even try talking to me with that tone; we're definitely not friends any longer," Ivy said angrily, "I am not here because I want to; I am here because I need to, so you will listen to us."

"Listen to you?" Reva laughed with hidden fury, "you burst into my kingdom, nearly kill the Trotter God, and almost start a great war between all kingdoms, but you want me to listen to you?"

"It didn't die, right?" I asked, "the Trotter God."

"No, *he* is not dead," Reva said, "luckily he only got hit by a shard of ice and not a sword, because that would've certainly killed him."

"At least it wasn't a living creature," I sighed with relief.

"Oh, he very well is one," Reva looked me dead in the eye.

"What?" I murmured, looking at Ivy, "why didn't you tell me?"

"Oh, that doesn't matter, Krell!" She rolled her eyes.

"Both of you, shut up and get to the point!" Reva yelled, "tell me what you want and then leave my kingdom."

"The shadows escaped," I said.

"At least make up something believable," Reva laughed, "you expect me to believe that?"

"Look, Reva, he is telling the truth!" Ivy yelled.

"Do not call me Reva!" Reva shouted at Ivy, "that is not my name anymore. My name is Kyra."

"Kyra? What even is that?" Ivy sighed with annoyance.

"Many things have changed since you left," Reva (or Kyra) explained.

"Kyra," Ivy said her new name, "you need to believe us. I saw these creatures with my own eyes—this is no joke."

"They have been destroying the lands piece by piece, and your kingdom is next," I explained, "please, you have to evacuate the light elves of your kingdom before anything bad happens."

"You think I will believe you after everything you've done? After everything your father's done?" Kyra yelled, "tomorrow I'll send you back to your kingdom. This is ridiculous."

"Reva," Ivy paused after realizing she didn't use her new name, "*Kyra*, I know everything that happened in the last few years has been a complete mess, and you don't trust me anymore, but this is real, and we need your help."

"No," Kyra simply said, "I'm sorry, but I'm not falling for your tricks."

"Reva..." I sighed, realizing too late I had called her the wrong name.

"I won't hurt you, but tomorrow morning you will be exiled from my kingdom," Kyra said, "I'm not gonna deal with you anymore."

Kyra stormed away, letting out a big sigh and leaving Ivy and I alone in the dark, gloomy, and freezing cells.

"That didn't work," I chuckled nervously.

"Reva has changed," Ivy shook her head in confusion, "I mean, *Kyra* has changed."

"What was she like before?" I asked, "and why did she even change her name?"

"I don't know why she changed her name, but I do know she hated her old one. She was greedy, jealous, and egocentric—she didn't even care about the people in her kingdom! The old Reva wouldn't even give us a chance to leave."

"People change over time. They all do."

"There is only one thing that remains," Ivy chuckled, "she's hard to convince."

"Maybe we can persuade her in some other way?"

"The only way to do so is by showing her an actual shadow."

"But maybe there is another way! The *tikh bracelets*!"

"Those tiny reincarnation things that the Zumba tribe wears?" Ivy asked, "that won't work."

"But it worked on me! It helped me realize that Reyna was telling the truth, so maybe it can help convince Re— *Kyra*," I said, searching for a solution.

"Yes, but how will Kyra know Reyna is a member of the Zumba tribe?"

"You're right," I sighed.

"You should get some rest, Krell," Ivy sat down, "you've been fighting monsters all day—you should be tired."

"I'm very tired, indeed," I laughed, "but I can't sleep with all these worries. Where is Reyna, anyway?"

"She must be in another cell far from here, but right now you must get some sleep."

"Wake me up if something happens, please," I said.

Then I laid on the freezing floor, using my scarf as a pillow, and slowly falling asleep.

*****

"Krell," I heard my mother's soft, calming voice once I eventually fell asleep.

"Mother," I smiled.

It was strange dreaming the same thing twice: my mother waking me up by gently touching my cheek as she humbly smiled and spoke to me in a hypnotizing voice. Her clothes were different from the last dream; her dress was dark purple, and she wore a golden crown adorned with rubies and diamonds. I knew it was a dream, but it still felt so real.

"You need to hide, now!" My mother's smile faded as a sword appeared in her hands.

"Wha-what's happening?" I panicked, looking around with concern.

"The shadows are attacking!" She glanced at her weapon and sighed, "you need to hide under the bed, now!"

I ran towards it and kneeled to hide, but the castle shook abruptly, tossing my mother to the floor. I approached her and hugged her unconscious body, attempting to wake her up.

"Mom!" I yelled in despair.

She didn't open her eyes, so I had no other choice but to drag her under the bed just like she did with me all those years ago. I looked outside the window and onto the streets of the kingdom, but smoke and fire blinded me. That was when a dry thud was heard from outside the bedroom door, just as if someone were kicking it down. I tried recalling my sword, but it wouldn't come to my hands. I leaned toward my mother and grabbed the weapon she held, hoping it would protect me from the unknown danger stalking the castle.

"Krell?" My mother startled awake, but when I turned to look at her, the door was torn open and launched at me, knocking me down.

I screeched and hurled the fallen door aside, standing up and noticing Osrov—the Shadow King—in front of me. I thrusted my sword at him, but he disappeared into thin air and reappeared behind me, striking his knee to my back and forcing me to the floor.

"What do you want!" I yelled at him, trying my best to protect my mother.

Osrov appeared in front of me, ready to stab my chest, but I immediately rolled away and countered at his stomach. Everything went foggy at that moment, darkening my vision as if I were waking up. I tried shaking my head to recover my sight, and when I did, my mother had a sword deep inside her chest. I was the one holding the weapon.

"Murderer," I heard Osrov's voice from behind.

"You are not real," I crawled back, "none of this is real!"

"Oh, but it is," Osrov grinned, "I am, at least."

"What? No! I will wake up and everything will be over!"

"The dream will be over—the nightmare will never end."

"How are you here? How are you inside my dream?"

"You have until the afternoon to join me. If not, you'll suffer the consequences," Osrov commanded.

"I will never join you."

"Then suffer."

I sank into the ground like quicksand, but instead of feeling relaxation, I felt pure stress. The dream had ended, but the nightmare was far from over.

*****

"Krell!" Reyna shook my shoulders and slapped my face until I gasped awake, "you wouldn't wake up!"

"How are you…? How are you here?" I asked, trying to ignore the awful nightmare, "how did you get here?"

"She burned the walls of her cell with an ember and then got here, but it doesn't matter," Ivy explained with a confused look on her face, "what the hell happened to you?"

"I was sleeping. What are you talking about?"

"Your eyes were glowing purple, and your veins were darkening, just like the shadows," Reyna explained, "I thought you were dying!"

"I was just dreaming. I had a nightmare, but that was all!" I gulped, "I didn't turn purple or black; you must've seen wrong."

"What kind of nightmare did you have?" Ivy looked at me, clearly stressed.

"It was a stupid one; it doesn't matter."

"Answer me, Krell!"

"Fine! I was in the Shadow War with my mother. She was unconscious. Osrov walked in and started talking to me about how the nightmare will never end and that it would keep on going forever," I explained, not thinking much of it.

"Osrov dream-walked," Reyna sighed, glancing at Ivy.

"But it can't be; he only does it with other..." Ivy started saying and then realized, "oh, sh—"

"Can you please explain to me what the hell is going on!" I yelled, interrupting Ivy, "it was just a dream, that's it."

"Look, Krell," Reyna grabbed my shoulder, "Osrov can do whatever the hell he wants with certain people. He can crawl inside people's dreams and control them."

"So, we're not safe to sleep anymore? I mean, he can go into our dreams whenever he wants, right? Isn't that dangerous for us all?" I asked.

"Krell, Osrov can only dream-walk with other shadows, which means that..." Reyna didn't want to finish the sentence.

That made no sense. Just because I had dark magic inside of my body didn't mean I was a shadow. I mean, I certainly didn't look like those bloodthirsty monsters I saw back at the Nature Kingdom.

"What? Are you just going to stand there without saying a single word?" Ivy asked, standing up and raising her voice, "you're a damn shadow and you didn't care to even mention it?"

"I'm not a shadow!" I screamed, "I may have dark magic inside of me, but I am not similar to those monsters whatsoever!"

"Ivy, he isn't our enemy," Reyna sided with me, "nor will he ever be."

Ivy squeezed the hatchet she had taken from the bounty hunters before entering Trotter Mountain and looked at the ground. She let out a frustrated sigh and then glanced back at me.

"If you turn into one of those monsters, I will kill you," Ivy stated, "and that's a goddamn promise."

Chapter 15

No one spoke after Ivy. We all stood up and walked out of the melted cell. I didn't know where we were headed, but I was almost certain we would try to raid Kyra's castle. Still, after the small argument we had, I was too afraid to speak.

"I'm sorry, but where are we going?" I built up the courage to ask.

I didn't get an answer. Instead, Reyna trotted to the door at the end of the corridor—the one that could free us onto the streets of the Frost Kingdom. When it swung open, I appreciated a view I thought I'd never see in my entire life. Inside Trotter Mountain, surrounded by frozen lakes and resting below a horde of stalactites, lay an area covered in unbelievable amounts of snow. Although I had a pretty good idea of how the kingdom's interior would look, it was far more peculiar than what I had imagined. Instead of igloos, the villagers lived in stone cottages with lanterns outside that illuminated the otherwise pitch-black kingdom. There was a straightforward path that led to the village below, but on a small hill separated from the rest of the houses, I noticed a light blue castle with a titanium gate.

"We need to head there," Reyna pointed, "that way we can convince the Queen and take her with us."

"Take her with us? You need to remember we aren't kidnapping her," Ivy laughed, "we first need to familiarize ourselves with the kingdom and let the people know that we're here in peace."

"Yeah," I agreed, "maybe if we let the people of the kingdom know that we're here to help, they can convince Kyra themselves."

"Really? Convince the people of the Frost Kingdom?" Reyna mocked.

"Yes. It may work," I said, glancing at Ivy in confusion afterwards, "wait, the people who live in this kingdom aren't *trotters*, right?"

"Of course not," she chuckled, "Trotter Mountain and the Frost Kingdom are two separate things that happen to be in the same place."

"So, no trotters?"

"Light elves," she explained, "light elves inhabit this place."

"Alright, if we're gonna help them, then let's do it quickly," Reyna sighed, "follow me."

As Reyna grunted with each step, Ivy and I were talking a few feet behind her. She explained Kyra's personality further, especially her behavior during the Trotter War and how it somehow changed over the years. Kyra only cared about herself for a long time, so when she stole a precious artifact from the Trotter God, she blamed Ivy, starting the war that destroyed the Nature Kingdom and killed her mother. Kyra realized the war's risk after a while and convinced the Trotter God to end it.

Ivy was ready to tell me one last story when we heard a blood-curdling scream coming from one of the houses. It was an old woman, crying for help after her things were stolen by a gang of thieves.

"Go!" I nodded at Ivy and ran towards the lady.

"Young man, you have to help me!" Said the woman—who was a light elf—wearing a coat and a scarf to protect her from the cold.

"Where did they go?" Reyna asked the lady, worried for once.

"They went to the alley over there!" She pointed at a dark street with a dead end.

"We'll get your things back, don't worry!" I said before chasing the thieves.

Ivy tried to ask the woman more questions, but we were already long gone, so she dashed after us. The dead-end alley was right beside the crying lady's house, which was why we caught up to the gang in less than a minute.

"Hand back the things you stole, and we'll leave you alone," I caught up to the thieves in just a few seconds.

One of the thieves chuckled, turning around to reveal his scarred face and long white beard tied in braids.

"So, you're Krell, right?" The man asked, drawing a sword from a holder on his back.

"Look, we don't want any trouble," Ivy said, stepping forward, "just give the lady's things back and we'll be on our way."

"I don't like being called *lady*," I heard a familiar, yet mysterious voice behind me.

When I turned around, I noticed the woman who called for our help. She no longer looked defenseless, especially with the dagger clutched in her right hand. At that moment, I realized it was a trap—they wanted our money. Thank God we didn't have any.

"You don't want war, do you Krell?" The old lady scratched the dagger on the alley's walls, "I heard why you entered the kingdom in the first place. I heard how you're attempting to convince everyone to join you in this *quest*."

"If you need money, we don't have it!" Ivy yelled.

"They don't want money," Reyna murmured, "they want us."

"There you go, Reyna!" The lady chuckled.

Reyna was pale as if she knew who the woman was and the threat she posed.

"How do you know her name?" I asked.

"Your parents, Reyna," the lady's smile faded, "they killed my whole tribe. They burned it to the damn ground! And now that they're dead, you're the closest thing to revenge I'll ever get."

"How do you know my parents are dead?" Reyna asked the woman.

"Your *tikh bracelets*," she replied, "it wasn't hard to figure out."

She raised her sword at Reyna's throat, staring deep into her eyes as the weapon's tip began to scratch her skin. As soon as that happened, I recalled my sword and swung it at the woman's face, spilling blood. She screamed and collapsed to the ground as Reyna pulled out her bow and shot a thief in the chest, injuring him. Ivy immediately grabbed her hatchet and struck another one's ribs, leaving him on the ground either dead or unconscious.

"Help me!" The lady cried, holding her blood-gushing slashed face.

I was glancing at the woman in shock, wondering if I should aid her, but someone approached me and threw me to the ground, thrusting his large sword at me. The thief missed every hit, and eventually, the sword got stuck on the ground.

"Go to hell!" The thief yelled after realizing he couldn't fight back, "everyone go back! Retreat!"

The remaining members of the group looked at each other and hesitantly sprinted out of the alley, glancing back at the defenseless, injured lady before leaving her behind.

"Help me! Don't walk away!" She cried to her friends before glaring at us, "help me, please!"

Reyna walked over to her and held her daggers over the woman's body.

"Reyna," I gulped, "don't."

She glared back at me, tilting her head in annoyance. It was obvious she wanted to kill the lady, but I knew that if she did so, the consequences could be much greater than the satisfaction of murder. We locked eyes for a brief moment before she returned her attention to the dying woman.

"You will leave this place and never come back again," Reyna commanded, closing her eyes.

"You will go to hell, just like your parents!" The woman revealed a hidden knife and stabbed Reyna's leg.

"Reyna!" I sprinted towards her, but someone got there before me.

Ivy raised her hatchet, and without hesitation, bashed the woman's chest, sending her flying to the other side of the alley. When the danger was gone, Ivy knelt beside Reyna and used the same ax to cut the palm of her hand.

"Hey," I tried stopping her, but blood was already dripping down the street, "what are you doing?"

"It needs to be warm," Ivy said in pain, "my hands need to be warm for my abilities to return."

I remembered the way her hands were covered in blood when we fought the Trotter God, which made her powers return despite the low temperature. She was doing the same thing to heal Reyna, but something was wrong.

"No..." I remembered the first time I saw Reyna get stabbed—right when we escaped the Main Kingdom.

I recalled the blood dripping down her leg, but some green substance overflowed her wound when she lost consciousness. The exact same thing was happening to her again, which could've only meant one thing: Reyna was poisoned.

"We need to take her to Kyra, now!" I yelled.

"Why? I already healed her," Ivy wiped the blood from her hands.

"She's poisoned. The only way to stop poison from spreading is novo juice," I replied, carrying Reyna in my arms, "we need to take her to Kyra as quickly as we can!"

"Damn it!" Ivy grunted, "she could die—let's be quick."

As I carried Reyna up the tiny hill that led to Kyra's castle, Ivy had already gotten to knocking on the building's door, yelling for Kyra to come out. There weren't any guards outside the castle—mainly because the kingdom was very safe—but there was one person inside the castle, who was kind enough to open the gates for us.

"What in the lands are you doing here?" The person said with a mocking tone.

"We need Kyra's help!" I yelled desperately.

The door at the end of the castle hall was opened abruptly. Kyra stormed out of the room, wearing a dismally beautiful, dark, shiny dress with sky-blue shoes. She stood outside the door for a couple of seconds before sprinting towards us in distrust.

"How did you escape the prison?" She touched Reyna's forehead, sensing the poison within her.

"Help us," my voice cracked as I spoke.

She didn't ask further questions and took Reyna from my hands, carrying her into the room she was in, and placing her on a stone table.

"Will she survive?" Ivy asked.

"Probably, but we need a few ingredients from my shelf," Kyra examined Reyna's body, "the plants on the right shelf, the jar of juice on the left, and a knife—quick!"

I searched the right shelf, looking for the plant as Ivy approached the drawers at the other side of the room in search of the jar of juice. There were many books over the drawers, so I threw them to the floor until I revealed the orange glowing flower. Ivy seemed to have found the juice as well, which was why arrived at the stone table at the same time.

"Now we just need to mix the plant with the juice..." Kyra tore a few leaves and dropped them inside the jar.

"It's novo juice," Ivy smirked, "remember we used it to... well..."

"Oh, I remember it," Kyra laughed, grabbing the knife Ivy brought her.

Kyra raised it over the stone table and stabbed Reyna's leg while I watched in shock, wondering if it was part of the procedure. When I glanced at Ivy, she seemed okay with it.

"What are you doing?" I asked

"We need to open the wound for the novo juice to enter her body," Kyra explained, "it probably hurts, but it's better than her dying."

That was when Reyna woke up with a sudden gasp. Her eyes rolled dizzily, and her palms shook uncontrollably as she elevated her hands like a marionette and giggled like a child.

"*What... happened*?" She asked with a strange accent.

"What's wrong with her?" I noticed something was off and asked Kyra, who was staring at Ivy.

"Well..." Ivy didn't know what to say.

"There weren't any other accessible plants around, so I had to use a..." Kyra laughed nervously, "she's drugged."

"You drugged her?" I gasped.

"It was either that or let her die," Ivy said, "the effect is short; it shouldn't last more than an hour."

"An hour? The shadows will probably arrive in this kingdom by then."

"The shadows?" Reyna chuckled lightheadly, "oh, the ones that are going everywhere to kill every kingdom in the lands?"

She then tried pressing her wobbly legs to the floor, but as soon as she did, she tripped and hit her face on the stone table. I carefully picked her up, placed her on the table, and instructed her not to move.

"See, Kyra," Ivy said, "even if she isn't fully conscious right now, she still knows about the shadows. It's not a lie!"

"You need to believe us. If you don't come with us, the lands are doomed," I tried convincing her, but she shook her head and frowned.

"Maybe the shadows escaped, but I am not letting my people die in another war—not again!" Kyra replied, conflicted.

While we were all talking, Reyna was glaring at her hands and wrists obsessively, staring at something within them. She picked one of her daggers and tried to cut her wrist, but I sprinted towards her and tossed her weapons aside.

"You need to rest, Reyna," I grabbed her shoulders and laid her on the table. She closed her eyes and tried to sleep.

"As I was saying," Ivy looked back at Kyra, "we can't ignore this war. The shadows are coming, and they could arrive at any minute now. We need to be prepared."

Kyra shook her head again. She didn't want to lead her people to die in another war, but she still wouldn't let the shadows infest her kingdom.

"I will announce to my people that we'll evacuate the kingdom," Kyra sighed, unsure if it was the right decision, "we will shelter ourselves at some edge of the lands while we devise a strategic plan to defeat those monsters. I trust you, but for this to go well, I need *your* trust."

Ivy and I looked at each other and, without any hesitation, said: "we trust you."

"Then we need to get out of the kingdom before the shadows arrive—" Kyra walked to the balcony of the room, but a crash was heard from afar.

That was when I saw them. Thousands of shadows forced their way inside the kingdom as a chunk of the mountain was torn apart and launched into one of the many frozen lakes surrounding the village. Light elves screamed and ran to Kyra's castle, hoping she would save them, but the deadly creatures were already dashing through the streets of the kingdom, catching anyone who stood in their paths and transforming them. At plain sight, there seemed to be no escape from the Frost Kingdom, but there was a crater on top of the mountain created by the shadows that infiltrated the kingdom—our only way out.

"No... no!" Kyra cried as she walked to her balcony, hopelessly glancing at the chaos below, "everyone hide, please!"

She reacted exactly like Ivy did when the shadows first breached her kingdom's walls. They both wanted to protect their people, but they knew they couldn't save them all. It was overwhelming for both of them.

"Look, Kyra, you cannot save your people," I tried comforting her, but it seemed to raise her angst, "if you come with us, we can find a cure—or something to turn your people back to normal."

"Krell is right, we need to leave!" Ivy carefully jumped off the balcony and onto the stone streets of the kingdom.

Kyra couldn't even speak anymore, so she simply followed Ivy off the balcony as I rushed back to the stone table and startled Reyna awake.

"Shadows!" Reyna forced her eyes open and dizzily sprinted to the balcony.

Just as I was about to help Reyna get down, she stumbled over the ledge and fell face-first onto the streets. I sighed and leaped off afterwards, watching Ivy and Kyra help Reyna get back on her feet.

"Can we get out through that hole the shadows left?" I tried to come up with an idea.

"Definitely not, it's way too high," Ivy said, searching for another solution.

"There is one way..." Kyra began, holding back tears, "but you'll likely die if you dare to take it."

"*Dying* is better than turning into one of those... things," I shook my head, "tell us where to go."

"There is a frozen river at the edge of the kingdom—one that can take us to the other side of the mountain," Kyra explained, "the problem is that the river passes below Trotter Mountain, which means you won't be able to catch a breath for some time. Can you last two minutes without air?"

"Minutes!" Reyna laughed, trying to balance herself, "I can last hours! Hours and more and more hours."

"It has a pretty strong kick, huh?" I chuckled.

"We don't have time for this—we need to leave!" Kyra yelled at us and walked away, "get ready because you will be in freezing water for more than two minutes."

We sprinted down the stone street, following Kyra toward what appeared to be an exit, but could have become our grave in a matter of minutes. As we ran, shadows began tearing the kingdom apart, destroying houses and transforming villagers into bloodthirsty creatures. Children screamed as adults panicked and tried their best to save their kids—they were ultimately unsuccessful. Although the shadows initially ignored us, our luck ran out when two appeared above and hissed at us, ready for a fight.

Chapter 16

"They're here!" I screamed after noticing the shadows standing on our path, "what should we do?"

"Leave that to me," Kyra raised her hand, leading ice out of the ground and onto the shadows' body, freezing them up to the waist.

"I need my vines..." Ivy began, "Reyna, pass me an ember!"

"Ember, what's an ember?" Reyna drunkenly asked, dizzily pacing around, "ember? Oh, ember!"

She reached into her pocket and grabbed a little red stone that glimmered from the inside. She tried launching it to Ivy, but didn't have enough strength, so Ivy had to pick it up from the ground instead.

"What is that gonna do?" I asked, but she simply smirked.

Ivy squeezed the ember in her hand, shattering the small stone and momentarily lighting the entire kingdom in a scarlet hue. After the heat from the mineral passed over us, Ivy took a deep breath and glanced at her arms.

"Do it, Ivy!" Kyra yelled.

Vines emerged from the ground, crawling over the frozen shadows and crushing their limbs. Normally, Ivy's abilities wouldn't shred shadows into a million pieces, but with Kyra's ice, it miraculously worked.

"Look, Ivy," Kyra gulped after killing the shadows, "I know I've done a lot of messed-up things in the past, and you probably hate me for that, but right now we need to work together."

"Don't even start," Ivy said reluctantly, "I'm doing this just because I need to, not because I want to."

"That's cool that you hate each other, but we need to get to the lake to hold our breath for hours and hours and hours..." Reyna chuckled like a child.

"It's right around the corner," Kyra ran through the streets, leading us to the frozen lake.

After running for a few minutes and killing any shadow that crossed our path, we finally arrived at the frozen lake. The word "*frozen*" was an accurate way to describe what lay before us as it looked like there was no water left—only snow covering a giant block of ice.

"We need to break the ice, now!" Ivy screamed, but as soon as she stepped onto the lake, two shadows appeared in front of her.

They weren't ordinary shadows though—they were the shadow sisters—the same that appeared back at the Nature Kingdom, and the same who worked directly for the Shadow King. Their tongues rested outside their mouths, and they wielded swords sharper than their keen teeth.

"We meet again, huh?" One of the sisters said.

"I told you we would find them, sister!" The other one laughed.

"I know, but I didn't think they'd be convincing the one and only Reva—the Frost Queen! Or should I say Kyra?"

" It seems like she changed her name along with her whole personality, huh?"

"Oh, let's not even talk about that. Did you realize everyone in this *group* has mommy and daddy issues?"

Kyra looked at them in disbelief and anger, clenching her fists and panting heavily.

"Break the ice, find a way to enter the water, and get the hell out of here. I will try to stop them," I whispered to the others.

"We will try to stop them," Reyna took a step forward to stand by my side.

"They really sent the weaker links to us," one of the sisters laughed, "well, bring it on!"

Reyna was the first to strike. She jumped and sliced at the sister, but before the knife could reach her, she leaped back and swung her sword at Reyna's back.

"Oh!" Reyna exclaimed, touching the blood running down her back, "why did you do that?"

I dashed to the second sister before she could harm Reyna, trying to swing my sword at her chest. But of course, she jumped out of the way and kicked my face, knocking me to the frozen ground. The sisters were untouchable.

"At least bring a fight to us," she hit my defenseless body.

Reyna stood up and tried shooting arrows at the sister, but the sister caught them effortlessly and tossed them aside.

"I have a fabulous, incredible, awesome, amazing idea," Reyna stumbled away, drunkenly slipping on the ice and giggling, "distract them!"

"Distract them? I can't—" I began, but one of the shadow sisters pushed me back to the ground.

"Weak!" The other sister kicked my stomach.

"You need to embrace the darkness inside you," the sister said with a burning passion, "let it consume you!"

I felt the anger again. Every muscle in my body twitched, and the most horrible, dark, sadistic thoughts entered my mind. I wanted revenge—I wanted to kill the sisters—but I wouldn't let the darkness inside consume me.

"There you go!!" The sister noticed what was happening to me.

"Embrace your nature, Krell!" The other one kept pushing me to the ground.

But I couldn't. I took a deep breath and glanced at Reyna, who was standing on a small hill behind the shadow sisters. She pulled her bowstring, ready to fire an arrow attached to a glowing item.

"Embrace this, bastard!" Reyna released the string, hitting one of the sister's arms.

"Really? That's all?" She laughed as Reyna tilted her head.

Right in front of me, something exploded. A light glimmered over the lake, knocking both sisters to the ground and forcing me to squint my eyes to see what was happening.

"Ember," I noticed the broken stone on the ground, "genius."

Although Reyna was drugged, she was still smart enough to fight.

"Thanks, but we need to go and hold our breath for hours and hours," Reyna smiled, attempting to maintain balance, "come on!"

While the sisters were screaming in pain on the ground, Reyna and I ran towards Ivy and Kyra, who were still trying to find a way to break the ice and get us out of the infested kingdom.

"It's too hard!" Ivy kept striking her hatchet against the frozen lake.

"I tried moving the ice aside. It doesn't work," Kyra added.

"Well, we don't have much time!" I hit the ground with my fists and then tried using my sword, "everyone, help me!"

Reyna grabbed her daggers, scratching them on the ground, but it was impossible to get past the thick layer of frozen water. She tried using an ember to heat the surroundings, but it only managed to slightly crack the ice beneath us. Just as I stood up and asked if there was another way to escape the kingdom, a shadowy figure appeared behind us.

"I trusted you, sisters," the shadow's voice was deep and stuttered, "get up!"

"Yes, master," both sisters said simultaneously.

It didn't take long for me to realize that the one speaking was Osrov—King of Shadows—also known as the most menacing man in the lands.

"Osrov..." Kyra said in shock and disappointment.

Osrov walked towards us, slowly but menacingly.

"I won't let you hurt them," I stood in front of him with my sword in hand.

"Brave, brave Krell," he kept walking.

Each step he took caused the ice beneath him to start melting—not entirely, but quickly enough to break through the frozen lake in a matter of minutes. If he would just stand still for a while, maybe we could finally enter the water.

"I know what's inside of you, Krell," he crept closer, "I know the darkness you hold within. You can let it all out if you just join me."

Osrov grabbed my cheek and examined my puzzled face, eager for my answer to his proposal. Never in my life would I join such a sadistic creature.

"I may have shadow magic inside of me—I may even be a shadow," my voice cracked, "but I will never be *your* shadow."

Osrov pulled away and frowned. He was disappointed, yet not surprised. He turned around and walked away, glancing at the sisters momentarily before disappearing.

"Don't take too long," he whispered.

"Oh, we can't promise that," one of the sisters smirked.

"Come on, sister," the other chuckled, "let's kill them."

I thought they would walk in circles and strategize, but the twin shadows dashed toward me without hesitation, pulling my hair and tossing me to the other side of the frozen lake.

"Take care of the others," the sister commanded, running over to me and slapping my face, "I think I'll do a fine job with this one."

"Leave me alone!" I screamed, but the sister pushed my head to the ice.

"Embrace the darkness!" She held me down.

With my face numb by the cold, I realized that my fingertips were turning black, just like last time. The darkness was consuming me, but I didn't focus on that when I realized something much more important: the simple touch of my fingers was melting the ice.

"Just let it out, goddamnit!" The sister lost patience.

"Never!" I screamed, pushing her away.

I jerked her backwards, grabbing her neck and strangling her against the ice. A sizzling sound was heard, and with one final attempt, I shoved her onto the frozen lake.

Before I noticed it, I was already submerged in the freezing water, being dragged downwards by the strong current. The last spark of light I saw before everything went dark was the sisters looking at me from above and giggling, certain I wouldn't survive. I tried searching for the others, but all illumination ceased in an instant.

Every second I spent underwater, I felt myself getting weaker, and without the ability to breathe, it was ten times harder to search for an exit. Although I couldn't see my friends, I already knew they shared the same desperation—I just hoped they were alright.

Then a vestige of light shone upon me. It was minimal, but the most relieving thing I'd observed in a while. We had reached the other end—the outside of Trotter Mountain—but as soon as the light grew brighter, my hopes of escaping were dashed. The other side of the river was also frozen.

"No!" I yelled underwater.

I saw Kyra and Ivy swimming by my side, but Reyna was nowhere to be found. I wondered if the sisters had captured her somehow, but then I noticed her at the bottom of the lake with her eyes closed and mouth open.

"Reyna!" I yelled again, rushing to her rescue.

On the verge of fainting and dying, I dove down. I had no strength, but I reached the bottom of the lake and carried Reyna to the surface. A thick layer of ice prevented us from exiting the water, but before I attempted to break it, a silhouette appeared on the other side of the frozen lake. He used a large spear to crack the ice and his armored hand to drag Reyna and me out of the water.

"Thank you," I breathed heavily, lying on the ground, "so much."

The man stepped in front of me, but I couldn't quite see his face or clothing. I thought he was my savior until he struck me on the head, rendering me unconscious.

Reyna was blindfolded and tied before being hit with a hammer. Ivy was dragged from the lake and stabbed, and when Kyra tried to defend herself, someone struck her chest with a spear.

As I slowly began to fade away, I glanced at the armor of one of the many men. Three words written:

King Henrius' Army...

PART VI
PRISONERS

Chapter 17

I woke up, dizzily forcing my eyes open and gaining consciousness. My head hurt, and I noticed it was bleeding from the red liquid reaching my lips. I wanted to move but quickly realized I was strapped to a chair. Clearly, I was being held captive.

After fathoming the situation, I looked around the room, which had beautiful scarlet curtains, a golden chandelier hanging from the maroon ceiling, and a door leading to a balcony. There was a desk in front of me and a chair facing away. Someone was sitting there, but I couldn't guess who it was.

"Do you have any idea—any idea at all!" The voice was familiar, one my mind wanted to forget, "of what you've done?"

Then the chair turned around, and I saw my father. He was wearing his usual clothes, but it looked like he hadn't showered in days, especially with his beard covered in dirt and mud. His expression was also notable; he was angrier than usual. His eyebrows were lowered, his teeth clenched, and he didn't even have his crown on.

"Father," I gulped in fear.

"Don't you call me *father* again in your goddamn life," he slammed his hands on the desk, "you are not my son, you were never my son, and you will never be my son!"

"I know you are mad at me, but you need to—" I tried not to upset him.

"Listen to you?" He anticipated my words before I spoke, "why should I ever listen to you? Why would I ever believe anything that comes out of your goddamn mouth?"

"Because I have proof!" I yelled, "the shadows have escaped and destroyed two kingdoms—probably three already!"

My father turned around and laughed in disbelief.

"The shadows haven't escaped, Krell. Why won't you trust me?" My father tried to persuade me.

"Before I can trust you, I need a reason to do so!" I shouted back.

"And what is your reason for *me* to trust you?" My father raised his voice again.

I looked down, trying to think of an answer, but couldn't. There were so many things I wanted to say—so many things I'd held back for years—but I couldn't express them. I simply stood in silence.

"Exactly," my father glared at me in disappointment.

I looked him directly in the eyes.

"Listen to me, I don't need your help, nor will I ever need it," I found the courage to speak, "since I was born, you've blamed me for my mother's death and have hated me ever since. You have massacred thousands and left many more without homes. I have held a grudge against you forever, trying to trust you, trying for us to be father and son... but that stops now. You should be scared of me, King Henrius Kovner. I am coming for you, and I will get revenge for everything you've done."

"You really think a threat will scare me?" My father laughed.

"Oh, it wasn't a threat. It was a promise."

I stood up and left the chair from which I had untied myself moments before. The King looked at me with disdain as I noticed a tray with fruit and bread on the table beside the door. I grabbed it and left the room, my father standing in silence.

As I walked through the corridor, I reflected on everything that had happened. I had become my father's enemy after gaining the courage to stand up to him—*no, that didn't seem right.* The word "*father*" didn't seem right. Henrius Kovner wasn't my father, and he never would be, just like he said.

I stopped in my grandfather's room, slowly opening his door and noticing him lying in bed, probably asleep. It had been days since I had last seen him, and judging by my father's behavior, he likely starved him during those days.

I dropped the tray on his nightstand and tried to leave quietly, but I heard a soft voice.

"Grandson?" Said my grandfather.

"Hi gramps," I turned back around and closed the door behind me.

"Krell, you're so big now," my grandfather smiled, touching my cheek.

"I'm sorry, gramps," I kneeled down beside his bed, "I had to leave for a few days and couldn't feed you during that time."

"Oh, I know you left," he laughed, "the smell you have is straight out of the chilling breezes of Trotter Mountain, and the leaves you have stuck in your hair are only found in the beautiful oak trees of the southern shores."

"How do you know so much?" I asked as he stopped grinning.

"I..." He tried speaking, "I just remember the old days when I used to explore."

"Yes, but then my father became King and ruined everything."

"Don't blame everything on your father," my grandfather said, "the loss of a loved one is hard to take. Everyone grieves in their own way. It's sad that your father choose genocide as his way."

"But it's not fair!" I stood up, "he doesn't know what happens out there—he doesn't realize that there are good people outside this wretched kingdom."

"Look, Krell," he began, "no matter what your father does, it doesn't change who you are or how you see the lands. Remember, you will choose your own destiny."

I thought about it for a second. Just because my father acted that way didn't mean he could make decisions for me. It was time someone actually escaped the Main Kingdom and observed the beauty of the outsides.

"Now leave," he said, "I know you want to keep following your quest. Go, for once and for all."

"What about you, gramps?" I asked, wondering who would take care of him.

"Don't you worry about me, Krell," he giggled, "I am old and weak, but I can handle myself. Now leave, please."

I hesitated but eventually started walking away, trying not to look back. It was inevitable; I turned my head towards my grandfather, who was still glaring at me. I thought he would have his eyes closed by that moment, but he was still smiling in my direction as if he knew something I didn't.

"Thank you, gramps," I smiled and—for a split second—forgot all my worries, "I love you."

Chapter 18

After speaking to my grandfather and clearing things up for him, I shut the door behind me and started planning my next move. My friends were definitely in the dungeons—after all, they were captured by the same guards that brought me back to the Main Kingdom's castle. I could've sneaked into the King's chamber and stolen the dungeon's keys, but it was too risky. So, I decided on the safest option: visit the dungeons and consult with everyone else on what to do next.

I ran towards the main staircase but stopped upon realizing that three armored guards stood in front of the main gate, preventing anyone from entering or exiting. I sighed and walked back in disappointment until I remembered the stained glass window I'd broken a couple of days before. I recalled chasing Reyna through the rooftops of the Main Kingdom—intercepting her by crashing through a stained glass window and talking to her for the first time.

"Please tell me they didn't fix it," I kept repeating as I ran through the blood-red carpet.

After arriving at the stained glass window, I noticed a gray piece of cloth covering it to make it appear unbroken. Due to the wind blowing in that direction, it was clear the stained glass was no longer there.

I ripped the cloth and glanced at the village below, noticing all the market tents and stone houses I could potentially land on. However, since I left my grapple hook at the frozen lake of the Frost Kingdom, I'd have to find another way.

"Just don't look down," I sighed before stepping out the broken window and skidding on the narrow edge of the castle.

I kept sliding along the ledge, aiming to reach the balcony just a few feet away, where I could stop to rest before continuing. I gripped the wall with my nails and tried not to look down, carefully turning around and grabbing the ledge above me.

"Alright…" I laughed in relief.

Just as I thought it was safe to continue, a bird flew over my head and screamed in my ear. I flinched and jerked back, losing my balance, slipping off the ledge, and falling backward onto the streets of the kingdom.

I could've died. My journey could've ended; no one would've been able to save the Main Kingdom, and the shadows would've destroyed the lands. Thankfully, that didn't happen! I managed to land on the music room's balcony, which was on the first floor of the castle and had been abandoned since my mother's death.

Fortunately, the unexpected fall worked to my advantage as it brought me closer to the village streets. I climbed over the balcony's ledge and dropped onto the market below, where villagers sold food, drinks, and souvenirs. The strange thing was that there were portraits of my face at every stand and house around the market. Beside the portraits, there were signs that read:

FUNDRAISING TO FIND
KRELL KOVNER
Escaped the kingdom in an attempt to stop war

HELP US FIND OUR PRINCE
HELP US STOP THE WAR.
HELP US STOP NEGLIGENCE.

IF NO ONE STANDS UP TO MAKE A CHANGE, INJUSTICE WILL PREVAIL!

I was glad that the villagers of the kingdom actually cared about me, but I also felt guilt, mainly because the citizens who created those signs were most likely getting killed. Just as I thought I had the support of everyone in the kingdom, the owner of *Uncle Bob's*—the biggest, richest, and surprisingly cheapest store in the kingdom—walked towards one of the stands, ripped a sign off the wall, threw it to the ground, and spit on it.

"Hey!" The owner of the stand said, "that was mine."

"That little bastard broke a hole in my roof twice!" Bob shouted, "I hope he's been ripped apart by a trotter by now."

I wanted to yell at him, perhaps something like: "*he is still alive,*" or "*I won't die that easily,*" but everyone would start freaking out. So I stood in silence as I watched someone step on my face and insult me. Still, it didn't stop people from noticing.

"Prince Krell, you're back!" Someone said from behind, diverting all attention to me. Most villagers had a smile on their face, while others frowned with disdain.

As everyone began running over to me, I noticed two guards dashing through the streets, pushing people aside and grabbing their spears from holders on their backs. That was my cue to leave.

"Move, move," I tried yelling but couldn't get past a whisper.

The knights were getting closer, and after I thought I had lost them in the crowd, another one appeared in the middle of the street, alerting his companions to my presence.

"Oh no," I muttered and sprinted to a nearby alley.

Three guards were chasing me, and I had no other choice but to keep moving forward. Then five more appeared at the end of the alley with swords and spears pointed in my direction. Their faces were red, either from exhaustion or rage—most likely rage.

"Maybe we can talk this out, and..." I nervously laughed, but the guards didn't seem friendly at all, "oh, screw it."

I jerked my right foot towards the wall, lifting myself up as I pushed my other leg to the other side, leaping onto the roof of one of the houses. The guards couldn't replicate my moves, so they ran away to find another way to reach me.

"Get him!" One of them screamed, climbing a ladder to the roof.

"Crap," I muttered, looking back at the knights launching spears at me.

I had no other choice but to enter the house, which I thought was abandoned or housed a nice person—but no! As soon as I opened the hatch on the roof, I encountered an old woman.

"Who are you?" She angrily asked.

"I'm sorry! I'm Prince Krell—I don't mean to harm you, but..." I tried to be reasonable, but her expression remained unchanged.

"There is no Prince. Get out!"

Her hand slipped into one of her drawers, and she grabbed five plates, tossing them in my direction. One of them hit my face and shattered on my nose, making an awfully loud noise.

"What was that?" The trap door above me opened.

I hurried to the front door and kept running through the streets, following the path to the dungeons. I pictured thousands of guards chasing after me, but when I glanced back, there was nobody behind me—not even the old lady peeking out the door and cussing at me from afar. I was finally safe.

Although the dungeons weren't far away, by the time I reached them, I was panting and wheezing. If I had my grapple hook, it would've taken a couple of minutes to reach the dungeons, but of course, the guards didn't bother to bring my weapons when they captured me in the Frost Kingdom.

As I approached the dungeons and walked down the slippery stairs into the dismal place, I heard a chuckle behind me. When I looked back, I noticed a guard smiling behind his thick, silver helm.

"Foolish of you to come back here," he said, kicking me down the stairs. I rolled and collapsed down the steps until I crashed into the dungeon's door.

"My arm!" Was the first thing I screamed upon landing.

I thought it was broken, but after looking at it, it seemed perfectly fine. The guard jumped down the stairs and thrusted his spear at my chest, but I stepped back and recalled my sword. Normally, it would arrive in my hands instantly, but after a few seconds of waiting, the weapon was nowhere to be found.

"Are you expecting a sword to magically appear in your hands?" The guard chuckled as I kept my hand up in the air, waiting for it to appear.

"Yeah, kinda," I said.

I remembered keeping my sword at hand the entire time I rushed down the frozen river back in the Frost Kingdom. However, when the guards captured me, my weapon fell from my hands and was left on Trotter Mountain. It would probably take a few more attempts for it to reach the Main Kingdom.

The guard stepped forward, tricking me into thinking he'd slam his head against mine, but instead, he slammed his spear at my feet. Before I realized it, he was already trying to stab me on the ground.

"Just die, goddamnit!" He yelled as I rolled to my right.

When he went for his final thrust, I crawled away and raised my hand once again. I felt the sword getting closer, but when I heard a whistling sound from outside the dungeon, I knew it had arrived. The weapon flew down the steps of the dungeon and landed in my hands.

"That won't give you an advantage!" He growled.

I flapped my sword at the guard's chest plate, tearing it off, and kicked the weapon from his hands. By the time he realized what was happening, it was too late. I hurled the chest plate at his face, knocking him unconscious.

"Bastard," I panted, rolling my arm to ease the pain.

I hurried down the dungeon's hall, wondering if the creatures inside the cells would reach through the bars to grab me. Strangely, the only prisoners I saw were at the end of the hall in a single cell. One of the girls had dark horns and white hair, another wore a beautiful green dress, and the third had sparkly blue clothing and blonde hair that glowed in the dark.

"Reyna!" I reached the cell, noticing everyone else.

"Krell," she smiled.

"You finally arrived!" Ivy looked happier than usual.

"Yeah, the one who got us captured finally arrived," Kyra sighed.

"What do you mean?" I asked.

"It doesn't matter, but you need to get us out of here." Ivy squeezed her face through the cell's bars.

"We already talked about this, Ivy!" Reyna raised her voice.

"I can help you out! I can go find the keys to the cell and we can get the hell out of here," I searched for a way.

"Krell," Reyna depressingly sighed, "you really think it'll be easy to steal the keys from your father after you already did it once? He knows what you're planning, and it won't be as easy as last time."

"Then I'll find another way! They'll execute you, right? Maybe when they take you to the main plaza for that execution, I can intervene and save you."

"Krell..." Reyna murmured.

"Or I can convince my father..."

"Krell!" She screamed.

"What!" I shouted back.

"There is no other way! We will be executed in a few hours, and there is nothing you can do about it!" Reyna cried.

"But maybe there's a way to save us," Ivy interjected, "Krell just named a few ideas—one has to work."

"It'll only get him in more trouble," Kyra broke her silence, "if the guards find out he tried saving us, he'll be next in line for the guillotine. We can't put him at risk."

"I don't care about the danger; I only care about you!" I was convincing myself there was a way, but there wasn't.

"The best thing you can do right now is get out of here," Reyna gulped, "the guard you knocked out is already waking up."

I looked at the entrance of the dungeon and noticed the guard I fought moments ago. He was moving his head in circles, rolling his eyes, and drunkenly chewing the blood in his mouth.

"If we don't make it," Ivy coughed, almost crying, "avenge us."

"And please don't come out of your room when they execute us," Reyna added, "I don't want you to watch."

Without saying another word, I walked away, knowing that after they killed Reyna, Ivy, and Kyra, there was no one left to help me in the quest. I was alone, forced to stop the war by myself.

Chapter 19

The walk back to the castle wasn't long. There were no guards following or people recognizing me, so I simply paced home in silence. Problems crossed my mind, thousands of regrets and issues flooded my thoughts, and voices were screaming inside my head. Although they wouldn't shut up, I was still at peace somehow. I had one simple goal: *go to the castle and sleep.* I could have been thinking about how to stop the war, save my friends, or kill the shadows, but no—I just wanted to rest.

As soon as I reached the castle, no guard stopped me from entering. In fact, they seemed surprised I voluntarily stepped inside. Without exchanging a word, I walked upstairs to my room.

As I made my way up, I noticed my grandfather's room with the door halfway open and the curtains closed as usual. He was looking at me from the door's crack, expecting me to go visit him again—I didn't.

When I laid down on my bed, I closed my eyes immediately, wanting to fall asleep as soon as possible. Just when I thought I was at peace, someone abruptly opened the door and chuckled.

"We're going to have a lot of fun," the guard standing outside my room smirked.

It was Vernan, the knight I fought outside the Nature Kingdom, who got captured by a flying trotter. I thought he had died, but he stood there with a scar crossing his face from one eye down to his chin.

"You see this?" Vernan pointed at the scar, "you were the one who did it, and you'll pay for it."

I was too sleepy to even answer.

"Now get up and follow me!" Vernan yelled.

I followed him down the staircase to the castle's kitchen. Vernan handed me a sponge and commanded me to polish every plate, clean the dust off the walls, and scrape the dirt off the floor.

"Really?" I asked, "clean the kitchen?"

"It hasn't been cleaned in weeks—it certainly needs some help. What better way to do so, am I right?" He kept grinning.

And there I was, scrubbing the sink, plates, and the dirt gathered inside each utensil. When my sponge eventually got dirty, I tried asking Vernan for a new one, but he simply screamed at me to continue.

"How long do you expect me to... keep... scrubbing!" It had only been a couple of minutes, and I was already exhausted.

"I never told you to talk!" He yelled, "keep scrubbing."

I can't even describe my time cleaning the kitchen. I was simply pushing the sponge up and down as Vernan shushed me every time I talked or breathed heavily.

"There!" I yelled in satisfaction, "I finished."

It had only been fifteen minutes, but it felt like hours.

"Oh, you really think that was it?" He chuckled, "the bathroom beside the kitchen is still waiting."

"You have to be kidding me," I sighed, my smile slowly fading.

As I walked to the bathroom, I tried asking for a new sponge, but Vernan didn't care to provide one.

Saying that the bathroom hadn't been cleaned in weeks was an understatement. It looked like a wild trotter had entered and destroyed everything inside as he defecated all over the damaged walls. The floor was covered in what I hoped was water, and the toilet was clogged with at least ten pounds of poop. I had to clean it all with just a sponge...

I didn't know if Vernan actually felt bad for me after I stained myself with dirt—and other unpleasant things that I don't even want to mention—or if he got bored watching me clean the bathroom, but he told me to follow him to the next task. I simply hoped it would be more enjoyable.

He led me outside the castle, and we walked for several minutes towards the edge of the kingdom, right beside the steel wall surrounding it. If I was about to get murdered, no one would hear my screams.

Vernan stopped at a field and examined me from head to toe. I wasn't sure what he wanted to do, but I knew his intentions weren't good.

"Let's see if you can still fight without the help of your elf friend," he said.

"Wha—?" I tried to ask, but he punched me before I could finish the word.

"I have waited for this my whole life," he whispered, then shouted, "come out!"

Dozens of guards jumped out from nearby bushes. They didn't have spears, but even with their bare fists, they still looked menacing. If the punch across the face wasn't enough, one of them proceeded to kick me to the ground. I tried recalling my sword, but Vernan stepped on my arm.

"We're all using our fists, why should you use your weapon, Prince?" Vernan laughed alongside the other guards.

The next one to strike punched my stomach and hurled me to the other side of the field, where I was greeted by three more guards who kicked dirt into my eyes, temporarily blinding me.

"What are you going to do, Prince boy?" They all laughed simultaneously.

"Stop!" My voice suddenly changed tone—it became deeper.

I felt the rage again—bad timing. If I were to turn into a shadow at that moment, I would have no mercy on the guards, slaughtering them all. Or even worse, if some survived, they'd spread the rumor of my actions to the whole kingdom, and I'd be executed! I tried controlling it, but it was almost impossible with a guard kicking my face, another hitting my stomach, and the remaining shoving dirt in my eyes. As soon as I felt the darkness expanding through my body, I heard the sound of screaming and gurgling.

I opened my eyes, noticing the many arrows flying through the field and impaling guards' chests. They choked on their blood and collapsed over me.

Vernan was the only lucky guy with the chance to sprint away, avoiding all the projectiles fired at him. For a strange reason, the first thing I mumbled after seeing the dead guards beside me was: "*Reyna?*"

I mean, it was obvious that it wasn't her, but the way the arrows were shot—as well as the brutality—reminded me of her.

That was when the person who shot the arrows walked over to me and offered a hand. I couldn't see who it was because of the blinding sun behind her, but I could make out the figure of a short girl with a bow in her hands. I grabbed her hand and examined her dark skin, fur clothing covering her chest and legs, and drawings on her face that looked like tattoos.

"Thanks, um... What's your name?" I asked after getting up.

"The huntress," she mysteriously said, doing something I thought impossible.

She raised her hand and recalled my sword—the one only I was supposed to recall. She grabbed the weapon tightly and handed it to me as I accepted it in confusion.

"I'll be seeing you, Krell," she shot an arrow to a nearby house and grappled herself to its roof, disappearing.

What had just happened? First, an unknown woman showed up out of nowhere and saved me from some guards. Next, she recalled the sword that only I could recall and then told me she would be seeing me. Again, *what*?

But I didn't have time to think. I simply wanted to get to the castle again to sleep—and that was exactly what I did.

As I was lying in bed, I realized that—thanks to the guards—I wasn't sleepy anymore. Instead, I was worried. I knew my friends were going to die, and I couldn't do anything about it. I sighed and tried to fall asleep but couldn't.

I glanced at a plushie near my bed that I had since childhood and placed it inside my pouch because of how nostalgic it made me feel. Then I remembered something: the room below my bed that I'd discovered some days before.

Something drew me towards it. I couldn't tell if it was a hunch or an actual entity urging me to enter the room, but I immediately moved my bed aside and opened the trap door, stepping into the dark. Unlike last time, I left the hatch open, illuminating the gloomy hall for once. At the end of the corridor there was a door covered in webs, with peeling paint and no doorknob. It was clear it hadn't been opened in years.

"What is this?" I whispered after entering the room.

The chamber was lit by several lamps pointing at a display glass containing some sort of outfit. It was dark green with black tones throughout, covering the entire body of whoever wore it. Right beside the glass was a bow with the same emerald hue as the suit. There was also a quiver with metal arrows inside.

"This is..." I began.

"Amazing," a raspy voice behind me said: my grandfather.

He was wearing the same clothes as before, slowly limping towards me with the help of his walking stick.

"Gramps!" I gasped and approached him, "what are you doing outside your room? You can't walk!"

"Don't worry about me, kid," gramps said, "worry about that."

He pointed to the suit and bow.

"Do you know who it belongs to?" I asked him.

"Have you ever heard the legend of the lost hero?" He coughed, touching the display glass.

"That story they used to tell us when we were kids?" I recalled, "about the guy who fought the trotters back when they were a menace and suddenly disappeared without a trace? Yeah, I remember."

"That is his suit," gramps revealed, "it belonged to him. When he could no longer save the lands, he kept his suit hidden in this chamber. Sadly, the lost hero can't help the lands in this painful age..."

"Oh," I realized, "you're the lost hero."

"Sadly," gramps sighed, "I tried to fight the trotters, but my illness prevented it."

I was in utter shock. My grandfather turned out to be one of the most famous rebel heroes in the lands' history, and he had kept it a secret his whole life? Not only that, but he also kept his suit and bow right below my bedroom.

"But I don't understand," I tilted my head, "why didn't you tell anyone?"

"A great magician doesn't reveal his secrets."

"That saying is not for... You know what, never mind."

"What I mean is that if I revealed that I was the lost hero, I would have put you in danger. Many people loved me back in the day, but many others hated me. Those men would try to kill us if they ever knew I was the lost hero," he explained.

My grandfather paused.

"Now this suit belongs to you," he said.

"What? No! I... I can't take this," I wanted it, but it didn't seem right.

"You have a quest, Krell," he tripped into my arms and coughed, "you need it more than anyone."

I thought about it for a few seconds. I visualized myself in the lost hero's clothing, wielding a bow and defending the lands from any threat—becoming a hero. It all seemed unreal.

Then I heard a bell. It was the sound that blared through the kingdom each time there was a public execution. I knew it was time.

"Time is running out," gramps said, "so, what is your choice?"

I looked at him with a clear decision in mind.

CHAPTER 20

"Today, we stand united to witness the execution of Reyna of the Zumba tribe, Ivy of the Nature Kingdom, and Reva of the Frost Kingdom," said the black-hooded executioner, "for the crime of entering the kingdom without authorization and endangering the Prince. The penalty for each of these crimes is death by guillotine. Now, let us begin."

Reyna, Ivy, and Kyra's hands were tied with a chain. They kept staring at the ground, not wanting to see the blade that would soon sever their heads.

"The first to pass will be Reyna of the Zumba tribe," the executioner announced, pulling a rope that raised the blade.

Reyna couldn't speak. She accepted her fate and kneeled before the blade as guards locked her arms and neck in place inside the lunette.

"Any last words?" The executioner asked.

"I will see every single one of you in the deepest pits of hell," Reyna paused for a moment and then ragefully said.

"Very well," he released the rope.

The guillotine fell toward Reyna's head at a fast pace. She closed her eyes and awaited death, but instead, the blade stopped as soon as it reached her neck.

It was an arrow—a metal arrow that got stuck between the blade and the lunette before it decapitated Reyna. The bolt was so strong that not even the guillotine could cut through it. Then, two more projectiles were fired at the executioner's feet, knocking him down.

I was the one shooting arrows from afar, riding on horseback toward the main plaza. The shining green armor distinguished me from any recent hero the lands had seen, and although the outfit was neat, it lacked an original touch. That was why I had my scarf wrapped around my neck, covering my mouth and nose, hiding my identity.

I fired one last arrow in Reyna's direction, hitting the metal lock that trapped her head and arms inside the lunette. She pushed the blade away and grabbed her daggers from a nearby bag, killing some incoming guards.

"Who is that?" Kyra asked.

"*Krell*," Ivy smiled.

I kept shooting arrows at every guard I saw, and after finally reaching Reyna, I lowered the scarf and panted heavily.

"Did you just copy me with the bow?" Was the first thing she asked after I rescued her.

"I just saved you, and that's what you say?" I sliced the chains trapping Reyna's hands, but before she could thank me, a spear flew over my shoulder, "we need to go, now!"

I approached Ivy and Kyra, and—with the help of Reyna—cut their chains and set them free.

"Where did you even get that?" Ivy examined me from head to toe.

"Didn't that belong to the lost hero?" Kyra added.

"It's a really long story," I said, "and we don't have any spare time, so get to the horse, now!"

Despite the spears getting hurled at us, we managed to reach the horse safely. We galloped through the streets of the Main Kingdom, trying to avoid the guards attempting to bring us down while also evading any passing villager.

"Where do we go?" Reyna asked.

"We can try to reach the roof of that tall house at the kingdom's edge," I pointed at a round building the same height as the steel wall we needed to get through, "the horse might be able to leap over the wall and get us back to the outsides."

"You think a horse can jump over that colossal thing?" Ivy asked, holding my waist so she wouldn't fall off.

"No, but I can create a path of ice to get us up there," Kyra suggested.

"Too slippery—the horse will fall," Reyna replied, shaking her head.

I couldn't focus on their conversation as I was busy guiding the horse through the kingdom's streets and dodging guards thrusting spears at us. I found some stairs leading to the roof of the tallest house in the kingdom, but we still needed a plan to cross the steel wall.

"Think of something quickly," Reyna urged, turning around and drawing her bow, "I'll hold off the guards."

We all paused for a moment to observe Reyna. She passed her fingers over the bowstring and fired with great aim and accuracy. When she hit one of the guards, the arrow went through his skull and impaled the one behind him. Reyna then shot two more arrows at the legs of another knight, finishing with an arrow right between his eyes.

"Oh my..." I mumbled, glancing back until Kyra touched my shoulder.

"Krell, wake up!" She snapped her fingers.

It turned out Kyra and Ivy were talking to each other while I was hypnotized watching Reyna shoot arrows.

"Kyra and I will create a bridge made of vines and ice to get us across the steel wall and back to the outsides, fine?" Ivy explained.

Two seconds later, I was already guiding the horse across the narrow bridge they had created. It wasn't steady or safe, but the horse seemed to cross it with ease. The plan worked, but Ivy and Kyra forgot to find a way to safely land in the outsides after the horse crossed their makeshift bridge.

"What now?" I yelled after the horse leaped over the wall.

"I don't... Ah!" Ivy screamed.

My heart stopped. I certainly couldn't do anything in that situation, so all my faith lay on Ivy and Kyra. Just as I hoped, vines emerged from the ground and caught the horse, saving us from an otherwise deadly fall.

"You could've at least warned me!" Reyna jumped off the mount.

"That was terrifying," Kyra panted.

"Krell!" Ivy approached me, "how did you even get this? I—"

"Turns out the lost hero gave me his suit, huh?" I laughed, wondering if I should reveal what happened with my grandfather and the mysterious girl who called herself *'the huntress,'* but I remained silent instead, "I couldn't move on without you, so I saved you."

"You're brave," Ivy grinned as if reminded of someone.

"Very brave," Reyna added.

"Glad you're not drugged anymore," I mentioned.

"Yeah, the effect wore out a long time ago," Reyna laughed it off.

"A long time?" Kyra chuckled, "when you woke up, you were still mumbling random words to us."

"I don't rememb—" Reyna tilted her head.

"You're proving her point even more," Ivy patted her shoulder, walking deeper into the woods.

"Let's just rest for a while and then plan our next move," I followed her at a slower pace.

"Come here, now!" Ivy screamed suddenly.

We glanced at the trees, watching as a creature pushed Ivy into a log and began scratching her. It looked like a trotter, but it was engulfed in dark smoke. Once I saw its glowing purple eyes, I realized what it was: a shadow.

"Ivy!" I gasped, grabbing my bow and shooting the shadow, but it didn't seem to hurt it at all.

Ivy tried using vines to sink the creature into the ground, but it wouldn't work. Kyra launched ice shards at its feet, but every attempt was unsuccessful. It was clear that the shadows were more powerful than we thought.

Kyra attempted to strangle the shadow from behind, but it grabbed her and hurled her into a nearby tree—nothing was working.

"Hey!" I yelled as loud as I could, yet the shadow wouldn't stop attacking her.

"Get… off!" Ivy dropped to the ground and curled herself into a ball before grabbing the one thing she saw beside her: a rock.

It was sharp and bright with thousands of tiny crystals on its edges, clearly different from any rock I'd seen before. As Ivy threw the rock at the shadow, something odd happened. The black and purple hue of the creature started to fade, its eyes lost their brightness, and the reddish skin of the trotter slowly came into view. After the darkness escaped the trotter's body, it galloped away, screeching in fear.

"What... the... hell..." Ivy panted, unsure if she should feel scared, relieved, or confused.

I was still processing what had happened. Had we just transformed a shadow back to normal?

"That was a shadow, right?" Kyra asked.

"What kind of rock was that?" I followed Kyra's question.

"Reyna," Ivy called out, "care to explain what this is?"

"It's a rock," Reyna explained poorly.

"Obviously, but what kind of rock?" Ivy insisted.

"It's one pulled straight out of *your* kingdom," Reyna examined the stone, "my tribe stole it from the Nature Kingdom a few years ago and threw it out here because we couldn't find a use for it."

"The *zylika*?" Mumbled Ivy, "it looks so different."

"Where can we even find this *zylkikika*?" Kyra asked.

"It was *zylika*, but—" I corrected.

"Just like Reyna said, it's found in my kingdom—or whatever's left of it," Ivy interrupted, "maybe if we go back—"

"We're not going back!" Reyna shouted, "last time we were there, shadows almost killed us."

I wanted to return to see if there was some sort of cure, but I knew it was a dangerous idea. If we went there, we could get murdered or—even worse—transformed into shadows.

"I vote to go," I said, about to raise my hand, but it would look too ridiculous.

"It's not a vote. If we go there, we're doomed," Reyna insisted,

"At least we'll die seeking justice," Kyra said.

Reyna thought about it for a moment and then sighed in agreement.

"Okay, fine!" She rolled her eyes.

"Then we'll go to the Nature Kingdom to find that rock. But what will we do next?" I asked, unsure of the plan.

"We can head to where the shadows were kept after the Shadow War ended. They were contained in a prison at the edge of the lands for over fifteen years, and I've heard rumors that that place holds the greatest forge in the lands," Kyra suggested.

All the way over there? That place was on one of the edges of the lands and, from what I'd heard, it was definitely not safe. First, we needed to travel to a shadow-infested kingdom and then visit the place they had called *home* for the last decade? It was an outrageous idea.

"Can't we find another forge?" Reyna asked.

"You'll never find one like that," Ivy replied, "if we want to create a substance that will turn all shadows back to normal, that's the place we need to go. I mean, that's if the zylika works for people too and not only trotters."

"The only thing you need to be aware of, Krell," Reyna glanced at me, "if we can turn some of the shadows back to normal, we can't do the same with the sisters and Osrov—they need to die."

I thought about it for a second. If Osrov and the sisters needed to be killed for the lands to be saved, then there was no other choice. It was either them or the entire lands.

"Alright, I get it," I gulped, "let's go now."

So we made our way to the ruins of the Nature Kingdom, not knowing what awaited us inside and not knowing if we'd even survive the journey. However, with a possible cure in our hands that could transform all shadows back to normal, we knew we were the lands' only hope.

PART VII
THE FORGE

Chapter 21

I looked at the sky. The bright sun shone on my face, eventually getting covered by gray clouds as thunder rumbled from afar. When the sun hid, I felt a drop of water on my head, dripping down my cheek and rushing to my neck. I held the edge of the canoe we were sitting in and glanced at Reyna.

"It's raining," she said.

"That's never a good sign," Kyra gulped and began to row faster, "the water could get fiercer. More creatures could... rise."

"Those are myths," Ivy laughed, "rain doesn't summon creatures."

"I thought so too until it happened to me," Kyra said, "just keep rowing."

I leaned my head out of the canoe and examined the lake, noticing many fishes swimming below us, but no monster anywhere around.

"What exactly did you see when it rained before?" I asked Kyra.

"The water started rising above shore level, and a creature jumped out of the lake. It was morphed with dozens of trotters and fishes, and... It was horrible," she explained with fright.

I looked at Reyna, remembering the creature we fought some days before. It had the legs of a trotter king, the arms of a nympho, and the faces of many dead fish and trotters. When the creature rose from the water, I recalled little drops of rain falling from the sky.

"Krell..." Reyna mumbled, "do you remember?"

"I do."

"Explain, please," Ivy interrupted.

"We fought the creature Kyra fought," I said, lowering my eyebrows.

"The one the size of a trotter king? With tiny arms and a big awful face?" She asked.

I nodded, realizing everything. Every time it rained, the creature would rise again. But last time we encountered it, Reyna impaled a dagger into its head. We shouldn't have been worried about it, right? It was dead.

"Kyra, did you kill the creature when you fought it?" I asked.

"Yes, did you?" She replied.

"We did," Reyna gulped, "that means the creature regenerates each time it rains. Crap."

The canoe started rumbling, the earth around us shook violently, and every bird flying above disappeared along with their chirping. A creature circled below, pushing the water and scaring the fish away. We stood still, hoping it wouldn't notice us, but the monster jumped out of the water and tore the canoe in half. Reyna and I crawled onto the broken boat, crashing through the waves as Ivy and Kyra climbed onto the other piece of it.

"Krell, hang on!" Reyna screamed, trying to keep the broken canoe steady.

The creature growled, diving underwater again.

"Ivy, Kyra!" I shouted at them, unsure if they could hear me, "go left! There's a waterfall ahead! Left, left!"

"He said *left,*" Ivy repeated, "help me! Use your hands!"

They tried to paddle with their hands, but the current was too fierce, and the canoe was getting dragged by it.

"Stop staring at them and help me!" Reyna commanded, pulling a grapple arrow from her quiver and hooking it around a nearby tree on shore, "now help me pull."

We fought against the current, tugging ourselves closer to land, but I was too focused on Ivy and Kyra, who were eventually pulled by the water into the mist. I hoped they wouldn't fall down the waterfall.

"Pull harder!" Reyna screeched.

Just as we thought we would make it out alive, the same morphed creature arrived. It jumped between the tree and the canoe, snapping the rope of the grapple arrow and hurling us back into the stream.

"What do we do now?" I asked in despair, observing the waterfall ahead of us.

"Brace!" Reyna screamed, closing her eyes as we both crashed down the waterfall.

The wind blew on my face. The voice inside my head told me that I was going to die, and the water hit my body so hard it felt like landing on a boulder. I truly thought that I was dead, but when I opened my eyes, I realized I was underwater, still conscious.

"Reyna!" I said, submerged in the lake.

"Come on!" Reyna yelled underwater, pulling me to the surface.

"Reyna!" I spat water after taking a deep breath, "where are Kyra and Ivy?"

Then I heard a devious growl from afar. When I turned my head toward the sound, I noticed Kyra and Ivy fighting the monster on top of a cliff—the same cliff where Reyna and I battled the creature for the first time some days before.

"Come on, we've gotta get there!" Reyna held my hand and dashed to the bottom of the cliff.

"H-how?" I asked, "I don't have my grapple hook, and I sure as hell can't climb that stone wall with my bare hands."

Reyna glanced at the cliff again, trying to find a way for me to climb it, but she didn't seem to find one.

"Oh, screw it," she hesitantly said, collecting a few rocks and sticks from the ground.

"What are you doing?" I asked.

Maybe it might have seemed smart to others, but to me, she was just picking up sticks and rocks while our friends were getting killed.

"Look, do you see this?" She showed me the items as the growling from above the cliff grew louder.

"Sticks and stones?" I asked to make sure I was seeing correctly.

"I know it may seem dumb..."

"It does," I whispered.

"But," she looked deep into my eyes, judging me, "God, what am I even doing? Look, these sticks and rocks can transform into a grapple arrow, but for me to reveal my tribe's secrets, I need you to become an elf."

"An elf? What?"

"Just repeat after me," Reyna grabbed my shoulder and closed her eyes, "I wish to become an elf."

"Really, an elf?"

"Just say it, damnit!"

"*I wish to become an elf,*" I didn't hesitate any longer after Reyna shouted at me.

"Give my life for the Zumba tribe," Reyna said

"*Give my life for the Zumba tribe,*" I repeated.

"On all highs and all lows," she continued.

"*On all highs and all lows.*"

"And watch over our kind until Kumblesgard arrives."

"*And watch over our kind until... Kombelsgard*? Or is it *Kumtelsgard*?" I had heard the word before but didn't know how to pronounce it—or its meaning.

"Just keep repeating!" Reyna opened her eyes momentarily and then shut them again, "I will never share our secrets and will stay true to our tribe."

I then repeated it one last time.

"Come on, now let's get you the grapple arrows," she said, dragging me to a nearby oak tree.

She kneeled, still holding my hand, and used the other to peel off the tree's bark, collecting it. Then she reached into her pocket, pulled out a stone, and broke it in half.

"Now, I need you to memorize these words just in case you need more of these arrows," Reyna closed her hands around the sticks and stones, "*Thalik Moriko.*"

As soon as she opened them, a grapple arrow appeared inside.

"How did you...?" I smiled in disbelief, grabbing the arrow.

"Just hold on to this—it will be useful later," Reyna ignored my question and sprinted towards the bottom of the cliff.

When we arrived at the stone wall, I pulled out my bow and placed the grapple arrow on the string, aiming at the cliff's edge before firing.

"You've climbed stuff before, right?" Reyna asked, even though we'd climbed many things together.

"Yes, but never with a bow," I laughed nervously, "I guess there's a first time for everything."

As we started climbing the cliff, Ivy and Kyra were on top of it, fighting the morphed sea creature. It looked similar to when we had last seen it, but with two more arms and a variety of new heads.

"Damn it, this thing doesn't die!" Ivy used her vines to fend off the monster, but it rolled towards her and attacked with its dozen tiny arms.

"Over here!" I arrived at the top of the cliff and shouted.

"Took you long enough," Kyra grinned.

The creature growled and charged at me. I dodged and swung my sword towards one of its many legs, chopping it off. Reyna arrived seconds later, shooting an arrow at the monster and knocking it to the ground, giving us a clear advantage.

"Now!" Reyna commanded.

I fired a couple of arrows at the creature as Reyna stabbed her dagger into its chest, and Ivy slammed her hatchet at one of its heads. Even after all of that, the creature still wouldn't die, so an ingenious idea came to mind.

"This needs to work," I reached into my pocket and pulled out the sticks and stones Reyna had handed me, "*Thalik Moriko.*"

The spell Reyna taught me worked correctly, so when I opened my hands, a grapple arrow lay inside. I shot the stringed bolt at the creature, wrapping it around its foot and tripping it to the ground.

"Reyna!" I yelled, pulling the rope and attempting to drag the creature off the cliff.

She leaped on top of the monster and continued stabbing her daggers into its chest, but it didn't seem to weaken the creature at all. That was when the grapple arrow's rope snapped and hurled me away. Although my plan hadn't worked, Ivy and Kyra had another one up their sleeve.

"Over here!" Kyra fired ice shards at the creature.

The monster screeched and charged at her when two thick vines entangled its body and launched it into a tree. Ivy hadn't realized the tree had been knocked down until it was too late. As it began falling on top of her, she had no choice but to cover her eyes and scream. Oddly enough, nothing hit her body. Instead, water fell from the sky and splattered over her.

"What the hell?" Ivy opened her eyes as water dripped down her clothes, "who did that?"

"Kyra? Was that you?" Reyna asked before I could speak.

"It only works sometimes," she gulped shyly.

"You just turned that log into water! Can you really transform something solid into a liquid?" I smiled in disbelief, "why didn't you tell us?"

"Yeah, well I guess it's not something I brag about," Kyra sighed, clearly wanting to change topics, "and it rarely works."

"Thanks, Kyra," Ivy smiled reluctantly, "it also helps getting wet once in a while. My plants need to grow."

"You need water to use your vines?" Reyna asked.

"Wait, this is a lot of information to process. Kyra can manipulate water, and you need water to use your powers?" I asked, "what are you, a human sunflower?"

"A little bit more complex, but yeah," Ivy laughed.

"Wait!" Kyra gasped and looked around, "the creature."

I recalled my sword and glanced at the forest and rocky hills, but the morphed creature was nowhere to be seen. The only thing left of it was a trail of multiple feet and arms that varied in size.

"I guess we scared it away," I sighed with relief.

"Or it stopped raining and it went back to hiding," Reyna observed the clear sky, "either way, we were pretty menacing back there, especially you, Krell."

"Yeah, you and your grapple arrows were amazing," Kyra said, "you even managed to chop one of its legs off."

"Really?" I smiled.

I proudly laughed and cracked my neck, looking at the sun. I didn't know what I was trying to observe, but I did not expect to see *the huntress* on top of a hill, staring at me. She wore the same outfit and had the same face tattoos that camouflaged her hazel eyes. I still hadn't figured out why she was following me—or who she even was—but I knew she knew something I didn't.

"There she is," I realized, sprinting up the hill.

"Who?" Ivy asked.

"Krell!" Reyna called my name after I didn't answer.

"We need to go after him, now!" Kyra grabbed Reyna's hand and started following.

I felt like a tortoise chasing after a trotter, knowing that if I ever caught up to *the huntress*, she would disappear in seconds.

"I know you're here!" I screamed, "who are you?"

Then I reached the top of the hill, glancing at *the huntress'* eyes, which were glowing in an enchantingly dismal way. Her brunette hair was tied up behind her neck, and her freckles were still visible beneath her face tattoos.

"Why are you following me?" I gulped.

"Your mother," she said with a deep and menacing voice that somehow sounded comforting at the same time.

My heart sank. Every time I hear the word *"mother,"* I was reminded of how she was brutally murdered by the shadows sixteen years ago.

"You knew my mother?" I asked, "what do you know about her?"

"You will find out soon enough," *the huntress* said, "Krell Kovner."

In the blink of an eye, the mysterious girl disappeared as if she had never existed and was just a figment of my imagination.

"Krell!" Reyna came running behind me, "what happened? Why did you run away?"

“I’ll explain on the way, but we need to leave,” I said, recalling my sword as questions swarmed around me.

But before I could answer those questions, I needed to think about what had happened and how my mother might not have been the person I always thought she was.

Chapter 22

"You will find him and you will kill him, understand?" Someone inside the Main Kingdom's castle commanded.

"Yes, sir!" Guards yelled, bursting out of the room and marching outside the palace.

The King was sending all those guards to find me, even though he had already lost hundreds in that cause. He wasn't giving up and had no plans to do so anytime soon. All he wanted was to find me and kill me, or have me spend my lifetime rotting in the kingdom's dungeons. Obsession was corrupting him—he wouldn't let me go, even though he wanted me out of his life the second I was born.

"If I may interrupt, King Henrius," said the lone guard who remained in the room: Vernan.

"Make it quick," Henrius sighed irritably.

"Why do you need us to find the boy?" Vernan asked, "you wanted him out of your life, and now that he is gone, you won't let him leave."

"Are you questioning me?" Henrius clenched his fist around a glass of wine.

"I don't care if you're the king; I can question you if I want to," Vernan replied boldly.

"He's putting us in danger by escaping the kingdom. He's trying to recruit allies and start a war that isn't even real! If he follows that path, he will get us all killed," Henrius took a deep breath and provided a reasonable explanation.

"You mean the path Queen Lorrette was following? I mean, before Osrov killed her," Vernan antagonized the King.

"Don't bring Lorrette into this, you don't have the right to say her name!" He shouted, "she tried renewing these lands, not plunging them into ruin!"

"And are you following her decision of renewing these lands, or are you setting us back into a darker, more painful age?" Vernan questioned.

"Her motives died with her," Henrius sighed, clearly annoyed.

Vernan knew what he was doing—antagonizing the king and trying to bring my mother into the conversation even if she had nothing to do with it. He knew something no one else did and was ready to share it with the kingdom.

"I was one of Lorrette's finest guards, and I knew exactly what was going on with her and you," Vernan continued, "all the times she wouldn't speak at dinner or when she would refuse to leave her room. The only times she did, a scarf covered her beautiful face."

"Vernan, what are you—?"

"You abused her, Henrius," Vernan said unemotionally, "you thought no one would ever notice, but I did. I know you'd leave bruises on her, purple eyes, cuts, and scars. Those agonizing screams coming from your room were followed by Lorrette sending me letters asking for help. I was too afraid to aid her at the time, but now... I'm not afraid of you, Henrius."

"You think I would hurt Lorette? The only person I have ever loved in my life? She was my wife! She was the only thing that made me happy!" Henrius lowered his head.

"And what exactly happened when she was pregnant the first time?" Vernan continued, "you had a beautiful girl, but right after she was born, she died."

"You know we lost the baby," Henrius said, sipping on the glass of wine, "she died weeks before being born."

"Did she?" Vernan asked, "cus' if my mind isn't playing tricks on me, I was there when the baby girl was delivered. In fact, I even remember her crying—the glare of her beautiful emerald eyes before you took her away from Lorette."

"You're a liar—I would never have hurt my daughter!"

"Really? Maybe you just killed her right after she was born. You wanted a son to become King, not a daughter," Vernan reached the peak of his accusations.

The King smashed the glass of wine on the floor, grabbed a knife from his desk, and stabbed Vernan's leg. Henrius pushed him against the wall, pressing the knife deeper into his thigh as Vernan struggled to fight back.

"So, you heard screams like this when my wife and I were in the room?" Henrius stabbed him again, "or were they even louder, like if I was killing her?"

Henrius pierced Vernan's leg two more times, and in seconds, his agonizing screams echoed across the entire kingdom.

"Don't ever talk about my wife again, do you understand?" Henrius continued stabbing, "do you understand!"

"Yes..." A weak voice escaped Vernan's mouth as Henrius withdrew the knife.

The King was covered in blood, panting as he watched Vernan leave the room in pain. He tried limping but eventually collapsed and had to crawl instead.

"Dismissed," the King said.

Although Vernan's accusations were humiliating and targeting, the King knew deep down that everything he said was true.

*****

"So, there's basically a stalker who's been following you since the day you were born, or what?" Reyna asked as we all stepped through a forest with trees that seemed to touch the sky.

We'd been walking for a few minutes and I had already explained everything about *the huntress* to everyone. I did leave out some key details, such as what she said about my mother or the fact that she recalled my sword back at the field of the Main Kingdom. I was still trying to figure out her purpose, which was why I couldn't concentrate properly.

"Krell!" Reyna snapped her fingers, "were you even listening to me?"

"Yes. *Stalker, the day I was born,*" I said, "yeah, I was listening."

"No, but what I said after that," Reyna rolled her eyes.

"Uh-huh, I listened."

I wanted to end the conversation with her, so I began walking faster. I left her behind and joined Ivy and Kyra, who were walking and talking ahead. I couldn't hear what they were saying, but it seemed like they were getting along for once—they even giggled as they spoke. However, because of everything Kyra did in the past, I knew Ivy would never forgive her.

"Oh, hey Krell," Kyra looked at me and then gave Ivy a side-eye.

They didn't say anything to each other, but the way their eyes met, Kyra might as well have said: *"Ivy, stop talking, he's here!"*

"Hey," Ivy coughed.

"How long until we get there?" I asked, breaking the awkward silence.

"It's not far," Ivy replied, "twenty minutes at most."

Kyra and Ivy didn't ask me about *the huntress*, but it seemed like they secretly whispered about it as they followed the path. Reyna was a few steps behind playing with her daggers, while I kept pondering about the mysterious stalker. I had to figure out who she was and what her connection with my mother was, but because we were in the middle of a quest, it was difficult to concentrate.

"Now you want to talk?" Reyna approached me.

"What? Oh, I never said I didn't want to talk," I laughed awkwardly.

"So then what does '*walking away while I am asking you a question*' mean?" Reyna asked sarcastically.

"Uhm..." I mumbled.

"Don't worry, it's okay to get stressed," Reyna comforted, "you are clearly distracted by something else right now, but what exactly is it? *The huntress*? The shadows?"

"It's complicated."

"Well, according to Ivy, we have twenty minutes before we arrive," Reyna insisted, "can you tell the story in twenty minutes?"

"I really don't want to talk right now. Please leave me alone," I said, trying to walk away, but Reyna persisted.

"Look, listen to me," she said as we crossed a stone bridge over a dried lake, "I know what it's like to fee—"

Suddenly, Reyna was launched away as something beneath my feet hurled me to the other side of the stone bridge. As I opened my eyes and stood up in pain, I saw a *trolem* looking at me from afar. Curiously, the bridge we were crossing had disappeared as soon as the creature arrived.

"It's a *trolem*!" Kyra screamed.

I grabbed my bow and fired an arrow at the creature's eyes, stunning it for a few seconds. The sudden appearance of the *trolem* sent us all flying in different directions. Reyna and I were knocked backwards while Ivy and Kyra managed to reach the other side of the bridge before the creature revealed itself.

"Never trust stone bridges," Reyna muttered to herself.

The *trolem* roared and used its heavy tombstone hands to strike my face, flinging me away. The monster was more than twenty feet tall, and judging by how hard its hands hit my head, it certainly felt that way.

While I was still recovering from the sudden slam, the *trolem* ripped a tree from the ground and tried to crush Reyna, but she sprinted away and hid behind a bush. She drew her bow, but couldn't aim at the creature due to the dusty wind. With no way to defend herself, she approached me, grabbed my hand, and dashed away.

"Run towards our side!" Ivy screamed from afar.

A dry river separated us, and since the stone bridge had turned out to be a *trolem*, I was certain there was no way to reach the other side. Nevertheless, Reyna had a plan in mind. She slid down the mud and sprinted to Ivy and Kyra's side, hoping they'd help us, but they fled the scene.

"Krell, Reyna!" Kyra shouted, "the water from the river is blocked by boulders! Lure the *trolem* into the river and climb to our side before we let the water flow!"

"You hear that, Reyna?" I asked.

"Yes, we need to hurry," she started climbing.

Then the *trolem* slid down to the dry riverbed and roared, galloping in our direction.

"We got the boulders out of the way—the water is flowing!" Ivy warned as I turned around and noticed the cascade making its way toward us.

Without any time to spare, I shot a grapple arrow at the *trolem's* leg, knocking it down before climbing to safety. However, the water rushed closer, and despite my best effort, the creature caught up to me before I reached land.

"Krell!" Reyna screamed, but the stream dragged me away.

Kyra tried using her water manipulation to stop the flow, but the current was too strong. I was separated from the others, rolling and tumbling underwater as the *trolem* slammed its fists on my body. It all happened so quickly and was overwhelming. After almost thirty seconds underwater, I finally reached the surface and took a deep breath before being pulled back down and hitting my head on a boulder. I lost consciousness immediately. At least if I drowned, I wouldn't feel any pain.

Chapter 23

I woke up, confused, with water still dripping from my clothes. I managed to spit out the remaining liquid, but as it fell, I realized it was going… upwards? I glanced at my tied feet and noticed I was hanging upside down.

"You finally woke up," someone said, sitting on a bench in front of me.

Although I was head over heels, I could see the features of the girl who spoke. She had freckles and short red hair, similar to Ivy's. Her clothes resembled those of a light elf from the Nature Kingdom, and after noticing her pointy ears, I knew she was one of them. That could've meant she was a survivor of the shadow attack—she could've been willing to help us with our quest!

"Help me, my head hurts," I coughed.

"So did the heads of all the people your father killed," she approached me.

Nope. She definitely wasn't willing to help.

"Oh, please, I can explain," I begged, reaching for the rope tied to my foot.

"I-it's okay," I heard a familiar voice behind the girl.

When the blurry figure crept closer, I saw him. It was the light elf Reyna and I encountered in a shack back at the Nature Kingdom. I remembered how Reyna chased him around his home, attempting to murder him, and how the poor guy ran around and screamed for help. I was surprised that such a timid person could survive the shadow attack.

"Are you serious, Kharum?" The girl with freckles asked, "his father killed our grandfather."

"Yuh-yes, and h-he was ah-ah-also the one who told muh-me about the sh-shadows in the first p-place," the elf—supposedly named Kharum—said, "y-you remember, sister?

"Damn it," Kharum's sister muttered as she cut the rope hanging me upside down.

I collapsed to the ground and immediately crawled away, getting back on my feet with caution. I examined Kharum, who had different clothes from when I last saw him—he wore a brown robe that reached his feet and held a stick to defend himself. His sister—unlike her brother—wore rural clothes common amongst elves.

"You survived?" I asked.

"Yuh-yes," Kharum stuttered.

"Why are we even protecting him?" Kharum's sister rolled her eyes.

"Look, I know you can't trust me because of all the things my father did, but I swear I'm different," I explained.

"Isn't that what they all say?" The girl sarcastically smiled.

"Ivory!" Kharum shouted in fright, "h-he is not a threat!"

Ivory frowned with disgust, clearly skeptical. I didn't want to say anything else—afraid she would try to kill me—but even when I stood silent, her hazel eyes menacingly stared at me as her scarlet hair reflected the sun into my face.

"We won't be friends, but at the moment, there is no reason for me to antagonize you," Ivory hesitantly said, "come, we'll show you our camp."

She walked away, followed by her brother, who asked me a few questions to ensure I was doing alright. When Ivory mentioned "*camp*," I assumed she meant a single tent with two small beds for Kharum and her to sleep in, but as I got closer, I was pleasantly surprised. There was a tent, followed by another, and then dozens more behind it. At least thirty tents were scattered across the grass. Several light elves prepared food, others were playing games with the children, and the rest were sleeping inside their open tents. It didn't take me long to realize I was in the remnants of the Nature Kingdom after it had been destroyed by the shadows. I could see the destroyed castle in the distance and the torn shacks of the poor villagers of the kingdom. Although the home of the light elves was destroyed, they were still happily living in the camp, accepting a new reality.

"This is our kingdom," Ivory introduced, "at least what's left of it."

"A-after the Quee-Queen died, we tried to rebuild the kingdom. D-despite this not being much, w-we tried to make it b-better for the ch-children," Kharum said.

"The Queen? You mean *Queen Ivy*?" I asked.

"Yes," Kharum said on the verge of tears.

"She's alive," I revealed, "after the shadow attack, she escaped the kingdom with us. I was back with her and Reyna—you remember Reyna, don't you?"

For some reason I didn't want to mention that Kyra was traveling with us too. After the Trotter War, light elves and the Frost Queen weren't on the best of terms.

"She's alive?" Ivory smiled, "Kharum, we need to tell the others!"

"Th-th-that is great new-news!" Kharum leaped with joy.

"Maybe we can go look for her," I suggested.

"Later," said Ivory, "if you want to come to our camp, do so now. Eat something, restock, whatever you need. *Not* as friends though! I still can't forgive you for everything your father's done."

"Fair enough. Take me to your camp."

"There i-is a troffe tent r-right over there," Kharum stuttered, pointing at a nearby tent with smoke coming out of a small chimney on top of it, "they sell the b-best bread i-in th-the whole kingdom, trust me."

"Huh, I haven't had troffe in months," I smiled, already tasting the sweet and hot liquid of the troffe grains—I really liked troffe.

Kharum led me to the tent and unzipped it while Ivory kept glancing at me with a malign frown. The inside of the tent looked more like a shack rather than one of a camp, mainly because of all the chairs and tables, as well as the large bar counter. There was a man behind that counter who greeted me with strange hand signs.

"This is Erin," Ivory introduced, "if anyone from the kingdom should have survived the attack—apart from the Queen—it's him. He's the best troffe-maker these lands have ever seen, but he's also mute and deaf. No one is here to translate, so good luck talking to him."

He kept flinging his hands in a strange manner that I couldn't understand. Eventually, he sighed and made the sign of a crown atop his head.

"Oh, yes, I'm the Prince," I realized what he meant.

Instead of being startled by the fact that my father was Henrius, Erin simply gave a thumb-up and smiled, minding his own business. Overall, Erin seemed like a nice person, and with his long beard reaching the floor, dirty clothes, and bald head, he looked exactly how I imagined troffe-maker.

"Now," Ivory said, sitting in the chair next to me and lowering the cup of troffe I was drinking, "what do you know about the shadows?"

"They escaped, somehow," I explained vaguely, "they are targeting the weaker kingdoms before finally attacking the main one."

"Weaker kingdoms," Ivory laughed, "it's not our fault your father made us weak."

"He's not my father," I said, "he is, but we're so different... I can't even consider him a part of my family."

"He's still your dad, and he's still the man who murdered our grandfather," Ivory slammed her hands on the table.

"Muh-maybe we're being too r-rough on him," Kharum said.

"You really want to minimize all the pain he put us through?" Ivory shouted, knowing Erin couldn't hear her, "you are insane, Kharum."

She grunted and barged out of the tent, clearly infuriated. I sighed and rolled my eyes, wondering if people would ever stop seeing me as the son of a corrupt king and actually notice my true qualities.

"I'm sorry about her," Kharum managed to stop stuttering once Ivory left the tent, "she might no-not realize you're also a normal person like us."

"Yeah, many people tend to think that," I replied with a forced chuckle.

I took one last sip of troffe before hearing screams and gasps from outside the tent. Kharum and I exchanged glances, nodding and standing up from our chairs. I could hear Ivory yelling in excitement, with all the other villagers unzipping their tents and dashing to the camp's entrance. I didn't know what I was anticipating, but I certainly didn't expect to see Ivy, Kyra, and Reyna.

"You're alive, my Queen," Ivory smiled.

"And you are too, I'm glad," Ivy was relieved, and became even more excited when she saw me and screamed, "Krell!"

Even though Ivy was the first to notice me, Reyna reached and hugged me before she could. I hesitated for a second but eventually embraced her back.

"I'm so glad you're safe," Reyna laughed, "I thought you had drowned!"

"Yes, we luckily suh-saved him!" Kharum said.

"Oh! Light elf..." Reyna was confused, "out of all the people in the kingdom, you were the least likely to survive."

"That's all thanks to his big sister," Ivory said, scratching Kharum's head.

"On-only one year older!"

"A lot can happen in a year."

"Are you okay, Krell?" Kyra asked, "do you have anything broken?"

"I'm fine, Kyra."

"I tried freezing the water, but my powers couldn't do *that* much," she laughed, not thinking much of it.

That was when the ambiance changed. Everyone's expressions shifted; Kharum's smile faded, and Ivory frowned as gasps and murmurs spread among the villagers. Before Kyra could ask what was happening, Ivory reached into her pocket and pulled out a kitchen knife. As she approached to stab Kyra, Kyra raised her hands and shot ice shards to the ground, startling Ivory and all the other light elves nearby. Everyone drew their weapons and waited for Ivy's signal to slaughter the Frost Queen.

"She's good—she's with me!" Ivy stepped forward and yelled.

"Traitor!"

"Get back to your kingdom!"

"Go to hell, witch!"

Sadly, all the light elves were shouting those words at Kyra, who was standing with a staggering look, taking it all in. It was obvious that people from the Nature Kingdom wouldn't forget what happened in the Trotter War. To be honest, if I were one of them, I wouldn't forgive Kyra either.

"Why don't you answer for your crimes, coward!" Ivory screamed.

"Listen to me!" Ivy yelled, shaking nearby plants, "Kyra has done a lot of bad things, but now is not the time to confront her about it. There are shadows everywhere, infesting the remaining kingdoms, and we need to focus on them—not on Kyra! She's changed."

Kyra smiled back at Ivy when she finished speaking. The whole time they were traveling together, it seemed like they were holding a grudge against each other, but Ivy was sincere with her words—she meant what she said.

"Now, can someone please help us find any zylika that might've remained after the attack?" Ivy sighed, out of breath.

"Yes, my Queen," the light elves replied without hesitation and dashed away in search of the zylika.

The villagers would take a long time scavenging, so I glanced back at the others and asked what we should do in the meantime.

"We have some free time," Reyna agreed, "do you want to rest a bit?"

"There's a troffe tent nearby," I suggested.

"Yes, please!" Ivy immediately replied.

"My mom used to make troffe when I was younger," Kyra said with a forced smile, "let's go there."

When we entered the tent where they served troffe, I introduced everyone to Erin. Ivy and Kyra already knew him, but Reyna also got along with him pretty well—Erin even taught her how to cuss in sign language. We spent more than fifteen minutes drinking troffe and discussing various topics, but one conversation that caught my attention was about Kyra's father and my father being good friends. Eventually, their friendship fell apart, and a few months later, her father was murdered. When I tried asking about her mother, Kyra remained silent, unwilling to talk about her.

Ivy seemed aware of the issue between Kyra and her mother, so she changed the subject and began telling us how they used the novo juice for *fun.* I didn't understand until Kyra told her to stop, and they both laughed. From that, I had a pretty good idea of what they were talking about.

"Alright, alright, but..." Ivy said, laughing so hard that she could barely speak, "Kyra, do you remember that one time we got trapped in the Ah'Lah'Rra tribe camp?"

Kyra laughed so hard she almost fell from her chair. Erin was visibly scared just by watching them—if I were him, I would've thought they were screaming for help and not from laughter.

"I remember the leader from that tribe let us go after just ten minutes because he was so annoyed," Kyra cried with laughter.

"Who is this Allah-whatever tribe?" I chuckled, unable to keep a straight face with Kyra and Ivy wheezing uncontrollably by my side.

"A very dangerous tribe we're neighbors with," Reyna explained, "but wait, you survived them?"

"Yes," Ivy stopped laughing but kept smiling, "they said they were going to kill us and sell us on the black market, but because of so much crying and begging, they felt bad for us and let us go."

"They got annoyed; they didn't feel bad," Kyra corrected, "it's not like that tribe has any humanity left."

"Wait, is that the tribe that killed three elves and threw their bodies into the Zumba tribe camp as a warning?" I asked.

I had heard that story at least a dozen times when I was thirteen, but I never really thought much of it. I couldn't imagine Reyna having to experience all that—it must have been horrible.

"Yes, that happened. It wasn't nice, trust me," Reyna said, taking one last sip from her cup, "you need to be careful with those guys. If you walk near their camp, they'll bash your head in with a wooden plank."

"Yeah, I think I'm done hearing these stories," I sighed, "I want to keep the image of the outsides as beautiful, not some death trap."

"Yeah, you won't keep that image for long," Reyna chuckled and stood up, "now let's actually see if the light elves have the zylika ready for us."

When Reyna stormed out of the tent, dozens of villagers were already waiting outside with the precious little rock in hand. It looked like they had been waiting out there for a long time.

"Woah," said Ivy, "how long have you been out here?"

"We didn't want to enter because of your fight with the Frost Queen," one of the elves said, "we heard screaming and yelling. Hope you won, my Queen!"

"Oh..." Ivy glanced at Kyra and laughed, "we weren't fighting, don't worry. Now, can everyone please hand us the zylika?"

Immediately, the elves crowded us, throwing the rocks at our faces and screaming whenever their Queen accepted their gifts.

"Thank you," Ivy greeted, "thank you all."

That was when I heard a high-pitched voice below my shoulder. As I tilted my head, I noticed a little girl standing beside me with one of the zylika rocks tightly squeezed in her hand. She looked no older than eight years old and had pointy ears, a ponytail, and a blue dress. She seemed excited to talk to me as if I was a hero of hers.

"I've had this rock since I was a baby, but if you need it, here you have it," she said, handing it to me.

"Oh, don't worry," I replied, trying to speak carefully as it was the first time I ever interacted with a child, "you can keep it."

"But you said you needed it," she chuckled, "you need it more than I do."

"I think we have plenty already," I knelt, "but I have something perfect for you."

I reached into my pocket, grabbing the plushie I picked up back at the castle of the Main Kingdom. It was green—resembling a dog—and the buttons on its eyes made me realize it was the perfect gift for the little girl.

"It's great!" She hugged me, "thank you."

She ran back into her tent with the plushie in hand, giggling as she showed off her new toy to everyone. Although the shadows had destroyed her kingdom, there was still happiness within her. With that simple, kind action, I hoped I brightened the little girl's day.

"Krell," Reyna grabbed my hand and pulled me out of the crowd, "we need to go to the forge now."

"Can't we stay here a little longer?" I said, but she kept pulling me aside abruptly.

"No time to lose," she led me out of the crowd.

"Wait!" Ivory called our name from across the camp with Kharum by her side, "you can't get there on foot."

Ivy accepted the last gift from the villagers and stepped away from the multitude as Ivory approached us. I didn't know why, but I flinched each time she walked in my direction—the look on her face made it seem as if she was going to stab me.

"So, what's your idea then?" Ivy asked.

"You remember that flying serpent we gifted you some years ago? I think his name was Sersh. Anyway, his brother is not far from here. He's a *shackflyer* named Seroph," Ivory explained.

Yes! We weren't going on foot! That was probably the greatest news I had heard all day. Even better, I actually knew what a *shackflyer* was, so Reyna didn't have to explain it to me.

"What is a *shackflyer*?" Kyra asked.

"A flying serpent that has a shack on its back," Ivy explained before I could.

"Great!" Reyna smiled, "we can rest without wasting any time."

Ivory led us towards her house, which wasn't even inside the kingdom. She lived on the outskirts of the Nature Kingdom and would enter it to visit her brother every once in a while. Her home was very big, mainly because of the enormous backyard, which housed sheep, chickens, reptiles, and all sorts of homegrown plants. On one corner of the yard was the *shackflyer*, sleeping beside the pine trees surrounding Ivory's home. The shack on his back was also a pleasant surprise—it was bigger than the houses from the Main Kingdom. The cabin had two floors and was made out of pristine wood.

"You've kept good care of him," Ivy laughed.

"Trust me, I have," Ivory said, raising her hand and guiding the *shackflyer* our way.

"What was his name again?" I asked.

"Seroph," Ivory replied.

"And his brother's Sersh, right?" I asked, "he was a nice creature."

"*Was?* Did he die, Ivy?" Ivory gasped.

"Sadly," she bit her lip, "but he lived a good life."

"Guess that's what happens when you become friends with the Prince," Ivory grunted, "everyone around you dies."

All the light elves who handed us the zylika some minutes before were following us the entire time to Ivory's house. I wanted to say something to them, but first I had to consult with Reyna.

"Hey," I whispered to her.

"It's pretty cool, right?" Reyna giggled as the *shackflyer* walked closer, "I've wanted to fly one of these since I was a little girl."

"Yes, me too," I gulped, "but I wanted to ask you something."

"What is it?" We exchanged glances—I never noticed before, but similar to her clothes, her eyes were also green.

"Don't you think these people should travel to the Zumba tribe camp?" I asked, "so they can get food, beds, and weapons. They can wait there while we go to the forge."

"That's a good idea," Reyna replied.

"Everyone," I glanced back at the villagers and cleared my throat, "this place is dangerous. While it may be your home, you are safer leaving here and traveling to the Zumba tribe camp."

That made some laugh, others frown, and most smile.

"You can go through the river, find provisions, restock, get weapons—whatever you need," I added.

The villagers didn't hesitate. They sprinted to their tents and packed the necessary items to travel to their new temporary home while Ivy and Kyra looked at each other and chuckled.

"You can take Seroph—I'll go pack," Ivory walked away, "but remember, Prince, I'm doing this for my safety, not because you've become my ruler."

Ivory seemed sweet on the inside but clearly couldn't get over the fact that I was the Prince of the Main Kingdom. I just wished she could let it all behind—maybe we could become friends someday.

"Ready to actually rest in a bed after everything we've been through?" Reyna held my hand and guided me inside the shack.

"Glad to see a real one for the first time in my life," I forced a chuckle, "my bed at the castle was just a piece of rotten wood."

"Huh, then it'll be even better for you," Reyna said as we stepped inside.

The cabin was quite spacious, with an ample living room and a set of stairs leading to a couple of bedrooms on the second floor. Ivy and Kyra didn't even check the place out; they ran to the only room on the first floor, closing the door behind them. Reyna and I stayed in the kitchen, seeking some entertainment.

"Are you hungry?" I asked her.

"The two troffe cups were enough for me."

"Very well."

I was about to head up the stairs to explore what the shack had to offer, but Reyna grabbed my arm and handed me something from the table. It was a note that read:

> Hello everyone. My sister told me to write this note while she looks for things but i don't know if there will be enough ink for me to write. Our mother left for supplies and food because this winter has been cruel to us. ~~Dad stopped moving and breathing a few hours ago because he gave all the food to us~~. My fingertips are already freezing and the windows are stuck with ice.
>
> P.D. My sister told me that the letter wasn't good and she is now making another. I'm starving and I just hope the ice melts before anything worse happens.

"Oh," I sighed after reading.

"Oh," Reyna repeated, "who knows what happened to the kids."

"Who knows if they're even alive," I put the note down and looked at Reyna.

Then it hit me. Two kids—the eldest a girl and the youngest a timid boy. The kids freezing inside the *shackflyer* were Ivory and Kharum. Both their parents died in the chilling breezes of the Frost Kingdom many years ago.

"Are we thinking the same thing?" Reyna asked.

"It must've been hell for them," I said.

"Frozen hell," Reyna shook her head.

While we were examining the note and discussing everything Kharum and Ivory went through, Ivy and Kyra were sitting inside the master bedroom of the shack. Ivy lay on her back, lost in her thoughts as Kyra walked in circles, pondering what to say.

"So..." Kyra played with her hands, clearly nervous, "the *shackflyer* is really big."

"Why did you do it?" Ivy asked as Kyra lowered her head, "why did you start it?"

"I guess this talk was inevitable," Kyra lay beside her, "and I don't know what to even answer."

"The truth," Ivy said.

"I didn't have another choice," Kyra said, closing her eyes, "the Trotter God was going to destroy my whole kingdom if I didn't—"

"So you decided to destroy mine?" Ivy replied, sitting on the bed, "my mother died, Kyra! You were the reason she was killed."

They were discussing the Trotter War—how Kyra stole an artifact from the Trotter God and blamed it on Ivy, igniting a big conflict between kingdoms. Ivy's mother was one of the many casualties in the battle.

"Ivy, I know that it is hard to believe me after everything I have done, but I've changed," Kyra held her hand.

"And it hurts me so much," Ivy cried, "because after all you've done... you're right—you've changed. I can't force myself to dislike you because you've become a good person, Kyra."

"You're also a good person, Ivy," Kyra said on the verge of tears, "and—if you're ready—I think we could become friends again."

"I want to forgive you—I really do," Ivy hesitated, "but I don't think I can."

Kyra nodded and shed a few tears.

"But I'd like to try," Iv's voice trembled.

"That would be nice," Kyra smiled, standing up and walking out of the room, "I'm going to get some sleep—thank you."

Then she closed the door behind her. Ivy lay on the bed, trying to close her eyes and sleep, but as she rested, two words echoed inside her head, flooding her mind:

Thank you.

Chapter 24

Reyna and I began to explore the cabin. The *shackflyer* had departed moments before, and we had already seen most of what the place had to offer. We discovered three bedrooms on the second floor, a small dining room, and a tiny, claustrophobic basement where provisions were stored. That place was so terrifying that I had no intention of visiting it again.

The only room left to discover was the attic, located at the top of a spiral staircase and beyond a hatch. When we arrived, we found boxes full of wrappings, wood, and other building materials. Reyna approached one of them and grabbed a fresh apple.

"I've missed apples so much," Reyna said, taking a bite, "we used to have them every day back at my camp."

"In the Main Kingdom we'd buy them at *Uncle Bob's*," I recalled.

I didn't miss the arguments with my father or the way the guards would beat me up from time to time, but I missed the people from the kingdom. There was an elderly woman named Urbosa who would always gift me some of the apples that grew in her garden.

"Mmh!" Reyna said with a chunk of apple in her mouth, "I have an idea."

She smirked, grabbed another apple from the box, and pulled an arrow from her quiver. Doing something that seemed very stupid to me, she impaled the fruit with the arrow's tip.

"What are you going to do? Target practice?" I asked.

"Even better," she said, gently placing her head against the wall and closing her eyes, "I'm going to count to ten. You will hide, and if the apple hits you, you lose."

"You do have a lot of energy," I chuckled, opening the hatch to leave the attic.

"One, two, three..." She started counting as I scouted for a possible hiding spot.

After dashing down the spiral stairs, I turned right and entered one of the *shackflyer's* bedrooms. Before crawling under the bed, an idea came to mind, so I tossed my sword into the room's closet.

"Ready or not, here I come," Reyna finished counting and ran directly to the room where I was hiding in.

Falling for my trick, Reyna approached the closet after noticing my sword. As she opened the sliding door, I crawled out from under the bed and tackled her to the floor. She didn't hesitate and shot the apple-attached arrow at my chest.

"You lose," she laughed.

"But I got you first!" I complained.

"In hide and seek, you need to hide, not attack," Reyna said, lying on the floor, sighing and closing her eyes.

"Alright, but you have to admit that putting the sword beside the closet was a great trick," I said.

"It was *fine*."

"*Fine*? You fell for it!"

"And the apple still hit you," Reyna teased.

I tried standing up so we could return to the attic and play another round of the hiding game, but as I pushed myself up from the floor, Reyna grabbed my hand and pulled me back down.

"Stay," she simply said.

I didn't mind talking for a few more minutes, so I lay down and looked at Reyna, wondering what she wanted to do.

"It'll take some time for the *shackflyer* to arrive at the forge," Reyna said, "why don't we talk for a while? Ask me something."

"Like what?" I tilted my head.

"Anything."

"What's your favorite color?" Was the first thing that came to mind.

"Not that, dumbass. I want you to ask questions about the lands, not my favorite color!" Reyna giggled, "which is green, by the way."

Because Reyna didn't want to talk about her favorite color, I tried switching topics. But what should I have asked? There were thousands of questions I had about the tribes on the outsides, the kingdoms, the lands, and what lay *beyond* them. So, I chose the one I was most curious about.

"Kumblesgard," I decided, "what is it?"

"Great question," Reyna said, taking a deep breath as she thought of a definition, "it's the death of the lands."

"What?" My smile faded, "I thought it was some person or mythical creature, not an event."

"Yeah, that was the same reaction I had when I first heard of it," Reyna sighed, "there are so many prophecies of Kumblesgard, and supposedly, they will all come true one day. No one knows when or how, but the lands will eventually die."

"I just hope I'm dead by the time it happens," I chuckled.

"Based on my tribe's beliefs, every single one of us will experience Kumblesgard. You know, because we believe in reincarnation," Reyna explained, "but even if reincarnation doesn't exist, the lands below, above, and between will all cease to exist."

"What?" I asked, "what do you mean by lands below, above, and between?"

"Oh my... You don't know about the different lands?" Reyna gasped, "you've been living locked away indeed."

"Tell me!" I laughed, "what is it?"

"All of us live in the lands above," Reyna said, "but there are different lands that exist beyond the seas. Legends say there are secret caverns leading to the lands between, lying under our feet. No one has ever explored that place, but supposedly, if you enter it, you can never escape. And the lands below are... well, below. Different civilizations live there, and they helped the lands above during the last Kumblesgard."

"Last?"

"Kumblesgard has happened before—around 600 years ago. The civilization back then fended off the echoes and evaded the death of the lands, but it was said to be a mere warning for what was to come in the future."

We kept talking about Kumblesgard for some minutes, and that simple conversation made me realize how little my father had taught me as a child. I learned that the creatures who started Kumblesgard were called *echoes*, and they were pure evil created by the Gods with the purpose of ceasing life in the lands. After the lengthy battle of Kumblesgard, the lands managed to trap the echoes far from our reach. Although no one knew where the creatures were held, there were rumors that they lay beneath the land's volcano, where the Fire Kingdom was located.

"What else?" Reyna asked after explaining everything about Kumblesgard.

"The different tribes," I replied quickly, "the tribes around the lands."

"If I were to mention every single tribe in the lands we'd be here all day," she chuckled, "but fine, I'll talk about the main ones."

She told me a lot of details about the Zumba tribe, focusing mainly on how they hid from the King when the elvish revolution happened. Reyna said that when it occurred, her mom was pregnant with her, so they had to flee to the outsides, which were much more dangerous at that time. They sought Renna—the witch—who seemed to be a powerful sorcerer capable of curing everything and everyone. Renna had the ability to hide people's physical traits. She cast a spell on Reyna's tribe so they could sneak into the Main Kingdom once again as light elves—the dark elves were thought to be extinct from that moment on. Reyna briefly mentioned the Quora tribe, which was a peaceful group allied with the Zumbas. The last tribe she mentioned was the Ah'Lah'Rra, which I knew well because of the frightening stories they told us back in the Main Kingdom. As Reyna delved deeper into that subject, her eyes lost their spark.

"So, you've heard the story of the boys murdered by the Ah'Lah'Rra, right?" She asked, unsure if she wanted to continue discussing them, "they were some kids from my tribe who were scouting the outsides and got captured by the murderous tribe. They tortured them for hours before killing them and sending their remains back to our home. The tribe's actions only infuriated my mother, who set their camp on fire afterward. If you remember the thieves back at the Frost Kingdom, they were members of the Ah'Lah'Rra."

"Reyna, I'm sorry to interrupt, but why did your mother seek revenge and not the parents of the murdered boys?" I asked

"Because..." Reyna gulped.

She frowned, tilting her head and sighing. Tears rushed down her cheeks, indicating it was a sensitive topic.

"They were my brothers," Reyna said firmy.

"Oh," I gasped.

Reyna's brothers were killed by the Ah'Lah'Rra.

"It was so long ago, I don't know why I'm even crying," Reyna wiped her tears, "my mother didn't speak to me for two whole years after it happened."

"Why? It wasn't your fault."

"But it was," Reyna sighed, "I was being such a brat and ran away from the camp. My brothers had to chase me through the outsides, but the Ah'Lah'Rra caught up to them eventually."

"I'm so sorry," I said, grabbing her shoulder for comfort, "but still, you didn't know what would happen. It certainly isn't a reason for your mother to treat you like crap."

"Yet she still did so," Reyna sobbed, "I still remember the first time she spoke to me after the accident. She was drunk, and I was walking her back to her tent when snapped at me and said: '*I don't want to see your goddamn face ever again.*' And after that, she said something I'll never forget."

"What did she say?" I asked curiously.

"I don't want to repeat it, but it's the reason why I..." Reyna tried to tell me something, but couldn't, "nothing."

I wanted to know what she was talking about but didn't want to pressure her, so I stood silent instead.

"I've never told this to anyone, but..." Reyna hesitated for a moment, "sometimes—after everything my mother did to me—I guess I'm glad she's gone."

I didn't know what to say, but after a moment of silence, the only words that crossed my mind exited my mouth.

"Okay," I awkwardly said.

Reyna let out a small sigh before standing up and storming away. While it might have seemed disrespectful how she rushed out of the room without warning, I completely understood her. But before she could exit the room, I called her name.

"Reyna, wait," I said as she turned around and sobbed, "if I were you, I'd be glad she's gone too."

Chapter 25

After Reyna walked out of the room, I lay on the bed. It had a red quilt, a pristine white mattress, and was the size of a child's bed, but even with my feet dangling, I still had the greatest sleep of my life. The warm sheets wrapped around my body, the squishy, soft pillow below my head, and the sound of the *shackflyer* dashing through the clouds were exactly how I pictured paradise.

When I woke up, I realized we weren't soaring through the sky anymore, and with the dark mist outside the window, I was certain we had arrived at the forge. I stood up, recalled my sword, and trotted downstairs, where I was greeted by Reyna, Ivy, and Kyra gathered in the living room.

"Look who's decided to join us," Kyra laughed.

"Why didn't you wake me up if we had already landed?" I yawned.

"We tried," Reyna said.

"Trust me, we really did," Ivy chuckled, "but now that you're awake, I think we're ready to get out of the house and forge a cure for the shadows."

"Do you have the zylika ready?" I asked, adjusting my hood and preparing myself.

"We have everything we need," Ivy took a deep breath.

As we made our way to the shack's front door, I kept glancing back at Reyna, wondering if she would say something regarding what happened a couple of hours earlier. It was obvious she didn't want to discuss it, but I was still thinking about the conversation.

Then Ivy swung open the door, blowing a mystical wind in our direction and revealing the destruction around us. Darkness spread across the land, consuming the rotten trees, killing the grass, and decaying every house nearby. I squinted and stared into the distance, catching a quick glimpse of the forging table from afar. Swords and hammers were laid on its sides, lava bubbled from inside, and a gloomy substance crawled over it. If I were to guess, we would probably have to place our weapons in the forge and melt the zylika for it to work.

"God," I mumbled as the flying burnt grass obstructed my view.

"It's worse than I ever imagined," Kyra gulped, holding a sword made of ice that she probably crafted herself.

"Then let's get our weapons forged before any shadows try to stop us," Ivy said, walking briskly.

I was afraid to even move. My shoes got stuck in the goo on the ground, making each step harder than the last. I wanted it to be over as quickly as possible.

"When we reach the forge, we use the zylika and leave," Reyna said with a disgusted look on her face, "and if any shadows appear, we get the hell out of here."

I nodded, but truly, if any shadows appeared, it would only increase my motivation to forge a cure for them. Then I felt a strange sensation down my spine—a hunch. I didn't know what was happening, but I sensed something creeping closer… a dark entity…

"Wait," I stopped and focused.

Then, in my peripheral vision, I saw an arrow flying in my direction. I closed my eyes and caught the projectile with my right hand, breaking it in half as I glanced around and shouted in fear. We were under attack—but not by any simple human. We were being attacked by shadow elves.

"Run to the forge!" Reyna yelled in panic, trying to walk faster, but her feet sank into the goo with each step.

The shadows sprinted towards us. Trotters, trolems, and humans dashed out of the woods, all consumed by darkness.

"Both of you, run to the forge!" Ivy drew her hatchet and handed it to me, "Kyra, give your weapon to Reyna and stay with me to slow the shadows down."

"Ivy…" I began.

"Shut up and run!" She commanded.

"Please don't break it," Kyra handed her sword to Reyna, "and run as fast as you can. I don't know how long we can slow them down."

"Reyna! We need to go," I yelled.

We sprinted to the forge, which was less than a hundred feet away, but because of the sticky substance on the ground, it made it feel like it would take hours to arrive. Ivy's heavy hatchet wrapped around my arms definitely wasn't helping—I was even slower than before.

"Krell, focus and run!" Reyna panted.

I kept hurrying, but made little progress. I tried jumping, and although I thought it was a great idea, I tripped and collapsed on the ground, splattering the goo all over my face.

"You've got to be kidding me," Reyna sighed, pulling my head out of the substance and helping me up, "now, run."

"Thanks," I sighed with relief, but she was already rushing away by the time I spoke.

We were getting closer to the forge, and just as my hope peaked, a shadow elf tackled me to the ground and began choking me.

"Get off of him!" Reyna stabbed the shadow with Kyra's frozen sword, pushing it away. Although a fatal strike like that might've killed any other living creature, the shadow remained intact. We desperately needed the zylika.

"Run!" Reyna yelled, "run to the forge and take this."

She handed me her daggers, her bow, and Kyra's sword, adding twenty pounds to the already heavy load I was carrying. I was glad she at least kept her quiver because I couldn't handle any more weight.

Finally—without believing my own eyes—I arrived at the forge in a hurry, dropping all the weapons to the ground and panting heavily before focusing on crafting a cure.

"Alright, which one first?" I asked myself.

When I tried placing a weapon inside the forging table, I noticed that it didn't fit. There was something wrong with the forge—no sword or dagger could fit inside. I took the zylika rock out of my pocket and placed it on a little emblem in the center of the stone table, wondering what would happen.

"It's not meant for weapons," I mumbled.

After a few seconds, a strange liquid emerged from the bottom of the forging table. In a large flask I had in my pouch, I stored the fluid, grabbing another zylika and tossing it inside the forge.

Then I realized what I had to do. I tilted the flask and spilled a single drop onto my sword. When the weapon started to glow, I knew exactly what had happened—my sword had absorbed the zylika's power. After melting several rocks and storing them in flasks, I knew it was enough. I picked up the remaining weapons and strengthened them with the substance—even my own bowstring gleamed after the liquid was spilled on it.

For the first time in my life, I felt powerful, knowing I finally had a chance against the shadows. All fear vanished when I sprinted towards the shadow attacking Reyna and stabbed its chest. I didn't glance back to see if the darkness had faded away—I just kept walking.

"Your weapons are over there," I said.

Reyna stared at me for a few seconds before dashing to the forge and picking her zylika-engulfed weapons. A shadow trotter charged at me, but with one simple gash from my sword, I sliced it from its shoulder to its waist. I knew trotters weren't living creatures, so it felt satisfying to kill them in brutal ways that Reyna and Ivy would normally enjoy. Although I liked doing it, I would never do the same to living creatures—not to mention people...

"Krell!" Ivy screeched, fending off the shadows, "please tell me our weapons are ready."

"Go to the forge," I replied, "I've cleared a path for you."

"Do you really think you can handle all of them?" Kyra asked, backing away from the shadows.

"Don't worry, I can," I continued walking towards the horde.

Two shadow elves approached, so I shot arrows at their legs, incapacitated them. A trotter sneaked up behind me and knocked me to the ground, but I recalled my sword and slashed its neck.

"Have you ever seen him like this?" Kyra asked Reyna as they picked up their weapons from the forge.

"No," she replied, looking at me oddly, "never."

But I wasn't done. I flung my sword at five trotters and hit them all in the chest—even managing to cut one in half. More shadows were coming, but I struck them all with my sword, chopping up trotters in the process. That was until I heard a roar in the distance and was greeted by a shadow trotter king rushing my way.

I felt the rage again. At that point you might have already known what I was talking about, but every time I felt it, it came with a different sensation. The shadow within me wasn't coming out by accident—I was releasing it for mere pleasure. After murdering all the remaining trotters, I was consumed by wrath and wanted to explore the limits of what my abilities could do. What better way to do so than murdering a trotter king?

I screamed as hard as I could, feeling my burning skin and raging temper. The shadow within me emerged. I stabbed my sword into the ground and furiously glanced at the trotter king. I didn't know what I was attempting to do as if I wasn't controlling my body anymore. I drove my sword deeper into the ground, and an explosive wave blasted through the land, killing the trotter king and any other shadows nearby.

When my body transformed back to normal, all I could do was stare blindly at the slaughter surrounding me—the slaughter I had created. While it felt satisfying to release my wrath on those shadows, guilt consumed me afterward. The worst part was that Reyna, Ivy, and Kyra were all watching from afar.

"What the..." Kyra mumbled at a loss of words.

"Kyra, we can explain," Ivy began but was interrupted.

"You were a shadow this whole time and didn't care to mention it to us?" Kyra approached me and crossed her arms, "huh? I mean, he didn't tell us, right?"

"They knew, but I hadn't told you yet," I gulped.

"You all knew?" Kyra asked, shaking her head, "and you didn't even mention it? Unbelievable."

"Kyra, you don't understand. I know it is hard to process, but—" Reyna tried calming her.

"So what? We've been killing your species this whole time, Krell?" Kyra interrupted, "are you really on this quest to stop the war, or is there something else you're not telling us?"

"Kyra," I took a deep breath before speaking, "I don't know what is going on with the dark magic inside of me. I can't turn you into a shadow if that's what you're worried about."

"I'm not worried about turning into a shadow; I'm worried about what is happening to you!" She cried, "what is it? Are you immune? Can you use dark magic in your defense? I don't understand."

"As far as I'm concerned, no shadow has ever transformed me into one of them," I said, "but there is something my mother and father didn't tell me."

"Krell," Reyna touched my shoulder, "what exactly happened to you the day of the Shadow War?"

"I-I don't know," I said. I was a newborn baby—I couldn't remember what happened that night, "from what I was told, my mother hid me under her bed when Osrov killed her."

"Are you sure that's the real story?" Kyra asked.

"Maybe there is something else," Ivy sighed, "what if Osrov handed you some of his dark magic the day your mother died? I mean, you were in the same room as him."

"It wasn't an accident," Reyna said, biting her lip, "there is no way Osrov didn't plan all of this from the beginning. His escape from the shadow prison, his desire for you to embrace the darkness within, and what he possibly did to you the day he killed your mother."

"It's all part of his plan," I clicked my tongue with the roof of my mouth.

Everything I'd endured since the day of my mother's death was just a part of Osrov's master plan for me to join him. Judging by how I killed all the trotters moments before, his plan was definitely working. It was a matter of time before I joined his side. But I would never accept it, right?

"Sooner or later, I'll figure out what happened that day," I said confidently, "and what better way to do so than by facing Osrov myself. We need to go to the lands' volcano to end it all."

"Krell, trust me, this is far from over," Ivy chuckled, "even if we kill Osrov, what then? Are the four of us going to transform all the shadows back to normal? Can we even heal all the thousands that were affected? A war is coming, and it is inevitable."

"It might be inevitable, but we can slow it down by killing Osrov," I continued, "he's heading to the Fire Kingdom next—maybe he's already there."

"So then let's go," Kyra agreed.

Reyna devised a plan to infiltrate the Fire Kingdom and kill Osrov. First, we would need to take a boat to reach the lands' volcano, which wasn't easy. A huge lava lake surrounded it, but Kyra assured us she could craft an ice boat to take us across. The next part of the plan was to climb to the top of the volcano and rappel down into the kingdom.

"Wait," I interrupted, "where can we even find a rope?"

"Your grapple arrows, remember?" Reyna clarified.

"Oh, alright. Keep going."

Then, after rappelling down to the Fire Kingdom, we would breach the castle's walls and meet the King, who could help us lead an army against the shadows—if he was reasonable enough, unlike Ivy and Kyra. After that, Osrov would attack the kingdom, and we would kill him with the help of the zylika. If we got the chance, we might also defeat the shadow sisters. We'd do anything to delay the inevitable war.

Easy, right?

"Then let's not waste any more time," Reyna walked towards the *shackflyer*, who was taking a nap while we were at the forge.

When Reyna started walking away, I watched her discreetly limp as if she were hurt but didn't want us to notice. She held her waist and shrugged each time she took a step. I was about to approach her when I realized what she was hiding. There was a strange mark that sent shivers down my spine as soon as my eyes met her waist. It was an obscure spot on her skin made of dark magic, which could've only meant one thing: Reyna was turning into one of them.

PART VIII
SHADOWS

Chapter 26

I had an odd nightmare about Reyna. She was lying on her side on the floor, hugging herself as she trembled and mumbled strange words. I tried approaching her, but the closer I got, the louder she screeched. When I got on my knees and gently touched her shoulder, she turned around and screamed. Her face was deformed, her skin was tearing apart, and a strange gas was coming out of her eyes. Reyna was turning into a shadow, and there was no way I could have stopped it.

I woke up with a sudden gasp, immediately leaving the child-sized bed and shaking my head to clear my mind. After what I'd seen back at the forge, I couldn't stop thinking of Reyna—it had become an obsession. She was slowly turning into one of them, and worst of all, she was hiding it from us. I tried reassuring myself, insisting that the zylika was the way to cure her whenever the darkness took over, but what if it couldn't? It worked on a trotter, but would it also work on elves and humans? To distract myself, I went downstairs and joined Kyra, who was eating an apple in the kitchen.

"Couldn't sleep?" She asked after noticing me.

"Oh, I slept," I chuckled, "I just had a nightmare and wanted to clear my mind."

"You shouldn't be afraid of nightmares," Kyra said, taking a bite on the apple, "I mean, they aren't real, so why be scared of them?"

"Yeah, but when you're a shadow and Osrov can dreamwalk into your nightmares and kill you, then it actually becomes frightening."

"Guess you're right," she yawned, taking one last bite, "I'm gonna meditate some more, so if Osrov pops up in your nightmares, just scream or something."

"Thanks for the advice," I said sarcastically as Kyra walked to the second floor.

All that was left to do was wait for the *shackflyer* to arrive at the Fire Kingdom. I could have done so many things, nothing came to mind. I sat on the leather couch in the living room, and after pondering for a few minutes, the floor started shaking. I thought something had hit the *shackflyer* from below, but before jumping to conclusions, I glanced outside the window and observed as we hurried through the clouds and plummeted toward the ground. We were reaching our destination—I could finally catch a glimpse of the land's volcano.

It was massive, even bigger than Trotter Mountain, which I thought was the tallest mountain in the lands. A lava lake surrounded the volcano, but I wasn't focused on it—my gaze was locked on the volcano's crater. Smoke emerged from its summit, which might have seemed normal at first glance, but it wasn't. The smoke wasn't coming from fire or heat—it was pure darkness. It didn't take long for me to realize that the shadows were already inside the Fire Kingdom.

"Hey, everyone!" I shouted and then gulped, not believing my own eyes, "come here!"

Reyna was the first to arrive, tears streaming down her face, daggers in hand. I wasn't sure why she was crying, but it likely related to what I saw at the forge.

"There is no way..." Reyna sighed, noticing the smoke, "we need to retreat—we're not going there."

"Why? What happened?" Kyra asked as she exited her room.

She glanced outside, gasped, covered her mouth, and leaned on the window frame, cussing.

"Ivy, get out here!" I called for her.

"Yeah, I already saw what's going on," she said, rushing out of her room, "we're entering the kingdom either way."

"What?" Reyna asked, "you want to enter that place even though it's already infested with hundreds—probably thousands—of shadows?"

"Yes," Ivy declared, "we need to see if there are any survivors."

"And likely die in the process?" Kyra asked, "we won't enter that place. End of discussion."

"But remember when we said we were going to fight Osrov and the sisters in the volcano?" I questioned, unsure which side to take, "we need to stop the war."

"It's dangerous," Reyna gulped, "and we planned to recruit all the fire creatures to help us stop Osrov. By the looks of it, there's no one left to convince."

"We won't be certain until we see it with our own eyes," Ivy said, grabbing her hatchet and opening the *shackflyer*'s door.

I didn't care what Reyna and Kyra thought of the idea; I needed to enter the Fire Kingdom, no matter how dangerous it was. Osrov had to die that day—it was our only chance to delay the war.

"Fine," Reyna sighed, "I'll go, but if it gets too dangerous, we evacuate."

"You too?" Kyra reluctantly agreed, "I won't stay here doing absolutely nothing, so I guess I'm coming with you."

I recalled my sword and walked through the *shackflyer's* door, uncertain if we had made the right decision. The hot air scorched my skin like a dragon's breath. I glared at the lava lake surrounding the volcano, questioning whether to enter the kingdom or stay away.

"Just look at how messed up this place is!" Kyra insisted, "are you sure you want to enter?"

"Of course," I replied without hesitation.

After deciding, Kyra used her abilities to create a boat out of ice. The small canoe was supposedly strong enough to hold the four of us, but since it was meant to cross a lake of scorching lava, it didn't seem safe at all.

"It won't melt?" Reyna asked, dragging the boat to the lake.

"Not even the sun can melt my ice," Kyra chuckled, "have a little bit of faith in me."

"I'm not sure this is the safest way," Ivy hesitated, "but there's only one way to find out."

When we placed the canoe on the lava lake, it started making a weird sizzling sound as if it was about to melt. After a couple of seconds, the sizzle ceased, and the ice canoe stood still upon the lava.

"Who will go first?" I asked, but Kyra had already jumped inside.

Reyna and Ivy followed her, stepping onto the boat and sitting on opposite sides. I wanted to be the last one to get in just in case it couldn't hold much weight. It seemed safe enough, so I jumped on top and sat on one of the edges. Although the boat was freezing, it felt soothing when I lay on it.

"Now, how can we get to the volcano?" Reyna asked.

It would definitely take some time to get to the docks on the other side of the lava lake. With all the burning gasses evaporating on my face, I wasn't sure if I'd survive the ride.

"I can boost the canoe with my ice," Kyra proposed, "I had this whole plan in mind before we even got here, so trust me, it will turn out fine."

"Let's hope it works—I don't want to be boiled alive," Ivy laughed nervously.

"Burned alive," I corrected, "*boiled* is for water."

"That's not even true but whatever you say," Ivy gulped, preparing herself for the ride.

Kyra didn't even ensure we were ready—she just started propelling the boat with ice shards. I was the only one prepared for that abrupt start, so I didn't struggle to hold onto the canoe's ledge. In contrast, Ivy and Reyna almost fell off the boat and into the lava.

"A little warning would've been nice!" Ivy shouted.

"Takes the fun away," Kyra chuckled back at her.

The boat was going faster than I expected. I could see the lava below us getting pushed backward as the boat sped down the lake. Hopefully, we could arrive at the volcano before anyone noticed us.

"So..." I glared at Ivy, "have you ever been here before?"

"Many years ago," Ivy coughed, "but I'm sure the kingdom has changed a lot since my last visit."

"I didn't know that," Kyra said.

"It was after the..." Ivy hesitated, "you know."

"What is it like inside the volcano?" Reyna asked her.

Reyna's voice disgusted me. Not because there was anything specifically wrong with her, but because every time she spoke, I was reminded that she was turning into a shadow. She didn't want to worry any of us by revealing it, but I still knew what was happening. I wanted to cry and scream, but couldn't—I had to face it in silence.

"It's very different from the other kingdoms. You'll see what I mean later," Ivy explained.

"I think I want to vomit," I gagged.

A horrible sensation dizzied and disgusted me. Saliva filled my mouth, and I tasted the vomit rising in my throat.

"You wanna what?" Kyra shouted at me, turning around and noticing my green face and purple lips.

"Don't stare at us! Turn the other way around!" Ivy commanded with disgust.

"Are you alright, Krell?" Reyna approached.

Her voice made everything worse, even though she was just trying to help. I stuck my head out of the boat and vomited, but after I finished and wiped my lips, the sense of disgust remained within me.

"Krell, look at me," Reyna touched my face.

She was the only one who wasn't weirded out by what I did, and she didn't mind touching me afterward. Ivy and Kyra on the other hand, turned away and were unwilling to help me.

"What happened?" She asked.

"Do you think the zylika will really cure them?" I snorted.

"Is that what you are worried about?" Ivy giggled before realizing how disrespectful it seemed.

"Don't worry, Krell," Kyra reassured, "it cured that one trotter and probably healed the elves back at the forge."

"Yes, but we don't know for certain," I cried.

"Don't think too much of it" Reyna comforted, "why are you so suddenly worried?"

I wanted to tell her—I did—but it wasn't the right moment. If I could just talk to her alone, then maybe we could figure out a way to stop the darkness spreading through her body.

"It's nothing," I lied, "don't worry about it."

I noticed Reyna wanted to say something, but an unexpected sound interrupted her. It was like a growl, similar to that of a trotter, but it came from under the lake.

"I think your vomit woke something up," Ivy said sarcastically.

I looked around the lake, waiting for some creature to emerge from the lava, but nothing happened. Moments later, the grunting ceased, yet I still had the sensation that something was observing me from afar.

"What was that?" I asked.

"I don't know, and I don't want to find out," Kyra gulped, "I'll try to push the boat faster."

"Should we be worried about it?" Reyna asked.

The boat began to rumble. At first I thought it was Kyra's ice propelling the canoe through the waves of lava, but it felt as if the boat was about to flip. Then the lava from the lake started draining, and the growling intensified.

One large finger emerged from the lava, followed by four more of them. A hand rose from the lake—the biggest thing I had ever seen in my life. It was bigger than the castle in the Main Kingdom, larger than the gigantic vine surrounding the Nature Kingdom, and greater than Trotter Mountain. It was even longer than the volcano standing in front of us. If the hand was already thousands of feet tall, I couldn't even imagine the size of the colossus' body.

"What is that thing!" I screamed.

"Kyra, go faster, now!" Ivy yelled so hard that her own voice scratched her throat.

"Goddammit, Ivy! I'm trying, but the waves aren't helping!" Kyra struggled.

"We won't be able to reach the volcano—we need to fight it!" Reyna drew her bow.

"A bow won't kill that thing!" I told her.

The hand was made of molten rock, but lava dripped from its fingers. Reyna shot an arrow at the colossal limb, but it melted upon contact with its skin. I thought Reyna's plan was unsuccessful until an icy explosion blasted the hand, knocking two of its fingers off and launching them in opposite directions.

"Ember and ice," Ivy realized what Reyna did, "clever."

"The fingers!" I screamed as the two stones plunged into the lava lake.

The impact wasn't rough, but what followed was terrifying. A wave of lava made its way to the boat, ready to swallow us into the scorching liquid. I gasped and closed my eyes, unsure of what else to do.

"Crap!" Reyna braced.

In one final attempt to save us, Kyra took a deep breath and glared at the wave of lava rushing toward the canoe. When she screamed, a swirl of water surged behind her, protecting us from the approaching magma. What happened next was the most beautiful thing I had ever experienced. The waves of water merged with the waves of lava, splashing back to the boat after fusing.

"I need to rest," Kyra coughed and sat down.

"That was magnificent," I smiled.

"You need to teach me how to do things like that," Ivy laughed with relief and hugged Kyra.

"I bet you can do better things with your vines," she chuckled.

"We need to leave before it returns," Reyna whispered cautiously.

"I think we scared it off already," I grinned, "and, by the way, what was that thing?"

"That *'thing'* is a titan," Kyra panted, "I've seen many creatures, but the size and shape of that... It had to be one of them."

"Fire titan, am I right?" I asked.

"*Tan' Tan' Roo'* is his name," Kyra said, "according to the legend, at least."

"Then let's get the hell out of here before *Tan' Tan' Roo'* comes out again," Reyna commanded.

But because we couldn't get a single minute of peace and tranquility, *Tan' Tan' Roo'* emerged from the lava once again. The colossus was just a few feet away from the canoe, and as the magma slid down his body, I caught a glimpse of his rocky skin with yellow stripes. Unlike last time, the titan wasn't just showing his hand—the titan's head was sticking out of the lake. And he was furious.

"Holy..." I gulped.

"Kyra! Go faster!" Ivy screeched, breathing heavily as she observed the creature standing before her.

"I'll take care of him," Reyna said.

She used the same method as last time, placing an ember on the tip of her arrow and engulfing it with Kyra's ice. She shot the bolt at the colossus' eyes, hoping it would do something. When the ember exploded, she realized it didn't even make the titan flinch.

"Someone needs to get up there," Kyra said, stopping her efforts to propel the boat to the volcano.

"What?" We all exclaimed simultaneously.

"It's the only way," Kyra continued, "if we keep shooting tiny arrows at a massive titan, we won't be able to defeat him."

"I'll do it," I said.

"Krell, I know you're a confident kid, but not in a million years will you ever accomplish something like that," Reyna grabbed my shoulder and said slowly.

"It only makes sense!" I argued, "you can shoot arrows from below, Kyra can keep pushing the boat to the volcano, and Ivy can... I don't know, she can manage to do something!"

"Still, how will you get up there?" Ivy asked.

"I can create a path of ice to get him to the titan's head," Kyra suggested, "but he needs to go before the titan crushes us."

I prepared myself to face the most powerful creature in the lands. I knew it was suicidal, but still, I took a deep breath and leaped out of the boat, trusting Kyra with my life.

As soon as I took the first step, a platform made of ice appeared below me. It was slippery, but it held my weight almost perfectly. When I jumped again, another platform was created by Kyra.

"Kyra!" I shouted from above, "right and left, alright?"

She nodded. I kept jumping higher, trying not to look at the titan in front of me, but I still felt his warm breath all over my body. I yelled at Kyra each time I leaped, but after some time dashing upwards, I was too far away for her to hear.

"Right... left..." I kept repeating, although Kyra couldn't hear me anymore.

After several minutes of mindlessly jumping from side to side, I was finally high enough to start climbing the titan by myself. I drew my bow and shot a grapple arrow at his head, hooking it in place before wrapping my body around it.

"*Calm down, calm down,*" I kept climbing, trying not to think of the awful things that could have happened, "*think of something relaxing.*"

The first person who came to mind was my mother, but not even her memory could calm me in that situation. Then I recalled a special memory of Reyna and me. I remembered how we lay on the *shackflyer's* floor, laughing and talking to each other—spending time together. And just as my mind began to clear, I was reminded that Reyna would soon turn into a shadow. If the zylika didn't work, she'd be gone forever. *She would die.*

"No!" I gasped, opening my eyes, "*something else. Think of something else.*"

But before I could recall another relaxing memory, I realized I had already reached the titan's head. One more minute hanging on that rope and I would have gone mad.

After successfully reaching the peak of the colossus, I tried stabbing his head, but my sword couldn't pierce through the layer of molten rock shielding him.

"Reyna!" I screamed, but she couldn't hear me. Fortunately, she could see me.

I gestured a bow and mimed an explosion. She understood immediately and shot an arrow to where I was standing. Her aim was so accurate that the arrow landed right in my hand.

I clutched the bolt and hurled it at the titan's head. It exploded, creating a hole and removing the shield that had prevented me from damaging him. I was thrown back but managed to catch myself before plummeting down into the lava.

After the icy explosion—and a few additional swings from my sword—it became clear the titan couldn't endure any more pain, so he sank back into the lava. I celebrated, only to realize that without the titan's head, there was nowhere for me to stand. I plunged hundreds of feet into the scorching lake.

Before reaching the lava, I glanced back at the boat. Kyra and Ivy were talking to each other while I fell, and Reyna was the only one who noticed me. She made a split-second decision and did something I would have never thought possible. She fired a grapple arrow in my direction, calculating it perfectly so it went through my stomach and hooked itself on my back. She tugged the rope so hard that I was sent flying through the air, landing abruptly on the boat. I didn't feel the sensation of the arrow impaling me until I was lying on the canoe. It was a pain I had never experienced in my sixteen years of life.

"Make it stop!" I screamed in agony, glancing at the arrow piercing my stomach.

"Reyna, what the hell did you do?" Ivy gasped.

"I saved him!" Reyna cried.

"You shot him! What the hell is wrong with you?" Kyra yelped.

"I didn't do anything wrong, I swear!" Reyna panicked, holding back tears, "he was falling to his death! I had to do something!"

"He will bleed out," Kyra approached my dying body, "we need to take him somewhere!"

"Novo juice..." I weakly said, slowly losing consciousness.

"I don't have novo juice," Reyna sobbed, "I'm sorry."

"I know where to take him," Ivy said after examining my wounds, "but it needs to be quick. Reyna, put pressure on his wound—use a piece of clothing if necessary. Kyra, you'll help me breach the volcano's walls."

"How?" She asked.

"Breaking and entering," Ivy replied.

I was listening to their conversation but couldn't utter a single word. Trying to stay awake, I took off my scarf and handed it to Reyna so she could wrap it around my waist. It was funny how that was the second time my scarf had been used to cover a wound. I couldn't be humorous in that situation though—I was in pain and agony.

"How did you enter the kingdom last time, Ivy?" Kyra asked.

"It's a long story. I just hope Tyrose hasn't turned into a shadow yet," she replied.

I would've asked who Tyrose was, but my mouth was full of blood, so I couldn't speak at all. The only one who could actually talk was Reyna, but she remained silent. Clearly, she was the one to blame for what happened to me, but it wasn't really her fault. If it weren't for her, I'd be sizzling at the bottom of the lake at that moment.

"It's okay," I managed to mumble.

She smiled and leaned her head closer. I thought she was going to kiss me, but obviously not. That was disgusting to even think about. Reyna and I? Absolutely not. Anyway, she didn't lean in to kiss me—obviously—she went to my ear and said: "*thank you.*" There was something off about her—she had some issue—but I couldn't figure out what it was. Then I remembered everything I saw back at the forge and how Reyna was slowly becoming a shadow.

After the words Reyna shared with me, I lost consciousness, knowing my life wasn't in my hands anymore. I just hoped my friends would find a way to heal me, but since they were heading straight into a shadow infested kingdom, my chances were null.

Chapter 27

I had yet another nightmare. I was reliving a childhood memory, sitting on the castle's roof and sobbing after being grounded by my father.

I still remembered what happened at the lava lake—the way I climbed a titan before a grapple arrow impaled my stomach, and I lost consciousness. If a memory from my youth was flashing in my head, it could only mean one thing: I was dying.

"No..." I tried to speak, but the words wouldn't come out.

With my uncontrollable breathing and utter panic reaching its peak, I tripped and fell off the castle's roof. I closed my eyes and prepared to hit the ground, but I splashed into a river instead. My skin trembled, and my eyes twitched as I tried swimming out of the freezing water. Just as I was about to reach the surface, a hand pushed me down. Before I drowned, I opened my eyes and realized who the hands belonged to: *my father.*

Then I finally took the deep breath I had been desperately seeking. I wasn't in a dream anymore, but I was still soaked in freezing water. Blood no longer filled my mouth, but there was an unsavory aftertaste on my pallet.

"Drowning them always works," I heard an unfamiliar voice a few feet away from me.

"What? Who are you?" I asked, rubbing my eyes and seeing the figure standing in front of me.

It was a man who looked no younger than twenty. As much as I wanted to, I couldn't guess his age accurately because he was a different species. Molten rock covered his body, some of it even sinking into his hazel skin. He was taller than anyone I had ever seen, which made me realize he was from the Fire Kingdom.

"The name's Tyrose," he said with an accent that I had never heard before, "not *Tyrone*! Tyrose with an *S*, remember that."

"Where are my—" I began.

"Your friends?" He finished my sentence, "don't worry, they are in another room, talking and excluding me."

"Why am I wet?" I asked, glancing at the tub of freezing water I was lying on.

"You peed your pants," he said, waiting for me to laugh, "it's a joke. You know what that is? Of course not, I bet in the Main Kingdom they don't even joke."

"I understood your joke; it just wasn't funny at all. And who are you?" I trembled.

"What don't you understand? My name is Tyrose. Some people call me *Ty*, but please don't call me that," he explained, "the shadows are in this kingdom already. Don't worry, Ivy and your other friends told me the whole story."

"Ivy," I repeated her name, "how do you know her?"

"We were friends some time ago, but it's been a while since I last saw her. I'm glad I can meet her friends after everything that's happened."

I tried getting out of the freezing tub, but as soon as I stood up, the pain in my stomach intensified, so I relaxed and lay back down.

"Don't do that," Tyrose warned, "I wrapped a bandage around your stomach to stop the bleeding. If you move abruptly, your insides will pop out."

"Fine," I returned to my uncomfortable, icy water bed.

After sighing and crossing my arms, I heard the crack of a door. I was scared at first—in a kingdom infested with shadows, the sound of a creaking door was never a good sign.

"I really need a break," Reyna said as she walked into the room, rubbing her eyes.

It looked like she washed her clothes in Tyrose's house. All the dirt on her leather suit was gone, the leaves in her hair were removed, and the blood that had dripped down her wrist and fingertips was cleaned. I never knew where that blood came from, but I was almost certain that it was the shadows' fault.

Gladly, she wasn't the only one with a clean suit. With the cold water from the tub, the mud on my suit had already washed off, leaving only the dried blood stains on my scarf.

"Krell!" Reyna approached, kneeling before the tub, "I'm so glad you're alive. I'm so sorry for..."

"It's okay," I reassured her, "it wasn't your fault."

"It was her fault, but whatever you say," said Tyrose with his funny accent, "what was your name again?"

"Krell?" Reyna replied before I could.

"Krell! I need to remember that. Krell, Krell, Krell, Krell, Krell," Tyrose repeated.

"I think we all agree with you!" The door of the room burst open as Kyra walked in and smiled, "oh, hi Krell, I'm glad you're not dead."

"Thanks?" I responded awkwardly.

"Krell's alive?" Ivy followed her into the room, "that's pretty cool. Now, let's talk about how we're going to get out of here."

It seemed as if Ivy and Kyra didn't care about my survival. At least there was one person who truly cared: Reyna. She had been there for me since we escaped the Main Kingdom and was truly the best friend I'd ever had.

"We already talked this over," Reyna stood up, "if we don't fight Osrov, he'll become more powerful when he strikes the Main Kingdom."

"And if we fight him now, we will all die," Ivy argued, "we don't have enough warriors, and there are four shadows out there that are more powerful than all of us combined!"

"Four shadows? What?" I asked. It seemed many things happened while I was unconscious.

"They've grown stronger and now have more *'super-powered'* shadows," Kyra explained, "Osrov, the two sisters, and some girl with psychic powers who crushed half of the volcano while you were asleep."

"You fought her?" I mumbled.

"No, but we saw her," Tyrose interjected.

"In conclusion, Kyra, Tyrose, and I want to leave this damned kingdom," Ivy insisted, "Reyna is the only one who wants to stay, so it's three against one. We will leave the kingdom."

"No!" I shouted, "you were the one who wanted to enter the kingdom in the first place, and now you're afraid to fight the shadows?"

"I didn't enter because of the shadows," Ivy admitted.

She had lied to us. Initially, she claimed we needed to enter the kingdom to fight the shadows, but she had other unspoken purposes.

"This is about Tyrose, isn't it?" I shook my head in disappointment, "you convinced us all to enter the Fire Kingdom just so you could reunite with your old friend?"

"Don't bring me into this," Tyrose stepped back.

"I came here to see if there were any survivors! I wanted to get more allies to defeat the shadows," Ivy said.

"And now you're running from them?" I crossed my arms.

Ivy didn't speak after what I said, but she was noticeably enraged. Kyra tried telling me that it was too dangerous, yet I didn't even listen to her. I knew that if we didn't fight the shadows at that moment, many more lives would be lost—the lands could be doomed. Still, the majority of us wanted to leave the kingdom, and I couldn't argue against that. That vote could have decided the fate of the lands.

"The docks are not far," Tyrose planned an escape, "we could probably get there in less than ten minutes if we keep a quick pace."

"Will there be any shadows?" Kyra immediately asked.

"The shadows entered through the other side of the volcano—where there are no boats. They have yet to arrive in this area of the kingdom," Tyrose explained.

"Then let's go," Ivy said, walking out the door.

I tried getting out of the tub, but the sharp pain in my stomach stopped me. With one last effort, I pushed myself to my knees, lifted a foot, and crawled out of the freezing water.

"Krell!" Tyrose surprisingly remembered my name when he spoke, "there are a couple of rules you need to follow so you don't bleed out."

"Rules?" I asked.

"I couldn't sew your wound—blood is still coming out—so you need to change the bandages regularly. And I need... Reyna! You can be his assistant!"

"No," Reyna replied unemotionally.

"Whatever. Anyway, I'll give you some bandages, and every twenty-five minutes you need to change them," Tyrose handed me three of them, "you need to apply pressure on the wound so blood doesn't gush out. Then, Reyna will wrap the bandage around your waist and tie a little knot at the end. Preferably a nice knot—I don't like ugly knots."

"You're joking; I'm not going to be his babysitter!" Reyna laughed.

"Do you prefer me bleeding out?" I asked.

"To be honest, yes," Reyna teased me.

"I already explained everything, and I'm not doing it again, so please take care of him, R..." Tyrose paused for a second, "Reyna! That's right. Reyna, Reyna, Reyna, Reyna."

"Please keep track of time," I told Reyna, "I don't want to bleed out because you forgot to change my bandage."

"If you don't remind me, I won't do anything," she chuckled.

I held onto the walls as I limped out of the room and stepped onto the streets of the Fire Kingdom. I was immediately overwhelmed by its dismal ambience and dim lighting. The houses were made out of metal, there were no lanterns on the streets, and the volcano's inside was covered with a thick layer of rock, giving us the chance to freely roam over it.

"I'm so tired of Ivy and Kyra," Reyna approached and whispered.

"Right," I quietly replied, "we were supposed to come here to kill—I mean, *destroy*—the shadows. Now they're afraid to even come near them."

"I'm choosing not to snitch on you," Tyrose suddenly appeared behind us, "but remember, don't talk crap about people."

He chuckled and joined Ivy and Kyra, who were taking the lead. Tyrose seemed to be telling them where the docks were located and the places they had to avoid so shadows wouldn't cross our path. Even though Ivy and he were supposedly friends, I had barely seen them speak to each other.

"Now that he's gone," Reyna continued, "I feel like they are trying to make all the decisions for the group. It's like they don't even remember who warned and saved them from the shadows in the first place."

"I know, but let them be," I sighed, playing with my hands.

I kept wondering if I should tell Reyna that I knew she was going to turn into a shadow, but the thought made my stomach drop. Who knew how she would react if I confronted her about it.

"Reyna," I said involuntarily.

"What's up?" She replied calmly.

"Back at the forge, something happened," I began, unsure how to approach the subject.

"What are you talking about?" She stopped smiling.

"I know about it," I gulped.

"What? What do you know? What are you talking about?" She shook my arms desperately, "answer me!"

I was about to explain everything when the ground violently shook. Ivy, Kyra, and Tyrose quickly noticed what was happening, screaming for us to run towards them, but Reyna didn't follow their directions. She grabbed my hand and dashed to the opposite side, retracing our footsteps. As I was being dragged away, I glanced at the sky and caught a glimpse of a levitating shadow on the other side of the kingdom. It was a woman surrounded by gusts of air, almost as if she was at the center of a gloomy tornado. As I squinted my eyes to see her face, a boulder dropped from the sky onto the street we were crossing. I flinched and fell back, realizing that if Reyna hadn't yanked me away, the stone would have crushed me.

"Are you okay?" I heard Ivy's voice from the other side of the boulder. We had been separated.

"We're fine!" Reyna yelled to the others.

"You need to find another way around," Kyra said.

"Aye!" Tyrose whistled to get our attention, "if you go to your right, you'll find an alleyway. Keep going straight, and on the first street you see, turn left; the docks shouldn't be far from there."

"Fine!" I shouted, "see you there!"

"Remember the bandages!" Tyrose reminded us before they walked away.

And after an earthquake that separated the group, Reyna and I had to walk through a shadow infested kingdom we had never set foot in before. Worst of all, the street we were about to cross led directly to the shadow that caused the quake in the first place.

Chapter 28

Reyna and I had been walking for a few minutes. We were on the lookout for the street Tyrose had mentioned—the one that could safely get us to the docks. On our way there, I kept hoping there was no rubble blocking the path, and most importantly, no shadow crossing our way.

"Do you want me to change it?" Reyna asked, but I was too zoned out to understand her, "the bandage."

"Oh," I rubbed my eyes, "it stings a bit, but I think I'll be fine for a few more minutes. Besides, I thought you weren't going to be my babysitter."

"I won't," Reyna chuckled, "I just don't want you to die."

"That may be the nicest thing you've ever said to me."

"And now I won't say it again."

Reyna kept rushing ahead, seeking the entrance to the street leading to the docks, but she was unlucky. I wondered if I should mention what we talked about earlier—before we were separated from the others—but I felt a sharp pain in my stomach before I could speak. Looking down, I noticed my blood-stained clothes.

"Reyna, I think it's time to change the bandage," I leaned against a wall and slowly sat down.

"I just asked you like thirty seconds ago!" She replied, rolling her eyes.

"Yeah, well, thirty seconds ago my clothes weren't soaked in blood," I took a deep breath, "now help me change it."

Reyna hesitated before lifting my shirt and examining my stomach, recalling Tyrose's instructions. She unwrapped the bandage from my chest, staining her hands with blood as I grunted and panted in pain—it was really awkward. I remembered what Tyrose had told me and began applying pressure to the wound, but it wasn't enough.

"Do you need help?" Reyna asked awkwardly.

"I can wrap the bandage around if you'd like," I said, "just help me by putting pressure on the wound."

She placed her hand just below my chest as I leaned forward and tied the bandage around my stomach. After finishing, I tried to stand up again, but Reyna's hand was still gently pressed against my chest.

"You can let go now," I cleared my throat.

"Oh, right," she pulled away, "it seems like you did a good job."

"Couldn't have done it without you. As Tyrose said, it's a two-person job."

"He didn't say that but I guess that's what he meant."

I leaped to my feet and stood firmly, hoping the bandage wouldn't come undone with the sudden movement. When Reyna pushed herself up a few seconds later, I knew it was the perfect time to talk about *the thing*. Before we were separated from the others, we had started discussing it, but I hadn't made myself clear. I mean, how was I supposed to even start the conversation? *Hey, Reyna! I know you're a shadow, and I know you will die soon!*

"Reyna," I began, "do you remember what we were talking about before? You know, when we were back with the others."

"Oh," she looked at the ground and rolled up her sleeves, "so, you know about it?"

"I do," I sighed, "I saw it back at the forge and can't stop thinking about it ever since! I just can't stand the fact that you may die!"

"I'm not going to die, Krell," Reyna glared at me oddly, "it's something that's been happening for a long time, and maybe because you've never experienced it, you think it's worse than it is, but it isn't. It's personal."

"How can you *turning into a shadow* be personal?" I asked.

"Oh," she gasped, "it's about that."

"Yeah, what else?"

"Nothing. Don't worry about it."

I decided not to ask any further questions about what she thought I was talking about. I was more intrigued by what was actually going on with her infection and why it looked exactly like a mark from the darkness.

"So, what are you going to do with it? You're turning into one of them," I said as we continued walking.

"I'm not turning into a shadow, Krell," Reyna sighed wearily, "it's complicated, but I feel like now is not the time to explain what *that* is."

"Then you're not turning into a shadow? At all?"

"No, Krell. I'll explain later."

She wasn't turning into a shadow! That was probably the greatest news I had received in a while. But then, what was that mark on her waist? Witchcraft? Some kind of burn? Although I didn't know what it was, I was beyond ecstatic that Reyna wasn't becoming a shadow.

"Come on, let's get the hell out of he—" Reyna started saying when something interrupted her.

Strange, high pitched whistles were heard from across the street we were walking on. As the hiss grew louder, Reyna took a step back, clearly frightened. The sound crept closer, but due to the kingdom's dim light, it was impossible to glimpse the approaching creature.

"What was that?" I asked Reyna.

She didn't answer.

When the whistling ceased, another sound ventured inside my ears—the eerie music of cracking bones. My knees trembled as I wondered what monster could be hiding in the darkness. I took a step back when it revealed itself. A twisted leg emerged from the shadows as an arm slammed the ground and bent out of shape. We flinched, but before any word could escape my mouth, one of the shadow sisters crawled out of the dark.

"It's them," Reyna breathed heavily.

"*Them*?" The sister chuckled, "oh, I'm doing a little solo work at the moment. And now I'm actually allowed to kill you."

"Krell..." Reyna murmured.

"Run," the sister finished her sentence.

I turned around and sprinted away, shutting my eyes and hoping the shadow wouldn't reach us. I couldn't look back, but I heard her claws scratching the brick road and her mischievous laugh rushing closer to us. It was terrifying, especially because of what the sister had said before dashing our way—she was allowed to kill us.

"Come here, little pigs!" The sister shouted.

Curiosity eventually got the better me, and when I peeked back, I was horrified. The sister was crawling towards us with contorted knees, twisted elbows, and a distorted head staring at the sky.

"Help us!" I screamed.

"I'll gut you both when I get the chance!" The sister giggled maniacally.

I closed my eyes again, trying to concentrate, but I was too tired to continue. With my open wound and the heat of the volcano scorching my skin, I knew I couldn't keep running. We needed to rest.

"Run faster, Krell!" Reyna cried, determined to keep running for miles.

Yes, I was sprinting as fast as I could, but I came to a sudden stop after noticing the alley on the side of the street. It had to be the one Tyrose had mentioned—the one leading to the docks of the kingdom. Reyna seemed to notice it as well and stopped running alongside me.

"Finally, you start to accept your fate," the sister began walking on two legs.

As she crept closer, her limbs twisted back to normal. Her arms cracked, her legs twirled, and her head rolled back to its original position.

"Reyna," I wondered if we were thinking the same thing.

"Yes," she nodded.

The sister was standing just a few feet behind the alley's entrance, so we bravely decided to dash in her direction. For a split second, she thought we were going to fight her, but right before reaching her, we turned to the street on our right.

I began chanting victory until something pierced my back and hurled me to the ground. I rolled and noticed the sister sitting on top of me and searing her sharp claws into my skin. Luckily, she missed my wound, which was a few inches below my lacerated chest.

"Krell!" Reyna gasped and ran toward me, but something stopped her.

The volcano rumbled again, even more abruptly than before. Parts of the crater crashed over the kingdom, destroying houses and toppling castles. Despite the kingdom crumbling, the sister remained determined to kill me. She stabbed her claws into my chest and burst into laughter as I screeched in pain.

"Get away from me!" I shouted, recalling my sword and using its hilt to knock the sister away.

While she was stunned, I got back on my feet and hugged myself to stop the bleeding.

"Are you okay?" Reyna asked as she helped me walk away.

"Yes," I panted, "just a few scratches."

"I am going to ki—" the sister dashed our way.

Before she could reach us, a boulder fell from above, landing between the sister and us. The last time a rock fell from the sky, it separated us from the others, but this time it was our salvation—we were freed from the sister.

"This isn't the last time we meet," she yelled angrily from the other side.

"Come on. We need to get out of here," Reyna said, grabbing my hand and running to find somewhere safe.

We walked through the streets of the Fire Kingdom, trying to find a way to reach the docks and escape. I wondered what the kingdom was like before. Was it so disastrously dismal before the shadow attack?

I glanced around, observing the inside of the volcano and catching a small glimpse of the sky past the crater above. It was difficult to imagine that we were essentially walking on top of lava. I mean, there was a layer of rock where the streets and houses were built, but below that thin crust lay a pool of sizzling liquid.

"We should be moving faster," Reyna quickened her pace, "the others are probably at the docks already—waiting for us."

"But we need to be careful," I said, "I don't think you want to encounter that crazy shadow girl who was causing all those quakes."

"We won't," Reyna laughed nervously, "at least not if we hurry up!"

Reyna began trotting while I meticulously examined the beautiful—yet spine-chilling—kingdom. The houses around me had shattered windows and scratch marks on their dark-brown front doors. There was a smell of decay in the air mixed with gasses of fire and magma coming from underground. As I looked further into the streets, I caught a glimpse of the mines with pickaxes lying on the ground and blood splattered on the walls. There were obvious signs of a struggle, but no bodies were scattered.

"Krell," Reyna stopped and pointed somewhere, "I need you to boost me up to the roof of that house."

"Boost you up?" I asked.

"Yes, like, push me up."

"Oh, okay," I agreed.

I kneeled, straightening my back and waiting for Reyna to jump on it and climb to the house's roof. I didn't know why she wanted to get there, but I decided not to ask.

"What are you doing?"She awkwardly asked from behind.

"Boosting you up just like you said."

"You don't boost people up with your back," Reyna chuckled.

"Well, it's not like I've ever done this before."

"Just put your hands together and then push me up."

I placed my hands on top of one another and slightly raised them. Reyna took a small leap, stepping on my hands before mantling over the house's ledge.

"There we go," I panted, "now, what are you doing?"

"I'm trying to see where the docks are!" Reyna whispered from above, "and I think I see... Yes! I see the docks! I'll lead the way."

"Great," I opened my arms to catch Reyna, but she simply jumped down and landed with ease.

"We should get there quick—" Reyna began.

When she turned around and led the way to the docks, the house beside us collapsed. Smoke covered the street, blinding us both as stones crashed against us and flung us to the ground.

"Krell?" Reyna coughed and stood up

Then, a silhouette emerged from the smoke. It was the outline of a woman in a long dress, her arms raised to her neck, and her hair floating above her as if she were submerged underwater. When she stepped out of the haze, I realized it was a shadow—the very one responsible for the recent earthquakes in the kingdom. Although she was fully enveloped in darkness, the dress she wore retained its hue: a wine color adorned with white stripes around the waist and neck. However, what stood out most was the red stone embedded in her forehead, shaped like a ruby. Whatever it was, it seemed powerful.

"Reyna," I whispered, "what do we do?"

"Fight," she gulped.

Although the shadow couldn't speak, she seemed triggered by what Reyna said. She screamed, summoning a rush of air that pushed us both to the other side of the street. The air began to swirl around her, growing darker with each rotation. The shadow lifted her hand, and a powerful gust of wind surged in my direction. I managed to push my body into the forceful breeze to avoid falling, but after a few seconds, I found myself on the ground.

Reyna attempted to approach the shadow and stab her, but the wind was so fierce that it sent her spiraling backward. I tried shooting arrows at the woman, but once again, the wind deflected them. It felt impossible to even land a hit on her.

"Damn it!" Reyna cursed.

The shadow lifted her hand again, and two gusts of wind flew our way. The only thing I could notice through the chaos was that as soon as the air rushed towards us, the shadow was no longer protected by it. We needed to wait for the woman to attack before we could strike, which wasn't going to be easy. I got hit by both swirls because I wasn't paying attention, but at least I had a plan to defeat her.

"Reyna!" I shouted to get her attention, "distract her!"

She could barely hear me through the wind, but she seemed to understand. She ran in the opposite direction, shooting arrows at the woman.

"Here, asshole!" Reyna caught her attention.

I was crouched behind the shadow, waiting for an opportunity to strike. After Reyna shot dozens of arrows in her direction, the woman eventually launched a gust of wind toward her. The air surrounding the shadow was gone, so I recalled my sword and stabbed her back multiple times.

"And stay dead," Reyna shot one last arrow at her head, "why isn't she turning back to normal?"

"Should she?" I asked.

Before Reyna could add anything, the shadow's fingers twitched. She silently growled, dragging her feet and rolling her head. Even though it seemed like we had killed her, she was still very much alive.

"The stone on her head!" Reyna realized, "we need to destroy it!"

The shadow screamed, crawling away and aggressively stomping her hands on the ground. The earth trembled as the mud and debris rose over our feet and knocked us away.

"I'll get her from behind, Krell!" Reyna grabbed my shoulders and said, "distract her!"

It wasn't easy to do so. With her switch from manipulating wind to controlling the earth, she was truly one of the most powerful and mystical beings I had ever fought. I was certain that all her power came from the stone on her head.

"Here, you... stupid shadow?" I tried distracting her, but I was never good at insulting people.

At first, the woman wouldn't even acknowledge me, but after I hurled a rock at her, she glared at me with a deadly stare. I pulled out my bow and shot an arrow at her eyes, hoping it would give Reyna enough time to sneak behind her. As the dart flew through the air, the shadow caught it with one hand and broke it in half. Before I could think of something else to do, the shadow was already launching rocks in my direction.

"Krell, run!" Reyna yelled from behind the shadow.

Those two words were loud enough to catch the woman's attention.

"No," Reyna shook her head.

But the shadow was already looking at her. Rapidly, I grabbed my sword from the ground and dashed at the woman, screaming and ready to strike. I swung my weapon at the shadow's back and then stabbed her stomach, unable to remove the sword afterward. Reyna jumped to the woman and gripped her hand around the stone on her head. I could hear it cracking as Reyna pulled it out of her skin. Yet, the shadow was agile enough to push Reyna away—she wasn't able to remove the stone.

"Krell!" Reyna coughed, "she's weak!"

I stepped backward, pulling the string of my bow and shooting an arrow at the shadow's head. In the blink of an eye, the scarlet stone shattered into three perfectly divided pieces, which fell to the ground and lost their bright hue. The shadow began to vanish, and her body disintegrated, eventually becoming ashes—her only remembrance was the wine-colored dress she once wore.

As I glared into the cinders of the deceased shadow, I realized that there wasn't any hope left for her either way. She was entirely consumed by the darkness, so even if we tried healing her with the zylika, she could never have returned to normal. The same would eventually happen to the sisters and Osrov because there was no point in saving them anymore—they had to die. But it wouldn't matter, right? After all, they were shadows, not actual people. They were monsters—not people! I would never kill a human being.

"You did it, Krell," Reyna panted.

"You did most of the work," I said.

"What is taking so long!" Kyra came walking from the other side of the street, clearly in a rush, "we've been waiting for you at the docks for almost half an hour!"

"Oh, sorry, we were too busy killing a damn shadow!" Reyna rolled her eyes, "she had all this creepy witchcraft of air and earth."

"And we killed her," I said, "just the two of us."

"That's great," Kyra said sarcastically, "now, please come to the docks. We've been waiting too long. I even had to kill a shadow on my way here."

She turned around and led the way to the docks, which I hoped weren't far—I was way too exhausted to walk for another mile.

"Try running from a sister and fighting a *witch shadow*," Reyna said, rolling her eyes.

"You were chased by one too?" Kyra asked, "one of those creepy girls started fighting us, but we lost sight of her after a while. They're powerful, you know."

While one was chasing us, the other was fighting them. It seemed they already knew we were separated and wanted to take advantage of it. I merely hoped they wouldn't show up at the docks, which we had reached in less than five minutes. Three boats were on the lava lake, all tied with ropes to prevent them from floating away. In one of the cramped canoes, Ivy and Tyrose were sitting, having a conversation—or argument; I couldn't tell.

"You're back!" Ivy exclaimed, standing up.

"Aye! You're not dead!" Tyrose added.

"Thankfully," I sighed.

"Why? What happened?" Ivy asked.

"Let's just say that the shadow causing the earthquakes won't be a problem anymore," Reyna said with a forced smile.

"I'm not even gonna ask," Tyrose replied with a smirk.

I climbed onto the boat, which was comically small and meant for only three people, so we had to squeeze together. They were about to start rowing away from the kingdom when I hesitated and stood up. I couldn't leave the lands' volcano. *We* couldn't leave. Not yet.

"Sit back down, Krell," Kyra said, already aware of my intentions.

"I'm not going," I replied, stepping out of the boat.

"We already made a goddamn choice, so sit back down," Ivy commanded angrily.

"We came all this way to kill Osrov, and I'm not leaving until I do," I recalled my sword and readied my bow, "you can leave if you want, but I'm not coming with you."

"You know what this means, right?" Ivy raised her voice, seemingly forgetting we were in a place full of shadows, "if we all leave except you, you'll stay here and fight that bastard alone. And after that, what? You take a boat and continue this whole journey by yourself? We won't be there waiting for you. You'll be forced to go back into your wretched kingdom again."

"This is pretty dumb, kid," Tyrose added.

"Yes, Krell, it is stupid," Kyra agreed, "but if you really want to kill that guy, go ahead. You're alone, though."

"He's not," Reyna finally spoke and followed me out of the boat, "I'll come with you."

"Are you...?" Ivy sighed in anger, "you will die!"

"Then so be it," I said, walking away.

Reyna followed me with a smirk planted on her face. Ivy and Kyra yelled at us, aware we could die, but honestly, I didn't care. We were heading to the heart of the beast—both the sisters and Osrov would be waiting for us there.

"Fifteen minutes!" Ivy shouted, "fifteen minutes, and if you're not back, we will leave!"

And then we walked away, ready to fight and kill Osrov.

Chapter 29

Reyna and I walked upon the stone streets of the kingdom with our weapons in hand. I wanted to attract the attention of every single shadow around, which is why the tip of my sword gently scratched the ground. The houses around us were abandoned, just like those on the other side of the kingdom, but unlike them, these were utterly destroyed—some even lacking a front door. If Tyrose was correct, almost every shadow that infiltrated the kingdom should have been scattered on the street we were traversing.

"Come out here!" Reyna shouted to get the shadows' attention.

I loosened the grip on my sword, allowing it to slide down. The screeching sound of the weapon being dragged along the stones grew even louder. All that was left was for the shadows to arrive.

That was when a roar echoed from far away, beyond the destroyed houses—the shadows were coming. At the street's corner, dozens of gloomy trotters ran in our direction, ready to kill.

"All set?" I asked Reyna.

"This is what we came for," she smirked and dashed forward.

Reyna pulled the string of her bow and fired an arrow at one of the many trotters sprinting at us. The sharp projectile impaled the creature's head, crossing its skull and reaching another one behind. Simultaneously, I raised my sword and gashed a shadow from shoulder to waist. I was certain the trotter had died with that blow, but to make sure, I stabbed it in the chest one last time. Realizing most of the trotters were still at a distance, I decided to pull out my bow and take a couple of arrows from my quiver. When I fired, one bolt punctured a trotter's foot while the other struck another creature's chest. It didn't kill them, but it was a clear opportunity for Reyna and me.

"Krell, together!" She yelled, pulling out her daggers.

I dashed towards the two stunned trotters with Reyna just a step ahead of me. While she stabbed her dagger into one's chest,

I threw myself to the ground and tore the arrow I had fired from the other's foot. At the same time, Reyna punctured the torso of the trotter while I stood up and did the same to its neck.

"Grab your bow!" I panted, "let's shoot the remaining ones."

Six trotters were still alive a feet away from us. Reyna and I began raining fire on the creatures, shooting as many arrows as we could—she even used some of her special arrows, including a scarlet one that blazed the trotters' skin and another with a sharp tip. When she shot that bolt at a shadow's stomach, three keen claws emerged, killing it instantly.

"You need to give me some of those," I chuckled.

"You wish," she said, laughing.

After all the trotters were shot down—mostly by Reyna—we started picking up the arrows from the ground, still alert for any other shadow that might cross our path.

"You did good," Reyna said, placing the darts back in her quiver.

"I think you have some competition."

"I said you did well, not wonderful."

I laughed, but a few seconds later, a shadow dropped from the roof of one of the houses. Unlike the trotters we fought before, the shadow was an actual person—a woman who lived in the Fire Kingdom and had unfortunately been transformed into one of the monsters. I considered fighting her for a moment, but I had a better idea: we could use the zylika to turn her back to normal!

As I approached Reyna to share my thoughts, she fired an arrow at the shadow. It wasn't a normal bolt though—it was a grapple arrow. Before I knew it, the hook tangled around the woman's neck, and Reyna aggressively pulled the rope attached to the arrow. Suddenly, the shadow's head rolled to my feet.

"Ready, let's go," Reyna said without acknowledging her actions.

"What the hell was that?" I screamed at her, "you killed someone! Someone we could've cured!"

"Are you seriously going to start doing this all over again?" Reyna rolled her eyes, "I am an elf. Elves kill! Many people are going to die on this journey, Krell, and it is not our fault. It's how things go. *Kill or get killed*."

"We had a chance to save her, and you decided to decapitate her?"

"I will kill many more people in my lifetime," Reyna said, "and like it or not, you will too. Just like me, you will start doing it naturally. You will lose count of all the people you've killed. It happened to me, and trust me, it will happen to you."

"Maybe it will. But before that happens, you won't kill anyone."

"I can't promise anything."

"Please try."

Reyna rolled her eyes as if she wanted to ignore me, even though she knew what I said made sense. She walked through the streets, proudly stepping on the heads of the trotters we had killed. In contrast, I was carefully placing my feet in the gaps between the fallen creatures. Although I was somewhat disgusted by the sight of the deceased trotters, it didn't bother me too much—I liked seeing those creatures get what they deserve.

"Where do you think Osrov is?" I asked, trying not to step on any dead trotter.

"All the shadows are located on this side of the volcano," Reyna replied, "Osrov has to be near."

Then, after reaching the end of the street, we glanced to our right and noticed a large concrete area with no houses or buildings around it. In other words, the perfect place to find Osrov. The area resembled an arena, but lacked seats for spectators like the one in the Nature Kingdom. As soon as I stepped inside the ring, I knew something bad was about to happen.

"Prepare yourself," Reyna sensed evil.

"I'm ready," I gulped.

I was expecting Osrov to fly down to the arena, deliver a speech on why I should join his shadow army, and when I refused his offer, unleash hellfire on us. Instead, we were greeted by a less cordial and more frightening welcome.

"Look who comes crawling back to us, sister," I recognized the voice immediately.

"I thought I scared them back there with my contortionist abilities!" Another voice echoed through the arena, "surely I scared the boy, though."

One of the sisters dropped from above and landed a few feet in front of us. It was the same girl who chased us before—the one with a large tongue and taller figure. Seconds later, her twin arrived, ready to brawl.

"We're only here for Osrov," I said.

"So you're saying you didn't come back for us?" One of the sisters pretended to cry.

"He's only here for that bastard," the other sister rolled her eyes, "but before they can get to him, they have to go through us."

"Why won't Osrov fight us?" Reyna asked, "we've seen him twice, and he always sends you two instead of facing us himself!"

"When you're worth his time, he'll come for you," one sister replied.

"But before that, you're stuck with us," the other laughed.

They grabbed their weapons and stepped back. If killing them meant finding Osrov, I'd do whatever it took. I recalled my sword as Reyna raised her daggers.

"I go left, you go right," I whispered to her.

I rammed at one of the sisters, launching my sword in her direction, but she swiftly spun and dodged the flying weapon. Before I could recall, she grabbed my neck and lifted me from the ground.

"You think you're smart, huh?" The sister taunted as she choked me.

I opened the palm of my hand, summoning my sword through the arena and into my grasp. Surprised, the sister released my neck and stepped back, hissing. Meanwhile, Reyna was rapidly slashing her daggers and dodging the sister's attacks—she knew that if she kept repeating that process, she could eventually defeat the shadow. But I didn't have time to focus on how Reyna was doing—I was in a fight of my own.

I approached the stunned sister and slashed my sword at her. She shielded her body with her arms, but I still managed to slightly injure her. The sister screeched and kicked my ankle, throwing me to the ground and stabbing her small sword near my neck. I was lucky to flinch and move out of the way before the object reached me, giving me the chance to push my knee into the sister's torso and knock her away. In a split second, I decided to grab my bow and shoot an arrow at the shadow, piercing her shoulder.

"Did you think an arrow would hurt me?" The sister chuckled, unaware of what was about to happen.

There was enough zylika on the bowstring for the arrow to absorb it. Just as the sister tried to fight back, the pain kicked in, and she fell to her knees.

"Yes. That's what I thought," I said with a small grin.

"You're going to die, goddamnit!" The sister tore the arrow from her body and screamed.

She rushed at me aggressively, thrusting her sword. I sidestepped a few times, but the weapon still managed to reach my waist, cutting a piece of cloth off my suit. The next time the sister swung her weapon, I blocked the attack with mine, but she kicked the sword away and punched my stomach. I had forgotten about the wound on my torso; it was still open, and my bandage desperately needed changing. I swallowed the pain and tried not to show any weakness, but it was difficult. The sister attempted to slide her sword through my neck, but I pushed it away with one hand, yelping when the weapon cut my palm.

"Looks like you got even weaker," the sister mocked.

She quickly landed her next hit, swinging her sword at my chest. I immediately lifted mine and parried the attack, wending sparks through both our weapons. She was knocked back, so I stabbed her chest and hugged her tight to prevent her from pulling away.

"What is this?" The sister screeched, feeling the power of the zylika.

"Your weakness. And your doom," I said, digging the sword deeper into her chest.

"Seems like you've found... my weakness," she chuckled in pain, "but you've forgotten that I've known yours for some time now."

She surreptitiously grabbed her sword and impaled my hidden wound. I gasped for air, collapsing to the ground as the sister stood up and pulled my blade from her chest. She tossed it aside and stepped on it.

"Why don't you try recalling it now, Krell?" She pouted.

The pain I felt was indescribable. The sweat fell into my eyes, blurring my vision, and although I was at the verge of death, I kept trying to recall my sword. However, the sister's foot put too much pressure on it. My chances of survival were slim.

"Come on! Recall it!" The sister laughed maniacally, "come on, you little stupid pig, recall it!"

"Go to hell," I struggled to say.

"I'm already there," she abruptly pulled the sword out of my body while still stepping on mine.

She raised the weapon—ready to kill me—when an arrow flew into her chest. I looked around and saw Reyna grabbing arrows from her quiver and firing them at the shadow. The other sister was on the ground with cuts on her shoulder and face.

"You can wait, right?" The sister looked at me and then ran towards Reyna, "you're both going to die!"

Reyna screamed and jumped at the sister, stabbing her shoulder, but the shadow hissed and pulled herself apart. Before Reyna could strike, the sister swung her legs at Reyna's ankles, tripping her to the ground. When she tried to stand up, the sister slapped her face and dragged her closer.

"You already know what is gonna happen, right, elf?" The sister seared her claws into Reyna's chest.

I was too weak to do anything, but I still had one choice—it might not have been the right decision, but it was my best shot at survival. I grunted and let every emotion overcome me, feeling the anger and heat rising inside my body. When I stood up, the bandage around my stomach fell, but instead of my insides dropping, nothing happened—my wound had miraculously healed. *Embracing the darkness within me could heal me.*

"You will both die, pigs," the sister continued scratching Reyna with her claws.

I ran to the sister and slashed my sword at her. I struck her so hard that she was launched across the arena—if she hadn't braced herself, she would've been killed. Although I wanted to kill the shadow for once and for all, I wouldn't let the darkness overcome me. I turned around and tried transforming back to normal.

"I always knew you were a coward," the sister said weakly, "just like your mom."

"What did you say?" I stood still.

"Yeah, I still hear her screams," she continued, "she couldn't even defend herself when I gutted her."

That was when I stopped controlling myself. I was enraged—I wanted to kill the sister, and that was exactly what I intended to do. I turned and menacingly walked in her direction. She was already dying, so I wasn't doing anything wrong—I was just ending her suffering—right? I grunted and thrusted my sword at her as she screamed in pain and coughed black smoke. She begged me to stop, but I didn't listen to her.

"You are a monster," the sister gurgled, taking one last breath.

Then I delivered the final strike at her neck. She was instantly decapitated, and her head rolled to my feet. Just then, I realized what I had done. The sister's words were true; I was a monster. The only thing that could comfort me was the thought that she wasn't a living creature—she was a shadow, not a person! She was the monster, not me!

"Sister, sister, sister!" The other one cried, crawling towards the body.

Reyna stood up in shock. She was right when she said that sooner or later I'd become a killer. The only thing I could do was collapse to the ground and bawl.

"It's okay, Krell," Reyna hugged me, "it's okay."

"I didn't want to do it, it wasn't me!" I cried.

"It's not your fault," Reyna said, "she deserved it."

"I don't care if she deserved it or not! That wasn't me! I don't know what I just did!" I couldn't stop crying.

"You killed my sister," I heard a crying voice behind me, "I've been by her side my entire life, and you just took her away!"

I looked at the dead sister's body, headless and lifeless. I couldn't believe what I had done, so I stood up and looked at the sister's eyes, not knowing what to say. Even if she was our enemy, I couldn't help but feel guilt.

"I'm sorry," I wiped my tears.

"You shouldn't be the one crying here," the sister said with a shaky breath, "I'm not going to fight you, though."

"What are you doing, sister!" Osrov appeared behind her suddenly, "are you talking? You don't talk, I talk! You fight, I talk! It's a simple goddamn concept."

"They killed my sister," she cried, "*he* killed my sister."

"And I couldn't care less!" Osrov yelled, "she had it coming anyways. She deserved it."

"I hate you, Osrov," she whispered with anger.

"And you think I don't, sister?"

"Don't call me that again. I'm not a sister anymore."

Then she walked away. I wasn't sure if she would stay with Osrov or go her own way, but I knew I had ruined her life forever.

I wanted the sisters out of the way, but not like this. After the sister disappeared through the kingdom's houses, I realized we were standing in front of the true threat: Osrov, the Shadow King.

I took a step backwards as Osrov crept closer to Reyna and me. I didn't know what he was attempting to do, but I knew he was prepared for a fight. He didn't have any other lackeys to send our way, so only one option remained.

"Oh, no, don't be afraid, Krell," Osrov said with a different tone, "I just want to talk."

"Yeah, I already know what you want to say, and the answer is *no*. I'm not joining you, Osrov," I stated.

"I am giving you a chance, Krell. You already know what you're capable of, and to be honest, you're more powerful than I could ever be. Imagine what we could do together!"

"He's not joining you, bastard," Reyna interjected.

"I wasn't talking to you, orphan child!" Osrov shouted angrily.

"How do you know everything about us?" I asked, tilting my head.

The way the sisters and Osrov interacted with us was unusual. The sisters made jokes about Reyna's family, and Osrov knew everything about the darkness hidden within me. How could they know it all if we had barely interacted?

"Because I've been watching you, Krell," Osrov revealed, taking another step forward, "for a long, long time."

"Then you know how I got all this... power?"

"I do," he smirked, "and I can tell you everything about it if you just come with me."

"Krell, don't do it," Reyna whispered.

I glanced back at her and discretely winked. She understood and did exactly what I wanted her to do. I took a step forward and caught Osrov's attention by nodding and smiling at him. Reyna pretended to scratch her neck but quietly grabbed an arrow from her quiver, placing the tip near her bowstring to absorb the zylika's power. The Shadow King grinned, thinking I was going to join him, but not even curiosity could make me ally with such a psychotic creature. Reyna surreptitiously handed me the arrow, and I hid it on my back, ready to stab Osrov.

"We're going to be so powerful together," he said with a mischievous smile.

"Powerful? Maybe. Together? Never," I replied as I impaled Osrov's stomach.

I twisted the arrow abruptly and pushed it further into his skin until he pulled away and punched me in the face. I was thrown to the ground, having to crawl away as a last resort. Osrov was enraged—angrier than I had ever seen him. All he wanted was to fight with one single purpose: *slaughter.*

"You wanted to fight me? You wanted to see my goddamn wrath!" Osrov trembled with rage, "now you'll see what it is like being my enemy."

He started levitating—his feet lifted from the concrete ground as a giant sword appeared in his right hand. Moments after, a cloud of dark smoke circled around his feet, swirling and whooshing as he soared to the top of the volcano.

"And you, Krell," he continued, "I really, really hoped you would have lived to see the day the shadows conquered the lands. And now, you and your little elf friend will die *all alone.*"

"They're not alone, asshole," said a voice from afar.

It was Kyra with Ivy and Tyrose standing behind her at the arena's entrance, ready to fight Osrov, even though they refused to join us back at the docks.

"It took you more than fifteen minutes," Ivy smirked.

"This is a bad, bad idea," Tyrose whispered, standing back.

"How about now?" Reyna asked Osrov.

"Not alone anymore, but you will still die," he grunted.

Osrov was floating ten feet above the ground, his right hand holding a sword and his left resting near his waist. His eyes were burning red instead of white, and although his expression was hard to read, we all knew how furious he was. Behind Reyna and me was Ivy, Kyra, and Tyrose. Kyra wielded an ice-crafted sword which managed to chill the scorching environment. Ivy stood beside her with her hatchet in hand—the same ax she had stolen from a couple of bounty hunters outside Trotter Mountain. I was almost certain she couldn't use her abilities because of the high temperatures of the land's volcano. Lastly, there was Tyrose, who was clearly unsure of what he was stepping into. I had heard that people from the Fire Kingdom were really strong, but from what I'd seen in Tyrose, he was more of a healer than a fighter. With all the group finally reunited, we were ready to *kill* Osrov.

"Let's do this," I glanced at Reyna and nodded.

Kyra was the first to strike, firing ice shards at Osrov's feet, which were surrounded by a gust of air. But the wind was too mighty, pulling the small shards away and launching them into a nearby wall. Everyone thought the Shadow King would stay on his hovering cloud, but he jumped off and landed in front of Kyra. He raised his sword and slashed at her head when she braced and pushed him away. Osrov tried striking again, but Ivy intervened and swayed her hatchet in his direction.

"This ax? Against me?" Osrov caught the weapon and broke it in half with a single hand.

In a panic, Ivy stepped back without a means of defense, but Osrov didn't want to fight her—he wanted to get to me. In the blink of an eye, he teleported in my direction, and after standing motionless for a couple of seconds, he drew his sword and swung it at me. I was knocked back by the surprise, falling to the ground and having to crawl away from him.

"Hey!" Reyna screamed to get his attention.

While he was inattentive, I kicked his ankle and recalled my sword, pushing him to the ground. Reyna jumped on top of him and stabbed her daggers into his chest repeatedly.

"Get off!" Osrov summoned a gust of air that blew her away.

Reyna didn't seem hurt after being launched to the other side of the arena, so I returned my focus to Osrov and hacked my sword at his legs. He simply stepped aside and kicked me down, raising his sword over my head when Kyra rained ice shards on him. Ivy wasn't helping us in any way—too afraid to fight. Then I noticed the reason why.

"My powers won't work," Ivy breathed heavily, "there's not enough nature in this kingdom!"

"I have a herbalist friend who has his own garden," Tyrose suggested, "it's not far—I can take you there."

"Thanks," Ivy sighed, following him out of the arena.

"Kyra," Tyrose stopped to ask, "do you need ice or some'n?"

"I don't need to be somewhere cold to summon ice," Kyra replied, continuing to fire shards at Osrov, "*I am the ice.*"

With a light smirk, she kept attacking the Shadow King, progressively pushing him further and giving me a chance to recover physically and mentally. Kyra's face was red as a tomato, and her legs trembled with each step—I wouldn't have been surprised if she collapsed.

"First time... someone has put on a... challenge," Osrov struggled to speak, "but it won't be enough."

Despite the pain, he shielded his face with his hands and pushed his body towards the shards, shoving them away. I wanted to help Kyra but was still recovering from everything Osrov had put me through.

"Just die already!" Kyra screamed.

I tried to stand up and distract Osrov in any way I could, but fortunately, Reyna got ahead of me and flung one of her daggers at him.

"I tried being patient," Osrov said, pulling the dagger out of his shoulder, "I tried not to choose this. I tried not to fight! But it seems like war after all."

With a simple flick of a finger, sticky black goo emerged from the ground. The thick matter entangled Kyra and Reyna, trapping them both before launching them against a nearby wall.

They couldn't move or talk—the goo had covered their entire bodies, leaving only their eyes exposed. I thought Osrov would do the same thing to me, but he had other plans.

"I had a deal," Osrov began, "an agreement. But I don't care anymore. I am going to make you suffer, and your friends are going to watch every second of it."

I heard muffled screaming coming from the other side of the arena, mostly from Reyna. I was too tired to stand up for myself, but I recalled my sword. When I expected it to arrive in my hand, it was pulled in the opposite direction. It reached Osrov, and he proudly held it for himself. I thought I knew everything about him, but it seemed like he had more tricks up his sleeve.

"You thought you were the only one who could do this?" Osrov laughed maniacally, "you think you're special just because you can wield a sword? You're just a kid—a kid who's confidence will get him killed."

With my own sword, Osrov struck a blow at my chest. Little did I know it would be the first of many I would have to endure.

*****

"We need to hurry, Tyrose, where is this garden?" Ivy asked as she crossed the streets of the kingdom, trying to find the herbology place Tyrose had mentioned.

"It should be on the next street to our right," Tyrose said, "or was it left? Or did we already pass it?"

"Tyrose, this isn't a goddamn joke! We need to find it, or we won't make it there on time!" Ivy complained nervously, "wait, I feel something."

"What?"

"Just shut up for a second."

Ivy closed her eyes and took a deep breath. She began walking to the street on their right as if sensing something. The garden was a few houses away, and Ivy was heading directly toward it.

"Can I talk now?" Tyrose whispered.

"I found it!' Ivy said with relief.

She walked to the house, similar to all the others in the kingdom. The door was barricaded, so she went to the other side and entered through a broken window. Inside, there were all kinds of plants, from roses to bushes and vines.

"This is the house?" Tyrose asked, "damn is it messed up."

"This'll be enough," Ivy said, ready to guide all the flora out of the house.

"Wait," Tyrose stopped her, clearing his throat, "we really need to talk."

"Tyrose, I know things between us are messed up, but this really isn't the time to talk."

"It'll just take a minute."

"Yeah, but the others could get butchered in that minute."

"I—"

"Tyrose, I know we were something back then, but time has passed and I have changed."

"You just left so suddenly! I didn't get the chance to say goodbye or even give you a last ki—"

"I escaped your kingdom because I was done with what we had. I needed a break from everything! I needed a break from life and to return to the kingdom where I was Queen," Ivy interrupted.

"And what about me? Have you ever thought about how I felt?"

"I did, and it kept me up every night!" Ivy cried, "but I needed to leave that part of my life and enter a new phase."

"And when that phase is over, can we talk about our relationship?"

"It's more complicated than that. I don't think I even..." Ivy gulped, "I don't think I even like people... people like you."

"People?" Tyrose paused, "oh..."

"Yeah," Ivy sighed, "now you understand?"

"Yeah, I do," Tyrose said with lingering confusion.

"Alright, now let's get back to the others," Ivy stepped out the same window she entered through, "and not a single word to anyone."

"Don't worry," Tyrose followed.

*****

Blood was smeared all over the ground. I could barely open my eyes, and when I did, tears and sweat prevented me from looking at Osrov. The taste of blood on my pallet was repulsive—I knew I was about to die. The Shadow King wasn't even using a sword anymore; he was killing me with his bare fists. I tried blocking with my remaining strength, but his punches were too strong for me to endure. Reyna and Kyra were still strapped behind a pile of goo, watching me get beaten to death. I could hear their stifled cries, but when I glanced in their direction, Osrov's knuckles clashed with my face. As my head hit the ground, I heard something cracking—he had definitely messed up my jaw with that punch.

"Stop," I tried speaking without moving my mouth, "stop."

"You want me to stop?" He laughed at me, "I gave you too many chances for me to *stop*."

I tried crawling away from him, but he noticed my attempt and placed his foot on my back. I wanted to scream but knew it would tear my jaw apart, so I fought the pain in silence.

"There you go," I heard him say.

I didn't even know what he was talking about until I looked at my hand. My skin was changing color—I was turning into a shadow again. Judging by what happened last time, I wasn't excited about it. Oddly enough, I didn't feel my body burning once the darkness took over me, probably because the pain was concentrated on the many cuts and bruises I already had.

"I'm not your shadow," I said weakly.

"We'lll see about that."

He kneeled beside me and started choking me. The pressure on my throat was so intense that I was already fainting by the time he started. Although he kept trying to kill me, I knew his goal remained the same—he wanted me to join him.

"You know you can heal yourself if you turn into one," he said, "you don't want to die, do you?"

"If it means you go down, I'll go down too."

As soon as I said that, Osrov flew across the arena. I saw him get smashed against a wall and get pushed towards it with force. The things tossing him around were... vines?

"Missed someone?" Ivy entered the arena with her hands raised.

The liana bound him to the volcano's crust and crushed his limbs—he finally knew how it felt. The goo trapping Reyna and Kyra disappeared moments after, freeing them. We had been saved, but I was still on the ground, covered in blood and weakly breathing.

"Krell!" At last, Reyna could express her desperation.

"What happened to the boy?" Tyrose gasped.

"That monster tortured him!" Kyra yelled.

"Find a way to carry him or something. I can't hold him much longer," Ivy's vines kept pushing Osrov to the wall.

"Reyna..." I tried not to spit any blood, "I'm okay."

"You're definitely not okay," Tyrose got closer, "I'm a doctor, and... his wounds are too grave. I can't do anything."

"Really, Tyrose?" Kyra asked.

"This is like the fifth time I'm about to die today," I attempted humor, though no one laughed.

"Krell, try to heal," Reyna touched my cheek.

"No, I don't want to turn into a... a..." I was stopped by the blood overflowing in my mouth.

"You don't need to," she said, "try healing, not turning."

I closed my eyes and tried to think of myself *healing*. I didn't know if I was doing it wrong, but it didn't seem to work. Then I had an idea.

I thought about things that made me angry: my father, Osrov, the kingdom's guards—they made my blood boil. I was already getting consumed by the darkness until I cleared my mind and visualized the things that made me happy: my mother, Reyna, Ivy, Kyra, and even Tyrose, although I hadn't spent much time with him.

My wounds began healing in an instant. The scars on my chest sealed, my bruises vanished, and the swelling around my eyes subsided. The only remaining trace of the attack was the blood still soaking my clothes.

"When were you guys gonna tell me this kid's a shadow?" Tyrose asked.

"I was surprised too," Kyra said, "I'll explain it to you later."

"No rush or anything, but we really need to go," Ivy said, maintaining the vines in place.

"But we're going to kill him," I stood up, fully healed.

As I said that, the volcano trembled. My first thought was that the shadow we had fought before—the one that controlled wind and was incredibly powerful—had come back to life, but it seemed almost impossible. I turned around and noticed Osrov, who was shaking uncontrollably beneath the vines entangling him.

"Like you said, Krell," Osrov twitched, "if I go down, you go down with me."

"The volcano is going to collapse!" Kyra shouted.

"What? No! My home!" Tyrose screamed.

"Is your home more important than your life?" Ivy lowered her hands and took a few steps back.

"We need to go!" Reyna was the first to sprint away.

I knew it was painful for Tyrose to watch, but his whole kingdom was falling apart. I knew Osrov would survive the destruction, but what would happen to all the other shadows in the kingdom? Would the Shadow King leave them behind? I knew they were our enemies, but that didn't change the fact that some were real people.

I tried not to get distracted by the chaos, but curiosity overcame me, and I peeked at the cracking walls. Debris was falling from the sky as pieces of the stone streets tore apart, revealing the lava hidden beneath the kingdom. I wasn't really paying attention, and after looking at my feet, I noticed I was inches away from stepping into a pit of magma.

"Pay attention, Krell," Ivy said, pulling me aside.

I kept running. I hadn't asked where we were heading, but Reyna seemed to be taking the path back to the docks. I saw the boats from afar, all tied with ropes except for one, which was floating a couple of feet from the docks. Thankfully, it hadn't been pulled away by the current.

"My home," Tyrose gulped as the debris crushed his house.

He stood motionless for a long time and was eventually pulled away from the group—I didn't notice until it was too late. I was about to call out his name when dozens of shadows sprinted in his direction.

"Tyrose, behind you!" I shouted.

He was still hypnotized by the image of his destroyed home—so distracted that he didn't notice the creatures creeping up behind him. One of them threw Tyrose to the ground and singed her claws at his face.

"I'm coming!" Ivy ran back to save him.

By the time we arrived, the place was swarmed with shadows. Tyrose was trapped in a horde of the creatures, and with what I had seen, he definitely didn't know how to defend himself.

"Hit them!" I screamed.

"I'm a doctor, not a fighter!" He yelled back, trying to push the shadows away.

I glanced at the others to see if they had any ideas to save Tyrose, but Ivy was fending off shadows, and Kyra was stunned on the ground. There was only one person who could help me: Reyna. Every time I was in a struggle, she was the first to aid me.

Oddly, she wasn't around when I called her name—she was sitting on the boat with her head in her hands. What was she even doing? Tyrose was getting killed, and she was resting? I didn't bother to ask and simply came up with another idea.

"Tyrose, catch and swing," I told him, "don't kill, just attack!"

I blindly tossed my sword in his direction, but despite my best efforts, the weapon landed on the ground. All the shadows were kicking and pushing it in random directions—I couldn't do anything else. It all depended on Tyrose.

"Get off of me!" He pushed one shadow away.

He crawled and reached for the sword, but a shadow kicked it, and the weapon landed at the feet of another, who tossed it again. Tyrose had to find a way to retrieve the sword.

"Please," Tyrose closed his eyes and stretched out his hands, placing his faith in mere luck.

As a shadow began searing her claws into him, he felt something sliding into the palm of his hand. With his eyes shut, he thrusted the sword at the shadow, impaling her stomach.

"I did it!" Tyrose gulped and stood up.

"Run, Tyrose!" Kyra yelled, stepping onto the boat.

He sliced the sword at the shadows in front of him with his eyes closed, not wanting to see what he was doing. It was his first time fighting, and to be honest, he did pretty well.

"Thanks for the help," I rolled my eyes at Reyna after stepping on the boat.

"I—" she stuttered.

"Tyrose, come on!" I interrupted.

He ecstatically got on the boat, grinning at all of us and expecting applause. It took a while for him to realize that the sword he held wasn't his.

"Oh, sorry," he handed it back to me.

Ivy grabbed the oar from one side as Tyrose and I picked up the other one and rowed away from the docks. Similar to before,

Reyna sat at the edge of the boat, holding her head. What was going on with her?

"We did it!" I exclaimed in excitement.

But Tyrose wasn't as happy after the volcano crumbled to the ground. I wondered if the shadows were crushed along with the kingdom, but a cloud of black smoke rose from the back of the volcano moments later. Osrov and his shadows were still standing.

"What now?" Tyrose asked, "now that most of the kingdoms are destroyed."

"The kingdoms may be doomed, but their people aren't," Ivy replied wisely.

I was going to add something when I noticed a strange silhouette emerging from the crumbled volcano. I thought it was flying debris until a boat—similar to ours—appeared from the smoke, infested with shadows.

"Go faster!" I commanded.

"I'll try pushing the boat!" Kyra sat at the back and raised her hands.

Ice shards propelled the canoe away from the volcano. Still, the shadows were moving faster than us, mainly because there were twenty of them in a single boat.

"I didn't know they were smart," Tyrose paused for a second.

"Just row!" Ivy slapped his head.

"And Reyna, why aren't you doing anything?" I asked while rowing.

"I'm tired," she replied weakly.

We were nearing the shore, but the shadows' boat was dangerously close. Some of the creatures even began jumping at our canoe, attempting to bring us down, but we fought back and drowned them in the lava.

"Can you go faster?" Tyrose shouted at Kyra.

"Only if you start rowing for once!" She screeched.

When the shadows finally reached us, something emerged from the lava: two colossal fingers the size of a mountain. It was *Tan' Tan' Roo',* the titan we fought when we first crossed the lava lake. He knew someone was breaching his territory and was prepared to defend it at any cost. I stood paralyzed for a second, remembering the threat the behemoth posed. When I thought the rest of the titan's body would surface, his fingers slammed into the lava, crushing the shadows' boat and capsizing ours. Our canoe was torn apart, and for a split second, I thought we were going to plummet and die. But when I opened my eyes, I realized we had all safely landed on shore. The grass itching my skin, the bugs crawling all over me, and the dirt and mud staining my clothes reminded me how much I missed the outsides.

"We did it," Kyra stood up and sighed.

"My back hurts, but I guess we did," Ivy struggled to speak.

Tyrose looked back at his destroyed home, observing the ash and smoke hovering over the sea. *Tan' Tan' Roo'* sank into hiding once again, and thankfully, he actually helped us kill the shadows instead of fighting us again. Tyrose knew he couldn't turn back anymore—his kingdom was gone, and he was the only survivor.

"Are you okay, Tyrose?" I asked him.

"Yeah, I'm good," he turned around and wiped his nose, "let's just get out of here."

"Agreed," Kyra was walking away when something happened.

A scream was heard, followed by a thud as if someone had hit their head on a wooden plank. Reyna—who had been unusually quiet for the last few minutes—collapsed to the ground. There were no blood stains on her body, which led me to think some lava from the lake had reached her skin. Then I remembered something that might have caused her to shout so suddenly.

"Reyna!" I kneeled before her.

Her forehead was burning, and sweat ran down her face and arms. She was obviously sick, but—if my suspicions were correct—she was also turning into a shadow. I had noticed the marks on her waist back at the forge, and when I asked her about them, she avoided the question by saying: "*it's something else.*" I knew I was right—I knew she was turning into one.

"Is that...?" Kyra gasped.

"I think she's turning!" I yelled, "what do we do!"

"Don't you have something to cure that?" Tyrose asked.

"The zylika, yes," Ivy blinked several times, "don't worry, Krell, we can cure her."

"Can we?" My voice cracked as I asked, "we saw it work on a trotter, not on a person."

"It'll probably work," Kyra reassured.

"I have some of it here," Ivy said, taking out a jar of the healing liquid.

I was about to grab it when I felt a cold touch on my arm. It squeezed me tightly and pulled me to the ground. Reyna was still awake, and although her eyes weren't open, she placed my ear near her mouth and whispered two words that sent shivers down my spine.

The curse.

"The curse?" I repeated after Reyna lost consciousness, "the curse!"

I finally knew what it all meant! Back at the Nature Kingdom, Reyna had told Kharum and me about some curse on her bloodline placed by a witch called Remma or Reva—I couldn't remember, but that wasn't the point. Reyna didn't know what the curse's effect was, but she said: "*when it starts to take effect, it won't be pretty.*"

"What did the elf say?" Tyrose asked.

"The curse!" I replied, panting heavily, "she mentioned a curse before, and now she just repeated it!"

"Calm down, Krell," Ivy said, grabbing my shoulder, "what curse?"

"I don't know!" I cried, " we need to help her! She sa-said that it was from a witch! Rella? Remma?"

"Renna?" Kyra asked with a haunting look in her eyes.

"Yes!" I smiled, thankful she knew who it was, "you know who she is? We need to take her there!"

Ivy shook her head as Kyra turned around on the verge of tears, looking at each other momentarily afterward. I didn't know what was happening between them, and I didn't ask—all I cared about was Reyna.

"We're not going to Renna," Kyra gulped.

"It's our only chance!" I screamed, "if we don't find her, Reyna will die!"

"The kid's right," Tyrose said, "whoever this *Renna* is, she sounds like the elf's only salvation."

"Both of you don't know half of what Renna can do," said Ivy, "or who she really is."

"I don't care who she is, but Reyna won't die like this!" I yelled.

"We're not going with her! End of story," Kyra argued.

"What? Are you scared to go with her? Is she too powerful for you?" I asked.

"You're stepping on real thin ice here, Krell," Kyra quietly said.

"Why? Why are you so afraid? Why!"

"Because Renna is my mother!" Kyra finally shouted, "she is my mother! The abuse I endured during the fourteen years I lived with her is a pain I don't want to relive ever again! She murdered people, including my father, and she is the reason I changed my name from Reva to Kyra! After she was exiled from the kingdom—after years of torturing civilians—she fled to the edge of the lands to live a solitary life. And I promised—I swore on my goddamn life—that I would never see her again!"

"Damn," Tyrose mumbled.

"I didn't know that..." I said with shame, "I'm sorry, I didn't mean to—"

"It's fine," she took a deep breath.

"Did you know this, Ivy?" Tyrose asked.

"I did," she replied, "I was there when the whole thing happened."

Was healing Reyna important enough to revisit Kyra's childhood trauma? I understood what she was feeling, but at the same time, I wished she would agree to visit her mother. I wouldn't rob her of the decision, though.

"Is Reyna really going to die?" Kyra asked.

"If we don't do anything, yes," I said.

"Kyra..." Ivy tilted her head and stared at her.

"So, are we going or what?" Tyrose asked.

"I guess..." Kyra sighed, unsure of what to say "I guess it's time I had a mother-daughter meeting."

PART IX
THE CURSE

Chapter 30

After the shocking revelation, we walked towards the *shackflyer* in silence. Tyrose offered to carry Reyna, claiming he was *the expert of the sick*—but instead of trying to make her feel better, it seemed as if he was playing with a baby. On the other hand, Kyra was noticeably concerned. She had a look of anger, odd excitement, and severe nervousness. While Ivy attempted to comfort her, Kyra would simply change topics in hopes she would be left alone.

The *shackflyer* wasn't very far away, but by the time we got there, we were exhausted. The bruises and cuts from all the fighting started hurting after a while, and the blood staining my clothes was begging to be washed away. As soon as we opened the shack's door, I ran upstairs and prepared a shower. Tyrose laid Reyna on a couch, Kyra went to her room, and Ivy searched the kitchen for something to eat—I knew we wouldn't talk to each other for a while.

I undressed and placed the clothes in a bucket of water, which turned bright red as soon as I dipped my suit inside. After taking a shower and scrubbing my musty body, I searched the room's drawers and found various clothes, including a... *buffoon costume*? I ignored it and chose another outfit: a white shirt and beige pants that barely fit me.

With my new uncomfortable set of clothes, I was finally ready to take a nap. I didn't even dream—I simply cleared my mind and rested.

*****

"It's weird, right?" Kyra asked Ivy after she stepped into her room.

"Reuniting with that witch? It must be," Ivy sat down on the bed and sighed.

"God, why couldn't the curse be from another witch!" Kyra complained, "I mean, what are the odds?"

"Renna is one of the few witches in the lands, so it's not as surprising," Ivy chuckled, "what do you think happened to her? Do you think she even lives in that swamp anymore?"

"I hope so," she sighed, "if she's not there, she's dead."

"You're probably right."

"So, what about you and Tyrose? You never told me about him," Kyra changed the subject.

"I don't know anymore. We were kinda something many years ago, but now... it's different."

"Do you still like him?"

"Trust me, I don't," Ivy laughed, "it's been a long time since I've liked someone."

"I've never liked anyone, so... yeah."

"I don't think I can visualize you with someone," Ivy chuckled.

"I thought the same thing for you," Kyra said, "until today."

"You know I hear everything!" Tyrose yelled from the living room.

"Shut up and take care of Reyna!" Ivy grunted in reply.

"Already did!" Tyrose shouted back.

"Then tell the *shackflyer* to go to the swamp!"

"I don't know how to speak dragon tongue!"

"It's not... You know what, I'll do it," Ivy said as she walked out of the room, "talk to you later, Kyra."

Ivy gave the *shackflyer* directions, instructing him to go east and stop at the swamp where Renna, the witch, was supposedly located. Who knew what other dangers that place held.

*****

I slept for more than an hour. I wanted to rest some more, but when I woke up, I couldn't force myself to sleep again. The first thing I did was check on my clothes, which were still drowning in the bucket of water. Most of the blood had been cleaned off the suit, but my scarf still had reddish tones all around it. I changed clothes—mainly because the ones I was wearing were too small for me—and went to check on Reyna, who I last saw downstairs. Although I had plenty of time to process everything that happened, I was still worried. If Renna wasn't where Kyra said she was, what would we do? She was our only hope of saving Reyna.

"Tyrose?" I asked as I stepped down the stairs.

He was in charge of Reyna—checking her temperature, taking notes on the curse's effect, and watching over her. He was joyfully peeling an orange in the kitchen, but Reyna was nowhere to be found. Last I saw her, she was lying on the leather couch in the living room.

"Is this the food in the lands?" Tyrose asked, examining the fruit, "in my kingdom, we only eat edible rocks and salt. But I do have a friend who owns a garden, and one time he gave me some berries. Man, were they delicious!"

"Pretty tasty, huh?" I said, "do you know where Reyna is?"

"Oh, she's resting upstairs," Tyrose explained, "I laid her down on the leather couch, but it was really uncomfortable, so I moved her upstairs. She's alright, don't worry."

"Is the curse expanding?"

"Part of her arms and legs are covered in that thing," he said, "it looks as if she's turning into a shadow. Do you think it has any relevance?"

"I guess we'll have time to ask Renna once we find her," I sighed, "now pass me one of those oranges."

"This is the last one."

"But there were four when I last chec—" I began, "you know what, just give me an apple."

"Um..."

"Did you also eat the three apples?"

"There are pears left. I didn't like them, so there's like two left."

I opened a cabinet, which had one pear, two peaches, and a piece of moldy bread. I grabbed the pear and took a bite.

"What about you, Krell?" Tyrose asked, "you're a Prince, right?"

"I was, but I don't know anymore," I said, taking another bite, "and you, Tyrose? Are you part of the royal family?"

"If I live on the outskirts of my kingdom, do you think I'm part of it?" He laughed, "the Princess from the Fire Kingdom—Stella—was my friend some time ago, but besides that, I don't have any relation with the royal family."

"I hope they survived."

"They probably escaped as soon as the attack started," Tyrose said, munching, "still, the—"

I didn't understand why Tyrose stopped talking until I glanced at his chest. Blood dripped down his stomach, and a sharp metal sword protruded from his torso. Before I could scream, the blade was withdrawn, and Tyrose fell to the ground, gurgling as he choked on his own blood.

"The bounty changed," said the person who stabbed him.

After staring at Tyrose's unconscious body for a few seconds, I turned my head to the man, whom I recognized instantly. It was one of my father's bounty hunters—the same one Reyna, Ivy, and I fought at Trotter Mountain. We tried killing him twice, but his strange regeneration magic prevented it. Now he was back, angrier than ever.

"You," I gulped.

"Your father," he said, "he upgraded the bounty."

The man was distracted, giving me the chance to try recalling my sword. I knew he couldn't die, but that didn't mean I couldn't injure him. As soon as I raised my hand, he grabbed it tightly and hurled me away. I hit the countertops before standing up and picking up the knife Tyrose was using to peel the orange.

"As I was saying," the bounty hunter continued, "he upgraded the bounty. Before, it was a bland and boring *dead or alive*, but now..."

"Get away!" I yelled as he walked closer.

"Now, if I bring your heads, I get twenty million additional vanes!" He exclaimed.

I took a step forward, slashing the knife at his skin. Blood leaked from his arm, but moments later, the wound sealed shut. The man rushed at me with his sword raised to waist height, but I jumped aside and stabbed his chest. He grunted and pulled the knife out of his skin with ease, throwing it to the floor afterward. I recalled my sword, which flew through the walls of the shack, destroying some of them—that would certainly catch Ivy and Kyra's attention.

I leaped and slashed at the man, but he used his blade to parry and launch me backward. I tripped over the knife on the floor and fell, twisting my ankle. When I tried to stand up, the man pulled my hair and slammed my face onto the wooden tiles. My nose began to bleed, and my bottom lip split. I raised my hand to recall my sword, but the man forced his knee onto my shoulder. If I didn't act, he would break my arm and nose.

"Now for the price," I heard him say.

The next thing I heard was a sword scratching its tip on the floor. I knew it was time—he was going to decapitate me.

"Tyrose, what are you doing?" Ivy stepped into the kitchen and saw what was happening, "Tyrose!"

The blade was inches away from my neck when the bounty hunter focused on Ivy, distracted from his main objective. I reached for the knife beside me and stabbed the man's ear. He screamed and tumbled down, covering his wound in pain. For a moment, I thought his regeneration magic had stopped working, but when he pulled his hand away, he had no open wound.

"You will die!" He screamed.

Ivy was still paralyzed by what happened to Tyrose, so she wasn't any help when the man choked me and threw me out the kitchen window. I didn't fall off the *shackflyer*, but I was no longer inside to help Ivy.

"How did you find..." She cried, "*Tyrose*."

"It was easy enough," the bounty hunter grunted, "I found a stuttering elf around the Zumba tribe camp. He told me everything I needed to know."

"What did you do to Kharum!" Ivy screamed.

"Oh, he's fine. Only lost three fingers."

Ivy shouted and dashed towards the man. She didn't have her hatchet at hand, and there weren't enough plants or trees nearby for her to use to her advantage, so she swiftly grabbed the knife on the floor and took a step back, ready to fight. The man raised his sword and lowered it toward Ivy, but she dodged and forced the knife at his chest. As it touched his skin, the man took the knife from her hand.

"I've been doing this for decades," he said, "I know every trick."

Before Ivy could react, he stabbed her in the stomach. The knife pierced her body, but it wasn't bloody enough to satisfy the man. He shoved Ivy against a wall with the knife still inside her. I could hear the screams from outside the shack—they were utterly terrifying. The tip of the knife was already protruding the other side of her body, and still, it wasn't enough for the man. He twisted the knife in circles three times, lacerating almost half of her torso. She cried, but the bounty hunter kept rotating the blade, beginning to cut upwards. Ivy was inches away from death.

"Ivy!" Kyra came out of her room and screamed.

She used her abilities to summon ice on the man's legs, adhering him to the floor and freeing Ivy. The bounty hunter pulled the knife from her stomach, attempting to strike Kyra instead, but she was too agile for him. She drew her sword and decapitated him, holding Ivy and dragging her away from the dead man's body.

"Kyra... I..." Ivy tried warning her but couldn't speak properly.

"He's dead—you're okay," Kyra said, covering Ivy's wound.

Then, a knife suddenly pierced Kyra's shoulder. She collapsed and lay unconscious on the floor with blood dripping down her arm. The man had regenerated once again and injured the last hope we had.

"I'll come collect your heads later," he said, "I'm just missing one more..."

He reached into his pocket and took out a folded paper. He unrolled it, revealing several drawings of all of us. There was a sketch of Ivy, seemingly drawn a long time ago, one of Kyra, drawn masterfully, and another of me, similar to the ones scattered across the Main Kingdom. When the man turned the paper around, it revealed the last person on his list: *Reyna*.

"Where are you?" He muttered, walking up the *shackflyer's* stairs.

He whistled a strange tune as he took each step. The first door on the second floor led to a bathroom, so when he kicked it open, he was disappointed. He rushed to the second door and punched a hole through it—thankfully, the bedroom was empty. Only one door remained, and the bounty hunter knew the elf he sought was inside. He slowly approached it and carefully opened the door, trying not to make a sound. Indeed, Reyna was there, shivering on the bed and wrapping herself with blankets.

"It's going to be quick, don't worry," the man quietly laughed.

He raised his sword over Reyna, ready to take her head. He was about to lower it when Reyna pulled the blanket away and revealed the dagger hidden beneath. She stood up and pierced the man's throat, pressing harder against his chin and shoving him against a wall. The bounty hunter fought back by kicking her away and regenerating his neck. Reyna tried not to collapse, but she was weak—the curse was still expanding.

"A sick girl?" He noticed Reyna's coughing, "let me end your suffering."

When the man thrusted his sword at Reyna, she grabbed a pillow to shield her body. The blade perforated the cushion, and when it was ripped apart, feathers flew around the room, reducing Reyna's visibility.

She blindly swung her sword, hoping one of the slashes would catch the bounty hunter off guard. After the feathers settled, she noticed the man was nowhere to be seen.

"I'll get my reward!" He jumped from behind and pushed her to the floor.

Reyna's dagger flew across the room, bouncing off the wall and landing a few feet away from her. She tried crawling, but the man pulled her foot and tossed her away. He grabbed his sword and slashed at her back, but she rolled away and got back on her feet before any attacks could hit her.

"How did...?" Reyna tried speaking but couldn't stop coughing.

"For a dying girl, you seem to be holding your ground," he laughed, preparing his sword once again.

Reyna knew she needed to defeat the man before the curse prevented her from staying conscious. Without hesitation, she ruthlessly stabbed his eye. The bounty hunter cried, walking in circles and waiting for it to heal so he could keep fighting. Although he couldn't die, he could still feel pain, and Reyna was going to use that to her advantage. She shattered the man's head on the room's window, holding his torso outside the shack as she coughed and fought to stay awake.

"I hope your eye is healed by now," Reyna gripped the man's head, "I want you to see what awaits you."

When his eye regenerated, he realized the *shackflyer* was soaring over a swamp filled with bodies in the acidic water, creatures lurking around, and deadly animals devouring the meat left on human skeletons scattered about. If he fell into the swamp, his body would decompose immediately, and whenever he regenerated, the same thing would happen repeatedly. Eternal suffering—a fitting punishment for a monster like him.

With the little strength she had left, Reyna pushed the bounty hunter off the shack. She didn't ensure he fell into the water, but she was ecstatically relieved to have gotten rid of him. The man's screams were so satisfying that Reyna even giggled before collapsing in pain.

"Reyna!" I barged into the room, panicked.

I had crawled through one of the windows on the second floor after the bounty hunter hurled me off the shack—Reyna was the first thing I saw upon entering.

"I killed him, Krell," she coughed.

"You'll be alright, Reyna," I said, touching her burning forehead.

"Go to the others, I'll be fine," she replied weakly.

"There's a glass of water on the desk," I mentioned before exiting the room, "I'll be back soon."

The hallway was full of dirty footprints, including one on a door that had been kicked open. I was too afraid to walk down the stairs, especially when no sound came from below. I knew the man had either killed Ivy and Kyra or left them greatly injured, but I didn't expect the bloodshed that awaited me in the living room. I gasped and scratched my nails on the wall, feeling weak. I wanted to vomit. It was sickening. Ivy was less than five feet away from me, her entire stomach lacerated, and her torso smeared with blood that reached my feet. I couldn't see if she was breathing because something else caught my attention. Tyrose—who had been stabbed in front of me—was facing the floor with blood overflowing from his mouth. He seemed dead but was still gasping small, frail breaths. The last person I saw was Kyra, coming out of a room with a box in her hands. She had blood on her shoulder, but ice froze the wound—she was the only one conscious.

"Kyra!" I sighed with relief, approaching her.

"Don't worry about me, just grab this!" Kyra opened the box and handed me a needle and a thread.

"Ivy and Tyrose... We need to do something!" I cried, trying not to look at them.

"Exactly, so grab the damn needle and sew someone!" Kyra shouted.

"Sew? Like cloth?"

"Yes, Krell! Stick the needle in and seal their wounds!"

In my kingdom, whenever someone had an injury so severe, they would decapitate that person to make their death "*less painful.*" I was glad there was another way.

"I'll take Ivy," I said, grabbing the needle and kneeling beside her.

"I was going to—" Kyra began, "never mind, I'll take Tyrose."

Sewing someone wasn't something I thought possible, but if Kyra told me to do something, I'd do it without hesitation. I started by threading the needle and locating the wound. Blood obscured my view of where the man had gashed her, so I stood up and grabbed napkins from the kitchen. The moment the cloth touched Ivy's stomach, it became soaked in blood. I carefully removed the napkin, but she still flinched when I touched her—at least that meant she was still alive.

"Her back," Kyra said, wiping her nose, "she has a wound on her back."

I flipped Ivy over and noticed the cut on her lower back. When the bounty hunter stabbed her, the knife had completely pierced through—it was horrible to even think about. I took the needle and perforated Ivy's skin, threading it through the wound and sealing it from the other side. She grunted and shook but didn't wake up. I had to finish before she gained consciousness, so I kept sewing and cleaning the wound for more than fifteen minutes until it was finally tied up with the tiny string. Kyra did the same with Tyrose, finishing moments after I did.

"Is she alright?" Kyra asked after I told her I was done.

"She's breathing," I replied, "Tyrose?"

"He'll live," Kyra said, wiping her bloody hands on the floor, "who was that guy?"

"Bounty hunter," I said, "my father sent him."

"Not even Osrov posed that big of a threat."

"I know," I sighed, standing up "I'll go check on Reyna."

"You want me to come with you?" She asked.

"I'm fine. I just need to talk to her alone."

"I'm here for whatever you need."

I walked upstairs to Reyna's room and found her lying on her bed with feathers all over her. I chuckled and stepped closer, noticing her constant trembling and flinching. It seemed as if she was having a bad dream.

"Krell," she muttered with her eyes closed.

At first, I thought she was talking to me, but her eyes were sealed shut. She was calling my name in her sleep.

"Don't—" she shivered, "I'm sorry, I'm not a monster."

I was confused. Why would anyone call her a monster?

"Don't go!" She yelped, tightly holding her wrist, "I'm sorry."

"I'm here, Reyna. I'm not going anywhere," I squeezed her hand.

"Do you forgive me?" She mumbled.

"For what?" I asked, even though I knew she wasn't talking to me.

"I—" Reyna sighed and then stopped.

I remained with the doubt of what she was talking about but didn't want to wake her up, so I simply grabbed a chair and sat beside her all night long.

Chapter 31

My father was in his castle, lying on his bed and trying not to fall asleep. He hadn't rested in days and wasn't planning to do so anytime soon. Sending guards to go murder me must have been really exhausting, right? His eyes were already closing when someone knocked on his door. A guard entered the room quickly, clearly preoccupied.

"I never said *go ahead*," the King said, sitting up on his bed and looking at the knight.

"I'm sorry, Henrius," he bowed before him.

"It's *King* Henrius to you," he wanted to yell but was too tired to do so.

"Sorry, my lord, but it's urgent," the guard cleared his throat, "we scouted the outsides and spotted a *shackflyer* flying over the swamp area of the lands. We believe it might have been the Prince."

"He's not the Prince anymore," my father stood up, "and I sent a bounty hunter to collect their heads, so don't worry about it."

"That's the thing—he failed."

"Huh, I never knew that man could fail," Henrius remarked, "send men to the swamp and find Krell."

"Absolutely, and there's another thing," he continued.

"What now?"

"When we were scouting the area, we saw some... *creatures*," he approached the subject delicately, "I'm not assuming anything, but they looked like shadows."

"Shadows?" My father laughed, "I locked those things away years ago. There's no way they could possibly escape."

"I'm not doubting you, my lord, but... they certainly looked like those monsters."

"I'll check it out later. Now, leave," my father commanded.

The guard rushed out of the room and slammed the door behind him. My father stood still, looking out the window and pondering.

"Shadows," he chuckled, then paused, actually processing the words that came out of his mouth, "*shadows*."

I woke up with a warm touch on my shoulder. My eyes forced themselves open, and I tilted my head upwards. For a moment, I was confused, forgetting why I had fallen asleep in a chair, but then I remembered. Reyna lay asleep on the bed in front of me, shivering and sweating uncontrollably. The curse was spreading through her arms and neck, slowly consuming her.

"Krell," someone beside me said.

I turned around and grinned—Ivy was there, shaking my shoulders and smiling. Her clothes were still tinted red, and it was clear she was still in pain by the way she held her stomach.

"Ivy?" I stood up, rubbed my eyes, and hugged her, "are you...?"

"I'm fine, don't worry," she said, pushing me away, "Kyra told me you saved me."

"If you mean *'sticking a needle inside you,'* then yes, I saved you," I giggled, "is Tyrose doing alright?"

"We found a tiny flask of novo juice in the basement. I didn't use it for myself—I prefer my wounds healing naturally—but Tyrose did," she explained, "he's fine, but... it's better if you see."

She limped out of the room with her hand tightly pressed against her stomach. I followed her, taking one final glance at Reyna before closing the door and walking down the stairs. Ivy held onto the railing, trying to remain steady, but with her stomach recently gashed, it was difficult.

"I'm coming with you!" I heard Tyrose's voice from the living room, "the more of us there are, the better chance we have!"

"Someone has to take care of Reyna!" Kyra argued with him, "besides, you're not entirely healed yet."

"And Ivy is?" He crossed his arms.

"I don't need you to take care of me," Ivy said, arriving in the living room alongside me.

"Tyrose, you're alive!" I exclaimed.

"Exactly, and that's why I should accompany you," he used my words as an example.

When I asked what the argument was about, Tyrose flinched and fell to his knees. He grabbed his chest and grunted, closing his eyes and clenching his teeth. Reyna had told me that novo juice burned when applied, and that was definitely the case.

"That's why you'll stay here," Kyra faked a smile.

"And you can take care of Reyna while we look for the witch," said Ivy.

"I won't—" Tyrose began, then stopped and sighed, "fine! But if it takes you more than an hour, I'm searching for you."

"It'll be quick," Kyra said, grabbing her pouch and opening the *shackflyer*'s door.

The whole time we spent arguing, I hadn't realized we had arrived at our destination: a swamp. Just by the smell, I knew it wasn't gonna be a pleasant journey. Still, to cure Reyna, I'd do anything.

"I'm coming with you, right?" I asked.

"What do you think?" Ivy said, exiting the *shackflyer*, "now, come on."

Tyrose sighed as I grinned, recalling my sword and grabbing my scarf. The humid smell hit me as soon as I walked out the door, making me want to go back inside—not to mention the temperature, which was as hot as the Fire Kingdom. The swamp itself wasn't really a swamp. It was dirt, dead trees, logs, and shacks infested with fungi and mud. There was water in other areas of the swamp, but the area where we stood was completely dry.

"Not how I remembered it," Kyra pointed out, "easier to traverse, though."

"That smell," I said, using my scarf to cover my nose.

"Let's do this quickly," Ivy coughed, "we'll get to Renna, she'll give us the cure, and we'll return."

"I don't think it'll be that easy," Kyra replied.

"Can we walk while we talk?" I asked, "we don't have that much time, and I can't bear the smell anymore."

Kyra looked back at me and rolled her eyes, taking a step forward. Ivy limped behind her, holding her stomach in pain. I asked if she needed any help, but she insisted she was fine and could handle herself. It was weird not having Reyna by my side—since the journey began, she had been with me, but at that moment, she was unconsciously lying on a bed, slowly deteriorating.

Time flew by as we walked. I didn't know if it was because I was overthinking or because we were in a hurry, but within minutes, we had crossed half the swamp. I wish I could describe my surroundings, but I didn't want to appreciate the view myself. All I could say was that it looked lifeless.

"Where is Renna?" I asked, avoiding the muddy ground.

"It's just north of the village," Kyra replied.

"There's a village?"

"Supposedly," Ivy continued limping without help, "it should be around here, but I can't see anything through the fog!"

"I'm starting to lose hope," Kyra shook her head.

"She needs to be here," I said desperately.

When I took another step on the viscous ground, I felt a warm touch on my calf. I thought some mud might have splashed on my leg until I looked and screamed. A dirty brown hand emerged from the ground, pulling me down to my knees and sinking me into the mud. Ivy and Kyra gasped, taking a step back and watching as other hands surfaced and gripped my limbs. It didn't take long for me to realize they were the same creatures that attacked us on our way to Trotter Mountain.

"Krell!" Kyra tried to help me.

Another hand emerged from the mud, grabbing her legs and pulling her down. Ivy attempted to escape, but similar creatures reached out and dragged her beside me.

"Help!" I shouted before a hand seized my head.

Kyra and Ivy struggled to free themselves, but it was nearly impossible. Their bodies sank into the mud before they could scream for help. Moments later, my mouth and nose were covered—all I could do was helplessly stare at the remaining hands on the surface.

I was about to close my eyes and accept my fate when I saw a figure creeping through the swamp. The person walked slowly towards us, holding a small dagger in the left hand, with a hood and cape covering the upper body. The mysterious figure stepped in the mud and slashed with the dagger, severing one of the hands. When another emerged, the person simply stepped on it—I never knew they were so easy to kill. Eventually, she pulled down her hood, revealing long, dark, silky hair, tanned skin, and dark eyes. The girl kneeled and took a flask from her pouch. As if she weren't in a rush, she opened the glass, took the ashes inside, closed it, and then smeared the dust over the mud.

Instantly, the hands holding us disappeared into thin air, and the mud under our feet began evaporating. In the blink of an eye, I was lying in a deep hole in the ground alongside Ivy and Kyra.

"Thanks," I coughed and sighed in relief.

"What were those?" Kyra asked after taking a deep breath.

"Demon hands," said the girl who rescued us, "at least that's what we call them."

The girl's voice surprised me; it was incredibly high pitched. When I noticed how tall she was, I started wondering if I was speaking to a child.

"How old are you?" Ivy asked before I could.

"Does it matter?" She sat down on a broken log beside us, "I'm eleven, and I still saved your ass—"

"Eleven!" I exclaimed.

"You're the Prince, right?" She asked after analyzing my face, "and you're... Ivy, and you're... *the devil's daughter.*"

"Devil's daughter?" Kyra said, then paused, "oh, *devil's daughter.*"

"What does that mean?" I whispered.

"Renna," Ivy murmured back.

"Wait," I said, "do you know where she is? Renna?"

"Don't say her name!" The young girl shushed me, "but yes, I know where she is."

"Give us a location," Kyra stood up menacingly.

"You're looking for her?" She laughed, "you're making a mistake."

"We didn't ask for your opinion; we asked for a location," Ivy interjected.

"I'll tell you," she smirked, "if you do me a favor."

"We're not doing anything," Kyra sighed, looking back at me, doubting the idea, "we're not!"

"You'll never find her without my help," the girl said, "it's not as easy as knocking on her door and starting a conversation. Without me and my father's help, your search will be in vain."

"If it's quick, we'll do it," Ivy said.

"We're not gonna do it," Kyra complained before finally agreeing, "fine! Take us to your daddy!"

"I'm Yusra," she said, attempting to shake Kyra's hand, but she refused, "follow me."

Yusra guided us to her home, claiming it was the safest path. However, we encountered various trotters along the way. Surprisingly, the smell improved as we traversed the area. When asked, Yusra explained that most of the rotten bodies remained at the swamp's entrance because few ventured that far. We walked for over fifteen minutes until the little girl led us to a nearby village. There were shacks and houses made of wood and stone, but the only building that stood out was a white and blue dome at the far end of the street. Yusra told us not to enter through the main gate; instead, we would sneak through the back.

"Why?" I asked her.

"You don't want to catch any unwanted attention, Prince," she glanced back and continued walking.

I understood her. Bringing two Queens and a Prince into a hidden village at the lands' edge would alarm everyone. So, after walking around the outside barrier of the hamlet, we climbed over a wall that led to the dome.

"Now, follow me inside the palace," Yusra pulled a key out of her pocket and opened the back door of the dome.

"Is your father…?" I began.

"The sultan? Yeah," she replied proudly.

"What is a sultan?" Ivy asked, stepping inside the palace.

"Someone similar to a King. You'll see what I mean in just a moment," Yusra said, guiding us through the majestic monument.

"I expected her father to be a peasant, not a King," Kyra whispered to us.

"I heard you!" Yusra exclaimed without bothering to look at us.

We followed her through the corridor and up a spiral staircase that led us straight into the sultan's bedroom, which was covered in mosaics of various sea animals. As Yusra opened the door, two guards appeared behind us, grunting after recognizing our faces.

"Dad?" Yusra called out for him.

"Eh!" I heard a voice from inside the room, "my Yusra!"

The sultan rushed to his daughter and kissed her cheek. He was wearing a white robe adorned with pearls, something similar to a towel over his head, and multiple rings on each finger. His beard was so long it even touched the floor at times, which wasn't very surprising considering he was shorter than Yusra.

"Papa, *insanlari buldum*," Yusra said in another language, "*iş için*."

"*Aferın*, Yusra," her father chuckled, "*Onlarla konuşacağım*."

"What are they talking about?" Ivy whispered to Kyra.

"I don't know," Kyra murmured back, "do you think they're plotting our death?"

"Not likely," she said, "I hope."

"Hello, everyone!" The sultan laughed heartily, kissing Ivy and Kyra's hands, "my name is Mustafa! And I heard you're looking for *cadi*—the witch?"

"Yes, we're looking for Renna," I replied.

"Don't say her name!" Mustafa placed his finger on my lips, "she hears everything."

"Cut the crap and tell us what you want us to do," Kyra said aggressively.

"I need you to stop a civil war!" Mustafa smiled innocently.

"Oh," I clenched my teeth and gulped.

"Stop a civil war?" Ivy laughed nervously, "is this a joke?"

"Why would it be a joke?" Mustafa kept grinning awkwardly, "*bir şey söylemek*, Yusra."

"What my father is trying to say is that we need you to stop a rebellion," Yusra explained, "if it happens, my father and I could die."

"I thought the favor would be: *'pick up some flowers by the garden and bring them to us,'*" Kyra said, "not to stop a civil war!"

"It's going to be easy, especially for people like you!" Mustafa approached us, taking tiny, goofy steps, "the people of the village think one of the Old Gods is hidden in slumber in a cave nearby."

"An Old God?" Ivy asked, "is he there?"

"Of course not!" Mustafa wheezed, "those people out there—nymphos, most of all—believe anything they hear! They want me to start an excavation to find the Old God's tomb. Normally, I would listen to my people, but the tomb is in Ah'Lah'Rra territory, and I don't want to mess with them."

"So, what do you want us to do?" I asked skeptically.

"Assassinate their leaders," Mustafa smiled awkwardly, waiting for us to respond.

"Assasi—?" Kyra giggled in disbelief.

"We're not doing that," I said, about to walk out the door.

"Yeah, we'll go find Renna ourselves," Ivy agreed.

"Don't say her name!" Mustafa screamed, trying to remain calm, "we ask you wholeheartedly to do us this favor. We'll die if you don't do something."

"If *we* don't do something?" Kyra asked, "you are King here; you can protect yourself."

"You'll never find her!" The sultan yelled.

"I like those odds," I stepped out of the room.

"*Bok*!" He cursed in another language.

I was already rushing out of the palace when a blood-curdling scream was heard from outside. We all looked at each other and then out the window, wondering what was happening on the hamlet's streets. People were running around, seeking shelter as dozens of nymphos stood in line and drew their weapons, aiming at the village's gate. Guards, knights, warriors, and archers from the Main Kingdom had traced our steps to the lands' swamp.

"People from the villa!" One of the guards shouted, crossing the gates, "we don't want to disturb you, so let's do this quickly and nobody will get hurt. We were notified of a young boy's presence near this area, and we must know where he is—now!"

The citizens of the village stood petrified, glancing at the guards from the streets or their windows. The nymphos stood their ground by growling at the warriors and aiming their spears, ready to protect their home.

"We'll pay!" The guard announced, "a hundred million vanes to whoever turns them in!"

I glared back at the sultan, who was carefully listening to what the guard said. He clenched his teeth and looked back at us with an innocent smile.

"A hundred million vanes is a lot..." The sultan began.

"Papa!" Yusra shook his shoulders, "you're crazy! Öylece ölmelerine izin mi vereceksin? *Bize yardım edebilirler!*"

"Yusra, the money can help us!" Said Mustafa, "*isyancı liderlerin öldürülmesine yardım edecek!*"

"Are you going to turn us in?" Ivy asked, stepping back.

"Mustafa, don't," I added.

"The kid is here! Hey, guards, he's here!" Mustafa opened the window and shouted, alerting the guards.

"What the hell, Mustafa?" Kyra exclaimed.

"It is what it is, kids," he laughed back, shrugging.

I shook my head at the sultan in hatred as Kyra pulled my arm and rushed out of his room. We ran down the stairs and were about to exit through the same window we came through when a couple of guards from the village caught up to us.

"Get away!" Kyra screamed as the guards began dragging her away.

Before they could do the same to me, I raised my hands and cooperated with them. While Ivy and Kyra were yanked outside, I was safely escorted to the village's main gate.

"Look what we have here," one of the guards from the Main Kingdom chuckled upon seeing my face, "Krell Kovner."

"Is the King really so obsessed with me that he has to hunt me down to the furthest areas of the lands?" I asked, recalling my sword.

"He's just following the kingdom's rules," he replied.

That was when I noticed the nympho tied to a wooden pole beside the guard, trying to shake himself free. I didn't understand what was happening until one of the guards lit a torch and handed it to his captain.

"Leave the nympho alone," I commanded.

"*Nympho*," the captain of the guards repeated, playing with the torch, "if it were an actual living creature, you would say *'he'* or *'she,'* but no! You say *nympho* because it is not a person! It is an animal, and it will get slaughtered like one because it isn't an intellectual creature!"

"Neither are you, and nobody says a damn thing!" I shouted with rage.

"You've got an attitude," he chuckled, "and that attitude will kill many."

The guard unemotionally tossed the torch onto the wooden pole. It caught fire immediately, expanding its flames to the nympho's skin and burning him alive. Kyra raised her hands without hesitation and summoned a wave of water to extinguish the flames and set the poor creature free. When the nympho trotted back to his village, all his companions cried for battle.

"You people..." Ivy shook her head.

"Attack!" One of the nymphos behind me screamed.

Around thirty of them ran towards the guards. I took a step backwards—not wanting to get involved in the brawl—but an overwhelming amount of them rushed in my direction and pushed me closer to the guards.

"Slaughter them all!" My father's men yelled.

As I prepared for the battle, something unexpected occurred. A gust of wind swept us away, hurling us to the ground. The houses around us shook, the ground trembled, and everybody gasped in fear, unsure of what was happening. After being knocked down, I opened my eyes and saw Kyra, the only one still standing. Her face was full of fear and uncertainty as if she knew something we didn't.

"I think I swallowed a bug," Ivy coughed.

"What was that?" The captain of the guards shouted as he stood up.

Behind him was a figure. I couldn't quite make out the silhouette, but it seemed like a woman adorned with a hood.

"You did that?" The guard turned around, "you dare attack the King's guards?"

The woman crept closer without any weapon in sight. The only thing she had was a pouch full of flasks and jars of different colors.

"Why don't we show her why she shouldn't mess with us?" The guard laughed with his companions.

He raised his spear with pride, but as soon as he thrusted to stab the woman, a sharp sound was heard. The man gurgled, wrapping his hands around his neck as he dizzily attempted to walk—inevitably, he fell to the ground. The woman had slashed a blade at the man's throat twice in the blink of an eye, lacerating his face and killing him. One of the other knights charged, but the woman grabbed a flask from her pouch and poured some strange dust on her palms. When the knight raised his sword, she blew the ash at his eyes, engulfing his head in flames. I was terrified by the massacre, but Kyra seemed unaffected. Her expression remained unchanged.

"Go! Fire! Quickly!" An archer screamed.

They tried to kill the woman, but with a simple flick of a finger, the arrows were redirected back to the archers. Many were impaled in the neck, others in the legs, and most in the chest. By that point, most of my father's guards were already running, but some still believed themselves powerful enough to stop her. Two guards were dashing at the woman when she opened another flask and spilled a viscous liquid on their face. They screamed, and moments later, ice spikes and shards emerged from their bodies, ripping through their skin and tearing their eyes out. I admit, I closed my eyes when that happened.

"No!" A guard screamed.

He chased after the woman with his sword, but she took another flask and tossed it in his direction. The glass shattered upon impact on the guard's armor. He coughed, collapsed to the ground, and died shortly after vomiting blood. Every single knight, guard, and archer had fled, except for one who was on his knees, paralyzed. He trembled and tried to surrender by placing his spear on the ground.

"Please," he muttered, "I won't do anything."

She looked at him and tilted her head, reaching into her pouch for another flask. She opened the jar and dripped some liquid onto her right arm, mischievously grinning behind her hood.

"No! No!" The guard cried, closing his eyes.

The woman's arm shifted to a brown tone, growing and sprouting dirt. She glanced back at the guard and whispered a few words before smashing his head in—I had never seen someone murder with such brutality. Who was she?

Her arm returned to normal as she wiped the blood from her clothes, glancing in my direction afterward. Shivers ran down my spine as I imagined the merciless barbarities she could inflict on us. With a single step toward the hamlet, the nymphos gasped and fled to their homes in fright, leaving us alone with the mysterious person. Ivy was trembling, and Kyra was staring at her with a straight face—she hadn't shown any emotion since the woman arrived.

"Who are you?" I asked bravely.

She pulled her hood down, finally revealing her identity. At first, I was certain it was my mother—her green eyes, tiny nose, and black hair were identical, but there was something wrong with her face.

"Mother," Kyra mumbled.

Mother? Mother! That woman was Renna? When I first heard of her, I imagined an old hag with white hair, yellow teeth, and wrinkles all over her face, not a beautiful middle-aged woman! My jaw hit the ground when that word came out of Kyra's mouth.

"Renna," I gasped.

"Krell Kovner," she squinted her eyes and said my name, "and the girl's friend."

"Nice to see you again, witch b—" Ivy began.

"I don't have time for this," Renna interrupted.

She walked away, placing her hood back on and stepping over the corpses of those she had massacred moments before.

"If you really want to see me," she glanced back momentarily, "meet me at my cabin north from here."

And then she disappeared into forest.

Chapter 32

The people from the village were kind enough to provide us with supplies for our journey through the swamp. Some of them gave us gifts for *"saving their village,"* even though we never fought anyone—I guess scaring off the witch was enough to gain the respect of the nymphos. I noticed Yusra running up and down the streets searching for us, but we purposely ignored her. I knew she wanted our help, but did she really think we could stop a civil war after her dad betrayed us? No, thanks.

"I think the exit is this way," Kyra said, rushing toward it.

"Please accept our gift!" A nympho cried.

"Thanks, but keep it to yourself!" Ivy shouted back.

I wasn't used to receiving much appreciation from villagers, and although it seemed exciting, it was truly exhausting. People approached me, offering gifts and trying to get a hug (which I kindly accepted, but Ivy and Kyra declined). We were attempting to leave the village, but people kept swarming around us and blocking the path. Kyra pulled me away as soon as we reached the hamlet's gate, leading us back into the swamp.

"We need to get out of here before Yusra notices us," Kyra urged.

"She's just a little girl, though," Ivy remarked.

"A little girl whose father almost got us killed," she replied, "besides, she wants us to assassinate her father's enemies."

"Don't just walk away! What is wrong with you!" I heard a high-pitched voice behind me.

Yusra was running towards us with a pocket knife tied to her waist and a white hood. I thought she was going to stab me until she stopped and stood still.

"You need to help us," she begged, "you know I can die if this rebellion happens, right? My father can die! And you're just going to walk away? You're supposed to be the *heroes of the lands*!"

"Look, girl, we are no heroes," said Kyra, "and if we actually were, I'm sure we wouldn't help someone who betrayed us."

"If you want, don't help my father, but do help me!" She cried, "those people are dangerous. They will kill me whenever they get the chance!"

"That is not our problem," Ivy agreed with Kyra and walked away.

"Yusra, you can come with us if you'd like," I offered, "we are set up in a camp east of here, near the Main Kingdom. I don't know if we'll accept your father, but if things get messy in your village, you can find help there."

"What is wrong with you?" She shook her head, "I don't want to move out; I want my father to be safe! You're a joke."

She turned her back on us and sprinted away, tears streaming down her face. I felt like a monster for not helping the little girl, but what else could I have done? At least I gave her the option to join us and protect herself from the rebellion. Still, I couldn't help but feel guilty. That simple choice could have cost Mustafa and Yusra their lives.

"It was our only choice," Ivy said, touching my shoulder, "c'mon, we need to move north."

I hesitantly turned around and sighed, ready to keep walking through the swamp. I had to close my heart to what had happened, so I followed Kyra and focused on our one and only goal at the moment: *finding the witch and curing Reyna's curse.*

With each step we took, the oddly viscous liquid from the swamp seeped into my shoes—it was gross, but it didn't seem to bother Ivy or Kyra. Renna said we could find her north of the village, but to be honest, I was frightened to see her again. What she did to the knights back at the village was horrifying, and I was terrified she'd do the same to us. I hoped she had some mercy—after all, I was her daughter's friend.

"She won't," Kyra said, "she doesn't see me as her daughter."

"What?" I looked at her oddly, "did you just read my thoughts?"

"You were talking out loud," she explained, "mumbling, but loud enough for me to hear."

"True," Ivy added, "and what she did to those knights back there? I can do it too. Maybe I'll give her a taste of her own medicine."

"Please, don't," I said, "let's try to solve this peacefully without spilling blood."

"Renna? Peaceful?" Kyra laughed, "my mother may be many things, but that isn't one of them."

"Look over there," Ivy interjected.

She pointed at the tall trees on our left. Dark autumn leaves flew past us as a chilling breeze blew in our direction and called our names. Renna's home had to be there. The dark forest matched her dismal style, and I knew Ivy and Kyra were thinking the exact same thing. Without a word, I hypnotically stepped toward the trees.

"Hold on, Krell," Kyra said, standing a few feet behind me.

I stopped and waited for Ivy and Kyra to reach me. Shoulder to shoulder, we began making our way to the heart of the beast: Renna's house.

We walked for twenty minutes without speaking. The birds chirped in an odd tune as trotters limped around the area, completely ignoring us—something was wrong with them. The swamp eventually merged into solid rock, giving us a chance to clean our shoes and wipe the acid off our clothes before continuing. Not far from there, a shack built with rotten wood lay surrounded by several leafless trees. Ropes were tied to their branches—some with people hanging from them. Kyra sighed as Ivy held her hand. By their expressions, I knew we had arrived at our destination.

"You can stay outside if you'd like," Kyra said, taking a step toward the shack.

"We're with you on this," Ivy smiled, hiding her uncertainty, "even if it's dangerous, I'll come with you."

"It's scary, but yeah, I'll also come," I gulped as my stomach tingled.

"When we get there, let me do the talking," she instructed us, "this is my mother, and I know how to speak to her. Don't say anything unless I tell you to."

"Fine," Ivy nodded.

When Kyra opened the shack's door, an unpleasant smell wafted out. The inside was as creepy as the outside. Webs were hanging on the edges of the hut, shelves full of potions and liquids that I couldn't look at for long enough without feeling a sensation of disgust. What caught my eye almost immediately was Renna, staring at us from the other side of the shack.

"Took you long enough," she grinned as her giant nails scratched the countertops.

"Renna, give us the cu—" I completely forgot what Kyra had told us beforehand.

"Krell, shut up and let me do the talking!" She screamed.

"You have the same temper as when you were a kid," Renna licked her lips, "and the same old, annoying, high-pitched voice. Cool hair, by the way. Looks like you've cut it all off—it barely reaches your shoulders."

"So my enemies can't pull it," Kyra replied, "remember you taught me that, mother? Or have you forgotten all those years we spent together?"

"Those years mean nothing to me."

Renna turned and opened a cabinet behind her, searching for some sort of potion. Why was she doing that in the middle of a conversation? Kyra didn't think much of it and kept talking.

"I won't waste more breath on you, so I'm gonna spell it out for you," Kyra began, "the Zumba tribe curse you cast on them many years ago? Does it ring a bell? Well, we need you to cure it."

"What makes you think I will give you the cure? What makes you think a cure even exists?"

"Because I've seen you heal curses before, and if you don't fix this one, we're going to have to do this the hard way."

"Oh, scary!" Renna chuckled, opening another cabinet, "aha, here it is!"

Renna took a small potion from the drawer and walked to the other side of the shack, pouring the liquid into a dusty flask.

"This curse begins to take effect when something rare happens," she explained, "it starts when someone in the Zumba tribe finds their purpose in life or when they fall in love. So if you know anything about that, you have your answer. And before you say anything else, I didn't know you had so many diverse friends, Reva! I mean, the Nature Queen, an elf, and even the Prince of the Main Kingdom himself! It's great that you're finally socializing after all these years! Oh, and also Tyrose."

"How do you know about him?" Ivy asked, tilting her head in confusion.

"I know everything, including where Reyna and him currently are," she grinned, "I can send hundreds of trotters their way with the snap of a finger. It would be a real pity if they got to them, considering the *shackflyer's* door is unlocked at this exact moment."

"You goddamn b—" Kyra drew her sword.

Before she could attack, Renna opened the flask in her hands—the one she had been working on since we arrived at her home—and tossed it our way. Dust stained the air, temporarily blinding us. Kyra was the only one expecting the sudden attack, so when I forced my eyes open, she was already chasing her sword after Renna. Sparks flew between blades as they tried to kill each other, and although Kyra wanted us to step back and let her do all the work, I couldn't bear seeing her struggle—neither could Ivy.

"Get off of her!" Ivy punched Renna.

She pushed the woman to the ground and ripped the sword from Kyra's hands. She desperately plunged the blade into the floor, but Renna rolled away and reached into her pouch. The blade got stuck on the wooden planks, and when Ivy pulled it out, Renna flung a flask at her.

"Wha—" Ivy tried to speak, but the words wouldn't come out, "I can't breathe..."

She dropped, clutching her throat and gasping for air. Kyra shook her shoulders, trying to figure out what spell the witch had cast upon her, while Renna stood back, laughing maniacally.

"Ivy, breathe!" Kyra yelled.

"Don't you think she's tried that already?" Renna chuckled.

"I'll help you!" I said, aproaching Ivy and Kyra.

"No! Hold Renna off while I figure out what to do with her!" Kyra replied angrily.

"Come on, boy, show me what you've got," the witch pointed her blade at me.

I was so frightened that I could have bolted out of the shack and escaped the swamp at that moment. My hands trembled, my eyes twitched, and my voice cracked as I stood petrified, staring into the witch's eyes. It seemed Renna took advantage of my fear when she ruthlessly smashed my face against the wall and slashed her sword in my direction. Before I could be sliced by the witch, I rolled away and recalled my sword, but she wouldn't stop chasing me.

"Recalling spell?" She coughed, surprised, "haven't seen that in years."

Meanwhile, Kyra was still trying to find a way to rescue Ivy, but nothing she did was working. She was running out of ideas.

"Please," Kyra pleaded, placing her mouth on Ivy's to see if anything happened—no luck.

She was turning purple. Her eyelids shook, and her muscles twitched as if she were choking on something. However, when Kyra placed her fingers inside Ivy's mouth, she noticed something was off. The airflow inside her body was perfectly normal, but there was some sort of barrier preventing it from exiting her mouth.

"It won't come out," Kyra mumbled, "there's another way out..."

Kyra was struck by an idea. She gripped a wooden plank on the floor and pulled it abruptly, tearing out a splinter. She hesitated before stabbing Ivy's chin with it. The tiny stake pierced her upper throat, blood dripping down her neck as her expression changed. She was in pain, but something was different—she was breathing again.

"Yes!" Kyra sighed with relief.

The spell had somehow broken, and Ivy began breathing normally. Kyra took a piece of cloth from a nearby table and placed it around her neck to stop the bleeding.

"Holy..." Ivy coughed, gasping for air, "my throat... What happened?"

"You couldn't breathe, Ivy."

"What?" She grinned, "did you kiss me?"

"It didn't work, so I had to figure out something else. That's why..." She paused for a moment, awkwardly glancing at Ivy's wound, "you know, your neck."

"So, you did kiss me?" Ivy chuckled.

"Yes," Kyra replied, "you're welcome for saving you, by the way."

"I mean, thank you, but why is Krell fighting that witch all by himself ?" Ivy pointed at me.

"Oh, crap! We need to help him!"

As Ivy and Kyra argued about how they saved each other and *kissed*—I heard that part but didn't really understand it—I was surviving Renna. Yes, *surviving,* because I didn't even try to fight back. All I did was dodge her thrusts and block her swings.

"Are you really that weak? Just fight!" She screamed.

Before the witch could attack again, I noticed a shelf beside me. Without hesitation, I pushed it in her direction and bolted away afterward. The rack collapsed near her, flinging flasks out of the open drawers and onto the floor, where many shattered.

"My potions!" She cried, "they are highly flammable."

Flames engulfed the wooden floor, but Renna used a potion from her pouch to extinguish the fire. Although it was relieving at first, shivers went down my spine when the witch turned around with an enraged expression.

"Get away!" Kyra yelled, stepping in front of me, "your fight is with me, Renna."

"Is it really?" She asked, "then why is your friend also trying to kill me?"

"Krell, Ivy," Kyra gulped, glancing back at us, "stand back. I can handle this."

"But, Kyra..." Ivy began.

"Step back," She repeated.

"We can help," I said.

"I know," she shook her head, "don't."

Renna smirked, wiping the blood from her cheek and panting. She wasn't even wielding her sword anymore. She tossed it aside and reached for her waist, unwrapping her belt.

"No weapons," she instructed, "just fists."

"Fine for me," Kyra replied, discarding her sword and preparing.

She was the first to strike, sprinting towards her mother and attempting to tackle her to the floor. When Renna punched her in the face, Kyra was forced to step back and recover—she wasn't used to fighting without weapons.

"Kyra," Ivy started to approach.

"No," I stopped her, "we need to wait."

Renna jerked her fist at her daughter's face, sending her to the other side of the shack. As Kyra stood up, Renna kicked her in the stomach and jumped on top of her, choking her afterward. I wanted to interviene and save her, but knew I wasn't allowed to.

"You think you can just come into my house, destroy my stuff, and ask me for a cure for a curse?" Renna continued, squeezing her daughter's neck, "then you're wrong!"

Kyra was already fainting when she noticed a wooden stake—the one she had used to stab Ivy's throat—lying a few inches away. As a last resort, she grabbed the sharp object and impaled her mother's eye. Kyra freed herself and crawled away, but Renna still had the stake deep inside her eyeball.

"Kyra, are you okay?" I asked, helping her walk away.

"Don't faint, please," Ivy added, "I really don't want us to kiss again."

"I'm fine," she panted.

"We agreed not to use weapons," Renna stood up in pain, muttering angrily, "and this is what you do? This is what you do, goddamnit! This tells me everything I want to know!"

Ivy, Kyra, and I stood together, holding each others' hands, ready for what was about to happen. Renna walked away and grabbed a bandage from one of her drawers, wrapping it around her eye and forehead. She picked her belt from the ground and tied it around her waist again.

"Give us the cure and nothing will happen," I said cautiously.

"Oh, it will happen," Renna breathed heavily, "it will."

The first flask she launched was aimed at Kyra. When it shattered on her chest and dripped the liquid through the cracks in the floor, hands appeared below us and began pulling us to our knees—the same hands we had encountered multiple times before. Luckily, the effect didn't last long. Renna was so enraged she kept hurling more and more flasks in our direction. One of the small jars collapsed over the hands entangling our legs—they were poisoned and killed by the liquid inside. We were freed, but another container was thrown at me moments after. Before I had the chance to run away, I was cast to the other side of the shack and strapped to the wall with a strange goo.

"You will die!" Renna cried.

After another spell reached Ivy and paralyzed her body, Kyra was our last hope, and she knew it. She managed to evade every single flask thrown at her with one simple goal in mind: *grab the sword she had tossed away moments before*.

"You destroyed everything I had! My beauty! My eye!" She threw glass after glass until there were none left, "how can I live without my eye? You ruined me! You ruined your goddamn mother, Reva! Because even if you don't want to accept it, that's your real name! Reva! Reva! Reva! Your name is Reva, not Kyra!"

"My name is not Reva!" She screamed.

With no more flasks left for Renna to launch at her, Kyra finally collected her sword from the floor. She tightly gripped its hilt and charged towards her mother, who was ready to take the hit—she didn't even care anymore.

"My name is Kyra!" She finally slashed her sword at her mother.

The witch gurgled after her shoulder was gashed. Her chest was bleeding, a piece of her throat was pierced, and her stomach was cut open. Kyra panted heavily, staining her clothes with blood as she disappointingly glanced at her mother.

"You killed me," Renna spat blood.

The dark goo that trapped me to the wall vanished into thin air, along with the spell that petrified Ivy. Renna was bleeding out and could no longer control her magic.

"Where is the cure?" Kyra asked unemotionally.

"Why should I tell you?" Renna gurgled, fighting to stay alive, "I'm dead anyway."

Kyra breathed heavily and desperately marched to a shelf, grabbing a jar of novo juice from one of the drawers and showing it to her mother.

"I'll give you some of this," Kyra kneeled before her, "you'll survive. Your eye won't return to normal, but you'll live. You can still follow the quest for immortality that you're so eager to accomplish."

"Right shelf; the third drawer," she said weakly, "black jar."

Indeed, when I searched the third drawer, there was a black jar with a note that read: "*Zumba Tribe Curse*." It had to be the cure, but what if it wasn't?

"How do we know this is the right one?" I asked.

"Because I need the novo juice..." Renna coughed, "*now*."

"I can tell when she lies," Kyra said, "she's telling the truth."

Kyra tossed the novo juice to her mother as I placed the cure in my right pocket. I heard when the witch dripped the liquid over her body, but I didn't really see it as we were already walking away by then. Kyra was sobbing, fighting the temptation to look back.

"You stupid kids," Renna cried, "you know you're making a mistake, right?"

I looked at Kyra, wondering if she would actually turn around and argue with her mother, but she kept walking in the opposite direction.

"Don't turn your back at me!" Renna screamed, incapacitated on the floor, "you come here, take my eye, my beauty, and my home! You can't walk away! You've always been a disappointment. Ever since your father and I created you, I knew there was something wrong with you, but I couldn't quite figure it out. Now I know what it is—you're a monster who kills and destroys everything in her path!"

Renna continued as Kyra closed her eyes, trying to ignore her mother, but it was difficult.

"Don't you dare come back here again, Reva! Don't you dare say my name or think about me again! I hate you!" She paused, then chuckled, "and you know what the worst thing is? At the end of the day, I'll outsmart you and outlive you. I have enough potions to live for centuries, and you—on the other hand—will die! When you're buried six feet underground, I'll sit at your grave and laugh! I'll laugh for hours and hours!"

Tears streamed down Kyra's cheeks as she gulped and then frowned, her expressions shifting. She wasn't sad anymore—she was furious. She turned around and looked directly at her mother's eyes, menacingly walking inside her home once again. Placing her hand on a shelf full of potions, she tilted her head and licked her teeth.

"Highly flammable, you said?" She grinned ragefully.

"No... no!" Renna screamed.

Kyra pushed the shelf without hesitation. Drawers opened, shattering flasks on the floor and drenching them with viscous liquids. It didn't take long for the wood to catch fire. By the time Kyra began walking away, the shack was already engulfed in flames. Renna searched her pouch for something to extinguish the blaze, but she had wasted all her flasks against us. The fire spread through the yard quickly, destroying the plants and trees surrounding the hut. Years of plantations were consumed by smoke, and all the medicines that could have made Renna "*immortal*" were gone.

"I'll come back for you!" Renna said, still inside the burning shack, "I will!"

Then the roof collapsed on top of the witch, crushing her frail body and likely killing her. Ivy stared at the flames in awe, squeezing Kyra's hand, which pulled her away seconds later. Although Kyra had caused the death of her own mother, I knew she didn't feel guilty about it. I wondered how it felt killing a family member—*a parental figure.* Was it as satisfying as it seemed? By the looks of it, it definitely was because Kyra was smiling as it all happened.

Chapter 33

I did my best to comfort Kyra on our way back to the *shackflyer.* We walked for over two hours, and although I tried changing topics and ignoring what had happened moments before, we were still haunted by Renna's death. I was worried about Reyna and Tyrose, who were alone back at the *shackflyer.* Renna mentioned she had the power to send trotters their way at any moment, so if she somehow survived the burning shack that collapsed over her, she could have done so. But I didn't have time to worry—in the lands, worrying would only get you killed.

On our way there, we passed Yusra and Mustafa's village. Ivy suggested we stop there, get supplies, and continue, but Kyra and I both refused. After everything that happened with Yusra and her father, the last thing I wanted to do was steal from their village. I hoped the little girl would accept our offer and follow us to the Zumba tribe camp, but I knew she was too stubborn.

Some of the "*demon hands*" almost grabbed us on our way back, but I luckily spotted and avoided them before another tragedy occurred. Besides tripping and falling into the acidic, disgusting mud, our return was pretty peaceful.

"No trotters around," I said, breaking the silence, "that means Renna didn't send them here, right?"

"It also means she's probably dead," Kyra sighed with uncertainty, "I don't know how to feel about it anymore."

"If you hadn't done what you did, she would've returned to kill you," Ivy echoed my thoughts, "it's not easy losing someone, though."

"I didn't lose her. I killed her," Kyra said unemotionally.

"Why did it take y'all so long!" A funny voice screamed from afar, "do you know how long I've been waiting? It's almost nightfall! You have the cure, right?"

"Tyrose!" Ivy exclaimed, approaching and hugging him, "are you alright? Did anything happen?"

"Nothing happened. Why would anything...?"

"It doesn't matter. Is Reyna alright?" I asked.

"It's complicated. You have to see this," he said, gulping and guiding us to the *shackflyer.*

It wasn't far, just a few hundred feet from where we stood. Tyrose mentioned that while we were gone, he fed the *shackflyer* and even became friends with him, which was unusual. When we arrived at the shack, he led us to the second floor bedroom, where Reyna was lying on a bed covered in feathers.

"Couldn't clean all the feathers, so don't mind it," he cleared his throat and approached Reyna.

When he removed the sheets from her body, I saw the deplorable condition she was in—the curse had consumed her entirely. Her arms, legs, and part of her face were tinted a dark purple, and if it weren't for her constant twitching and mumbling, I would've thought she was already deceased.

"Reyna…" I touched her burning forehead.

I took the cure out of my pocket and read its label once again to ensure it was the correct one. Smoke emerged as I opened the lid, filling the room with a mystical aroma.

"Let's just hope it's the one," Ivy sighed.

I placed the flask on Reyna's mouth, tilting it steadily and forcing her to drink. She tried spitting it out, but I pressed the jar against her mouth, ensuring she swallowed every drop. After finishing, I tossed the flask away and waited patiently.

"Why is nothing happening?" I asked after a few seconds of silence.

"It'll probably take a while," Kyra replied, "let's just wait some more."

Reyna's expression and skin color remained unchanged—most importantly, the pain wasn't gone. She mumbled my name and twitched, speaking gibberish as she tried to force her eyes open, but the curse wouldn't leave her body.

"I dunno, she doesn't seem alright," Tyrose said.

"Reyna listen to me," I cried, shaking her shoulders, "Reyna, wake up!

"K-Krell," she mumbled, "I'm s-sorry."

"Reyna, wake up!" I yelled.

With a sudden gasp, she sat up from the bed and breathed heavily. Her veins changed color as her pupils shrunk and her shivering ceased—at last, she was back. I hugged her tightly and laughed, resting my head on her shoulder.

"Reyna!" Ivy smiled with relief, hugging us both.

"Oh, please, not a hug," Kyra rolled her eyes.

"I don't mind hugs," Tyrose said, embracing us.

"W-what happened?" Reyna asked.

"A bunch of stuff," I chuckled, shedding tears.

"The curse? You… took it away?" She asked.

"I don't want to reveal how much effort it took us, but you're cured," Kyra grinned and then awkwardly stared at us, "don't force me into hugging you. I don't like hugs."

"Not even after everything that's happened?" Tyrose asked, "after your friend just woke up from her deathbed?"

"Don't make this a usual thing," Kyra sighed, deciding to hug us all.

And we kept hugging for a long time, celebrating the fact that Reyna was healed. From that moment on, I wasn't letting anything happen to her again.

I chatted with Reyna as the *shackflyer* took us back to the Zumba tribe camp. I explained everything that happened with Renna, including the shocking revelation that she was Kyra's mother. Reyna was surprised but promised not to mention it around Kyra because it was a sensible topic. I also narrated our encounter with Mustafa and Yusra, which still weighed on my mind. Although Reyna assured me I made the right decision by not helping them, it didn't alleviate my guilt. Finally, we discussed the bounty hunter who ambushed us, and I praised Reyna for defending herself against him. She fought marvelously for a sick person.

"I'm so glad you're back," I smiled.

"I was never gone in the first place," Reyna grinned back, "but I'm glad too. Just tell me, why did the curse suddenly start taking effect?"

"She gave us a lame explanation, but I think it starts whenever someone finds their purpose in life," I recalled the witch's words, "or when they find true love."

"True love?" Reyna laughed, "doesn't sound like me."

"Yeah, I figured that out," I chuckled, "so, you have a purpose then?"

"A great one. Killing shadows? Amazing."

"Whatcha doing, honeybuns?" Tyrose barged into the room and interjected, "it's something one of my teachers used to say when I was twelve. Anyway, we're about to land, so be prepared cus' it might be rough."

"What? We've arrived already?" I asked.

"It was shorter than expected," Tyrose yawned, "get ready because we're leaving the shack as soon as we get there!"

Tyrose closed the door behind him as Reyna sighed, looking at me momentarily. Her eyes were teary—probably because of all the pain she had been put through—but there was something odd about her. I couldn't quite figure it out, but she was different.

"Is something happening, Reyna?" I gulped.

"Like what?" She asked.

"I don't know. Anything that may bother you," I replied, "you can talk to me, you know?"

"I know," she sighed and then coughed, "but that's a conversation for later, and I have to get ready. See you later."

Without saying anything, she left the room. When she closed the door, I noticed a single teardrop fall from her eye. I wished she could tell me what was going on, but I knew I couldn't force her to talk. She was hiding something, and I was determined to figure it out sooner or later.

The landing wasn't as rough as I expected. It was surprising, yes, but I didn't tumble across the room as the *shackflyer* crushed the trees upon arrival. I wished I had rested for at least a couple of minutes before going downstairs, but Tyrose was desperately yelling at me to come to the kitchen as soon as we landed.

It didn't take long for us to regroup in the living room and exit the *shackflyer.* Tyrose tried feeding an apple to him, but he refused it. I wondered if he trusted us as much as his previous owner, Ivory.

"I recognize these trees," Reyna examined them, "my camp is near."

We had no other choice but to follow her through the trees. I wondered if Reyna actually knew the path, but after seeing the silhouette of a fortress in the distance, I chuckled joyfully. We had arrived at the Zumba tribe camp, and it didn't seem abandoned because of the smoke coming from inside.

"Kharum, did you take my goddamn lunch!" I heard Ivory's voice from inside the camp.

"I-I-I didn't know i-i-it was yours," Kharum replied with fright.

"That's it, I'm taking the chicken you killed," his sister said.

"B-but Iv-Ivory! I huh-hunted that chicken muh-myself," Kharum gulped.

"An-an-and I duh-duh-don't care!" Ivory mocked him.

"Why do you always have to muh-muh-make fun uh-of me?"

"Because it's the only thing that makes me laugh!"

"Queen Ivy!" Kharum noticed us and walked out of the camp gate.

It seemed the survivors from the Nature Kingdom had indeed followed my commands and traveled to the Zumba tribe camp. When the light elves heard their Queen's voice, they emerged from their tents and knelt. It was strange, especially with all the elderly worshiping someone younger than them.

"Woah, alright, slow down! We're alive, great! You can all return to your tents!" Kyra said sarcastically.

"When you said you were Queen, I didn't imagine all this," Tyrose chuckled, "so what? They gon' hand you gifts now?"

"Maybe," she replied, "but I don't think so. They already did that last time."

"I'm just going to my tent," Reyna yawned, rubbing her eyes, "let me rest, please."

She was still behaving oddly, but I couldn't bring myself to question her. After everything she had gone through, I knew she needed a good night's sleep.

"We have food stored if you're pleased to take some," Ivory smiled at her Queen, then looked at me with a frown of disgust, "you can rest tonight, but tomorrow morning, we must strategize a plan."

"K-Krell," Kharum stuttered, approaching me, "huh-help me, pluh-please."

Kharum walked away, gesturing for me to follow him. The way he spoke made me think he was in danger, but truly, he just wanted help arranging things in the camp.

"What do you need, Kharum?" I asked, stepping inside a smoky tent.

"I need you to huh-help me with these a-acorns," Kharum said, "huh-help me cruh-crack them for the sou-soup I'm muh-making."

He gave me a handful of acorns and handed me a tiny knife. Not too long ago, I was fighting the most powerful witch in the lands. Little did I know that a few hours later, I'd be cracking acorns to feed the people from the Nature Kingdom. An unexpected turn of events.

I noticed the way Kharum used the knife to cut the nuts, struggling to hold it steady. It seemed odd until I noticed a bloody bandage wrapped around his right hand, covering his palm and three of his fingers.

"What happened to you?" I asked, preoccupied.

"Oh," he gulped, "I-I-I-I... A muh-man ambush-ambushed us on our wuh-way here. He was look-looking for you."

"He cut your fingers?" I paused.

"He wou-would've killed muh-me if I didn't tell him your location," he looked at me with guilt, "huh-he found y-you?"

"He did," I sighed, realizing he was talking about the bounty hunter who ambushed us at the *shackflyer*, "don't worry, that man is no longer a problem."

"I-I'm glad you're nuh-not dead."

"How have the light elves been doing?" I switched topics, cracking another acorn.

"It's good. They're going through a lot," Kharum replied.

"You didn't stutter," I smiled at him, "good job."

"I didn't? I-I didn't!" He grinned back.

"Have you been stuttering your whole life?" I asked.

"I-it's been eleven years sin-since I've spo-spoken normally," he struggled to crack the acorn, "this one-one tuh-time in the *shackfl-shackflyer*, my sister and I were truh-trying to survive a winter. T-the winter that took our parents."

"I read the note," I confessed, "the one inside the *shackflyer*."

"Oh," he sighed, "the two weeks we were stuck on the chilling outsides of the Frost Kingdom, I couldn't speak properly. I got so accustomed to stuttering because of the cold that I couldn't stop doing it when we left. My stutter always reminds me of those times..."

"Kharum," I interjected, "you know you didn't stutter, right?"

"What?"

"You're doing good."

"I-I guess I am," Kharum said, cracking the last acorn, "i-if you see Ivory, tuh-tell her that I'm suh-sorry for taking huh-her lunch."

I handed him the acorns I had cracked, and he tossed them into the soup he was cooking. I had never eaten acorn soup—and it didn't look tasty—but my stomach wanted something to eat. I took a sip before stepping out of the tent and noticed Ivory speaking to an elderly man. She seemed angry at him, but then again, she always looked angry.

"If you want food so much, then go grab it yourself, old bastard!" Ivory abruptly stood up from her chair and stormed away, "be grateful we saved you from those shadows!"

"Ivo–" I began.

"What do you want, Prince!" She interrupted without even looking my way.

"I just wanted to thank you for everything," I said.

"I'm still not forgiving you for what your father's done," Ivory sighed, glaring at me momentarily.

"I know," I said, "but Kharum sent me to tell you that he's sorry for taking your lunch."

"Oh," she chuckled, stopping in her tracks, "he still owes me his chicken, but I'll go talk to him."

Calmer than before, she slowly walked into her brother's tent as another person approached and spoke to me.

"Kid," Tyrose coughed, "I need some help with our weaponry. I would've asked Ivy, but she was busy with Kyra. And I can't seem to find Reyna anywhere... *weird*."

"You want to check the arrows?" I asked.

"Overall weapons," he replied, "follow me."

He led me to another tent filled with boxes of swords, hatchets, katanas, bows, and different arrows, including flame arrows, frosted arrows, poison arrows, hypnotic arrows, sleeping darts, and... *love arrows*? I didn't even ask what they were when Tyrose mentioned them to me.

"Ivory said there were 52 people in the camp, of which only 27 are capable of fighting," Tyrose began, "without counting us, obviously."

"So, we need to count the weapons?" I asked.

"Exactly!" Tyrose punched my shoulder.

"That hurt!" I exclaimed, but he didn't care.

I leaned over to the stash and counted a total of seven hatchets—one of them in a deplorable condition. On another small crate lay nine swords, but one of them was broken, so eight. Tyrose told me he counted ten bows and one dagger.

"That means we're missing one," I calculated.

"Nah, it rounds up to twenty-seven," Tyrose confidently said.

"No it doesn't," I chuckled, "seven and eight makes fifteen, plus ten, twenty-five, and then there's that one last dagger."

"So... *twenty-seven*?"

"No, *twenty-six*."

"It rounds up! Haven't you had math class before?"

"I don't think that's how it works, Tyrose," I laughed, "do you know where the other weapon might be?"

"Oh," Tyrose snapped his fingers repeatedly, trying to remember something, "I think I saw a little girl with a dagger in hand."

"What?" I tilted my head, "how'd she look?"

"Little."

"How little?"

"I dunno. Seven, maybe?"

"Sev–!" I shouted, then sighed, "I'm going to go find that kid."

I exited and was immediately greeted by Ivy, munching on an apple. She asked if I had seen Reyna, but I told her I hadn't since we arrived at the camp. I would check on her later, but first I needed to find that kid.

The camp was small enough for me to search, but I still had to enter the tents and ask different elves to locate the girl. An old man told me he saw a child roaming the camp with a sharp object in hand. When I asked him where he saw her, he couldn't remember the exact location, so I had to enter another tent to ask again.

"I saw her around Erin's troffe tent," a young man said.

It didn't take long for me to find her. A little girl with blonde hair and a dagger swinging in her left hand was extremely noticeable. What I hadn't realized was that shs was the same little girl I met back at the destroyed Nature Kingdom. I remembered giving her a dog plushie, but it seemed she had replaced it with a deadly dagger.

"Hey, hey, hey, girl," I trotted towards her, "what are you doing with that knife?"

"It's not a knife, it's a dagger!" The child yelled, then turned her head to me, "oh, Prince Krell! Um... you can have the dagger if you want."

"Thank you, girl," I said, taking the dagger from her hands, "do you still have that toy I gave you?"

"It's back at my tent—I can show you!" She pulled my hand.

"Not right now," I laughed, "I just wanted to make sure you were keeping him safe."

"*Her*! She's a girl!" The girl pouted.

"My mistake," I chuckled, "now, I don't know if you've been told, but where we are isn't entirely safe. You're safe inside the camp, but out there... it's dangerous."

"I know; my grandfather told me not to go out," she yawned, "but I won't! I know it's dangerous! And, oh! I meant to ask, did you use the zylika the people gave you?"

"We did," I knelt, "it's actually right over here."

I took the bow from the holder on my back and showed it to the little girl. She was in awe after seeing the sharp string attached to the pristine wooden arc. Just by her expression, I knew she'd become a warrior one day.

"Can I use it?" She asked immediately.

"Not right now," I smiled, "but when you grow up, I'll be happy to train you."

"Yes!" She jumped with excitement, "at what age?"

"First, your grandfather needs to give me permission, but I suppose at... *twelve*?"

"Twelve? That's a lot!"

"Time flies by," I said, "in the blink of an eye, you'll be slaying trotters with your own bow."

"I hope so."

"*Kirimato, yulaña ugahna, Sof*!" An old man trotted towards us, speaking another language, "I was worried sick, Sof! Why are you speaking with... *him*?"

"Don't worry, grandpa, he's just telling me how he'll train me whenever I grow up!" The little girl said joyfully

"Train you?" The man clicked his tongue, "now that's something I didn't expect!"

I thought he would yell at me for speaking to his granddaughter, but instead, he simply chuckled and told the little girl—whose name was Sof—to go back inside their tent.

"I knew she wanted to be a warrior ever since I took her to the kingdom's arena," the man said, "I can just imagine my granddaughter fighting trotters, clashing in arenas... I could even see her become... *a huntress*."

Huntress? Like the one that stalked me in the Main Kingdom and observed me on the outsides? I must have heard him wrong because why would he even mention her?

"A what?" I blinked several times.

"Oh, a... a warrior," he began walking away from me.

"No, no, you said *huntress*," I rushed after him.

"Pardon my spelling, young man," he avoided me.

"What do you know about the huntress!" I shouted.

"Kid, it's better if you stay out of this," the man whispered, looking into my eyes, "you don't want to know the dirty secrets your mother kept."

Then he stormed away, leaving me standing awkwardly in the middle of the camp with many people judging me for yelling at an old man. How the hell did he know my mother?

I rested for a few minutes afterward, sitting on a bench and appreciating the community that survived the shadows' attacks. The one thing that bothered me was that I couldn't see Reyna anywhere. I remembered Ivy asking me where she was, but I didn't give it much importance. Where the hell was she? I stood up and approached her tent—the only place I could imagine her hiding.

"Reyna, are you here?" I asked, quietly unzipping the tent.

There she was, facing the other way, murmuring and sobbing. She didn't hear me walk in, but as soon as I took a step forward, she gasped and moved her hands across her face, wiping away the tears. I crept closer and noticed her dagger drop to the tent's carpet. The silent thud was loud enough to catch my attention, and before Reyna could drag it away, I noticed the blood on the dagger—it wasn't dry.

"Krell, what are you doing!" She snorted, "you can't just walk in here!"

The first thing she did was roll up her sleeves, trying to hide something on her wrist. My eyes were quick enough to see the blood dripping her arm, staining her fingertips. Someone had cut her. There was no one else in the tent, but there was fresh blood on the knife and her wrist.

"Reyna, wha-what happened!" I asked, frowning.

"Nothing, Krell," she cried, her voice cracking.

"Are you okay? Are you—"

"I'm fine!" She shouted

"You have blood! You're bleeding, Reyna!"

"I know."

"What happened, Reyna? Who did this?" I asked as she paused for a second and then murmured.

"I did."

My heart sank when I heard those two words. The simple thought of it made me sick. Why would she be doing that? What happened to her? Since when? All those thoughts flooded my mind as I tried to comprehend the situation.

"Oh, Reyna," I gulped.

"Why did I tell you this?" She shook her head, standing up to leave the tent.

"Reyna, you can talk to me," I stopped her.

"I know! Just… not about this," she said with a shaky breath.

"Please, let me help you!" I insisted.

"I don't need help," her voice cracked, "sometimes there are things you can't heal. This is one of them."

"Tell me, Reyna," I said, "since when?"

"I…" She stared at me before replying, "I've been doing it ever since my brothers died. It was a form of relief that took away all my pain."

"How can it take away your pain and cause it at the same time?" I tried to understand.

"It turns the psychological pain into physical pain," she sobbed, "I thought I had finally freed myself from doing it, but then my tribe died and I felt the guilt all over again. You know, when everyone in my tribe became shadows—when my mother, my father, and my friends were all killed—I watched from afar, seeing them die without stepping in."

She covered her mouth and shuddered.

"I could've saved them! Every single day, I hear the same stupid words in my head telling me how afraid I am, how much of a coward I am, and that I'll never be enough! Then it returned."

"Reyna, you need to realize that you're enough," I said, grabbing her shoulders, "no matter what anyone says, you will always be enough. Don't listen to your mother's words or your father's! Listen to yourself!"

"I am the one putting those words in my mind! I can't even listen to myself anymore because I keep repeating the same things inside my head all the goddamn time!"

"Tell me, what can I do to help you? Tell me, Reyna!"

"I don't think you can do anything," she replied despondently.

"But *you* can," I told her, "just talk to me, Reyna. Don't stay quiet!"

"I want to, but I can't!" She cried, "I don't know who I am anymore; I don't know what to do. I'm scared, Krell. I feel like I don't even have a purpose in life."

"Yes, you do. You are Reyna from the Zumba tribe, and you are the bravest person I have ever met! You are caring, strong, and fierce, and should never let anyone take that away from you! Your parents should never make you feel like you don't matter—never! You are enough, and you will always be enough."

"Thank you, Krell, but I don't know if I can stop this anymore," she panicked, hyperventilating, "every single time I do something wrong, a voice inside my head tells me to do it again! You don't think I'm a monster, right?"

"Reyna, of course not. Why would you even think that?" I hugged her, beginning to sob, "I would never think that, and you should never think that, Reyna."

"I'm so sorry, Krell."

"Don't be sorry, Reyna. Just promise me that you'll never do this again."

"I can't," she cried, "I can't promise you that."

"Then promise me that whenever you feel the urge to do it, you'll tell me."

"I don't know," she kept crying, "I don't want to worry you anymore."

"I would spend my entire lifetime by your side just to make you feel better," I looked into her beautiful, emerald eyes, "and don't ever doubt that. So please, promise me that when you feel that way again, whenever you think of it, or whenever you feel like doing it, you'll tell me. Please, Reyna, promise me that."

"I..." She sobbed, then reluctantly said, "I promise."

I leaned in to hug her, and as she gently placed her head beside mine, tears fell on my shoulder. I couldn't believe she was in so much pain that I hadn't noticed. I felt like a bad friend for not helping her any sooner, but at least I found out before it got worse. The last thing I did was grab a rag to clean the blood off her wrist. I was worried she wouldn't feel comfortable with me doing that, but when I looked at her before wiping, she nodded and told me it was fine.

"Thank you, Krell," she whispered in my ear.

"Don't worry about it," I said, pulling the rag away, "it's getting late, and I really need to get some sleep. Is it okay if I leave?"

"Go sleep," she smiled, "and wake me up, please."

I was already heading out, pulling the tent's zipper to finally exit and get some sleep. That was until I heard Reyna's voice again.

"Hey, Krell," she looked at me, "I don't want to bother you any longer, but could you sleep here?"

"Yeah, sure, no problem" I gulped, turning around, "do I sleep on the floor, or…?"

"There's some space on my bed," Reyna said, "you can sleep here."

I carefully lay beside Reyna as she turned her body to one side of the tent, and I turned my head the other way around. I closed my eyes and tried to fall asleep, but Reyna's gente voice murmured something.

"Thank you," she said, rolling around to face me.

I turned my head toward her again and smiled, wrapping the blanket around my body. And then we both fell asleep in each other's arms.

Chapter 34

I had the best sleep of my life. After several hours of sobbing and comforting, Reyna and I fell asleep inside her tent. We had agreed to wake each other up, but when I eventually opened my eyes, she was no longer by my side. I yawned, unzipped the tent, walked outside, and noticed Reyna sitting on a bench, gently rubbing her wrist.

"You slept together?" Ivy approached me.

"Woah," I said, startled.

"I always knew something was going on between you two, but sleeping in the same tent?" She smirked, "be honest with me, Krell, what did you do? I saw you enter the tent before nightfall, and now you're exiting after more than ten hours with Reyna? Very suspicious, Krell."

"We didn't..." I sighed, "we did sleep in the same tent, but it isn't what it looks like!"

"I give you two weeks before you're together," she chuckled, "if you're not dead by then."

"You think we'll die soon?"

"Likely," she gulped, "anyway, Ivory had a meeting with everyone while you were asleep. She has a plan, but I don't think it's entirely safe."

"What is it?"

"She wants us to raid the Main Kingdom in a couple of hours," Ivy replied.

"Raid? We're not thieves!"

"Not because of that, but because she wants us to barge into the kingdom and warn your father about the shadows."

"Of all people, Ivory wants to do that?" I asked, chuckling, "she hasn't even forgiven me, and she already wants to talk with her biggest enemy? Besides, I think the King is already aware of the threat. He's just too stubborn to act."

"I heard you guys talking about me," Ivory arrived, looking at me oddly, "and for your information, I'm not forgiving you *or* your father; I'm only doing this because it's necessary. Judging by the fact that there are very few people in this camp—half of them elderly—we don't have enough warriors to defend ourselves when the shadows strike. It's our only shot."

"And if we die?" I asked.

"Then it'll be a better fate than turning into one of those things," she replied before walking away, "get ready, we leave in twenty minutes."

"*Twenty*!" I couldn't believe we were actually raiding the Main Kingdom, "what will we do with the kids and the elderly?"

"Ivory said it's better if we leave them here," Ivy sighed, uncertain of the plan, "they can take care of themselves, and if we recruit the Main Kingdom, we can come back for them."

"That is a really big '*if*.'"

"Do you have a better idea?"

"I guess not."

"Then deal with it, 'cause from now on, Ivory is our... army leader," Ivy laughed before leaving.

I was about to approach Reyna—who was still sitting on a bench—when Kharum came running towards me and began jabbering. I glanced at his bandaged fingers, which looked slightly better than before, as blood wasn't staining the white cloth wrapped around them.

"Krell," he gulped, "Ivory suh-said that she wuh-was gonna raid the Main King-Kingdom? I don't know if I'm cuh-capable of doing it, Krell."

"Who said you had to?" I asked, "old people and children will stay here."

"But I am twenty-three years old!" He cried, "I-I'm supposed to fight, no?"

"Not all people are born to fight—some have different specialties," I said, "for example, you may not know how to wield a sword, but you're a great cook!"

"You think so?"

"You make delicious acorn soup."

"Th-thanks," he chuckled, "I'll try to help puh-people pack up. See you later, Krell."

After Kharum stormed away, I finally had the chance to talk to Reyna, who seemed to be waiting for me as she discreetly looked my way while I was talking to Kharum. I sat down beside her and sighed, surreptitiously looking at her wrist.

"You don't have to worry about me anymore," she said, "I'm doing better."

"I know," I said, grabbing her hand, "I just want to be with you."

She pulled away and cleared her throat, taking something from her pocket.

"Remember the bracelets I told you about?" Reyna looked at me with teary eyes.

"The tikh bracelets? Yeah."

"While I was falling asleep last night, I started thinking about how much I care for all of you..." She began, "you're like my family, and I want you to feel that way."

She took the phosphorescent emerald bracelet out of her pocket and looked me in the eyes, wondering if I was ready for the commitment. I didn't even have to think about it. I simply nodded and let her wrap it around my wrist. I was going to have that bracelet until the day I died—or the day Reyna died. I hoped it never came to that.

"Is it too tight?" She asked.

"It's perfectly fine," I smiled.

"I would go hand out the rest of the bracelets, but I'm exhausted," she sighed, "could you give these to Ivy, Kyra, and Tyrose? See if they want them."

"Sure," I said, grabbing several and walking away.

Luckily, the three of them were talking outside a tent, probably gathering the last few resources to raid the kingdom. I interrupted their conversation and explained how the bracelets worked, although Kyra and Ivy already knew.

"And what are they for? I don't believe in elf stuff," Tyrose hesitated.

"Me neither, but it's for Reyna," I replied.

"If it can bring the five of us together or connect us in some way, then I'm up for it," Ivy said, raising her hand and telling me to put the bracelet on.

It took me a long time to pair the bracelets as I had to put four of them on each person. Tyrose was skeptical at first, but after explaining what it meant for Reyna, he decided to do it.

"If one of us dies," it felt strange to even say it, "we can use these bracelets to reunite in another life."

"And you actually believe that?" Kyra asked.

"At this point," I gulped, "it's better to believe in something than not to. You can at least have faith—you can escape the darkness."

I returned to Reyna afterward, gave her the other three bracelets, and talked to her for a while. She seemed completely drained, yet somehow stayed awake to speak with me. I had never seen her like that before, and because we were about to raid the Main Kingdom, I was worried.

Moments after, Ivory called us to the center of the camp. I was ready to cross the steel barrier into the Main Kingdom, but Reyna definitely wasn't. Ivory stood over a podium, cleared her throat, and began speaking.

"As you all may know, we will be breaching the walls of the Main Kingdom now. Everyone over the age of sixty must stay here, and those over fifteen can join voluntarily. Elders, take care of the children while we are away, and may all odds be in your favor."

She jumped off the podium and raised her sword over her head, leading everyone to the Main Kingdom's steel barrier. I couldn't do much, so I placed my trust in Ivory and hoped she wouldn't lead us to our deaths. People followed her, including

Ivy, Kyra, and Tyrose, who were close by my side. Like the night before, I couldn't find Reyna anywhere.

"Where is she?" I asked Ivy, trying to search for her as the crowd marching towards the kingdom pushed me forward.

"Reyna?" Ivy looked around momentarily, "she's probably near."

"Yeah, but where?" I insisted.

"Just keep marching. We have other things to worry about, boy," Tyrose whispered.

I hoped she was doing alright, especially after what happened last night.

"Ballistas ready?" Ivory asked as people began severing the trees standing between us and the wall surrounding the Main Kingdom. That was when I realized what was about to happen.

"Are they going to destroy the goddamn wall?" I shouted, my jaw dropping.

"Ivory got the idea while you were asleep. The ballistas will hook onto the wall and pull it towards us," she explained.

Before I could say anything else, the two ballistas were fired. I watched as the two anchors hooked onto the top of the steel wall and began dragging it down. I never thought the structure was so frail, but it hit the ground in just a couple of seconds, covering the air with dust and momentarily blinding us all. After hearing the screams of villagers and smelling a mixed scent of bread and rotten fruit, I realized I was back inside the Main Kingdom.

"Someone call the king!" I heard from the other side of the fallen wall.

As the smoke faded, I glimpsed the guards standing on the kingdom's streets, eagerly awaiting orders to kill. Ivory stood on the destroyed wall, raising her hands and speaking.

"We come here in peace!"

"Like hell you did!" A guard shouted.

"We want to see the king," Ivory commanded.

"Why would he ever want to see someone like you?" Another guard asked, trying not to gag.

I wanted to let Ivory do the talking, but after the knight said that, I felt the urge to step up. I cleared my way through the crowd and stood firmly next to Ivory.

"Bring him out," I stated.

After seeing my face, the guards didn't linger and ran to the castle in search of my father. I honestly didn't think Henrius had the courage or dignity to listen to us, but we were out of options, so we all waited for his arrival.

"Krell!" My father screamed from afar, the stomps of a galloping horse accompanying his voice.

"King from the Main Kingdom," Ivory looked at me with an *'I've got it from now on'* expression, "we are here to speak with you. No threats. No fight. Just a simple talk."

"You first destroy my wall, then you come here thinking I will find all of this *peaceful*?" Henrius yelled, "I will give you twenty seconds to speak, and then I will rain hellfire on all of you!"

"You know the shadows are here, father," I said as Ivory furiously glanced at me, "it isn't my fault your pride is too big to admit they've escaped your *'magical and impenetrable prison.'*"

"The shadows are not here! You really wanted all the attention for yourself, didn't you?" He jumped off the horse and grabbed his sword, "even spread those lies to the other kingdoms?"

"I have seen those monsters myself!" Ivy shouted.

"Quiet!" Henrius clenched his teeth, "you should've been executed many days ago!"

"What do you want, father?" I asked, "what will it take to convince you? If only you left your castle and saw the state of your kingdom, you would actually do something about it"

"If you really think I do absolutely nothing for my kingdom and just sit at my castle all day, then fight me!" Henrius drew his sword, "come on!"

"Kid, don't," Tyrose said, grabbing my arm, but I pulled away.

"And everyone else, don't you dare step in!" He commanded.

I recalled my sword and walked closer. Was he attempting to kill me, or did he just want to *teach me a lesson*? Either way, I wouldn't hold back at all.

"Ready?" I was going to ask, but my father swung his sword at my face.

I screamed, but he didn't stop there as he kept slashing over and over again. The first three cuts were at my cheek—one touching my forehead, and another almost reaching my eyes. He proceeded with three more strikes at my knee, leaving me incapacitated on the ground with his sword right beside my neck.

"Beg," he simply said.

"What?" I panted.

"Beg for mercy! Or do you want to die like this? Like a damn coward!"

"I won't beg."

"Do it!" He insisted, pressing on my neck.

"No."

"I am going to cut your neck right this instant if you don't beg!"

"I said *no*!" I screamed.

"Very well."

He raised his sword and took a blow at my neck. I closed my eyes and heard blood splattering, followed by another thud—the liquid began drenching my clothes. Then an awful scream blared from afar: *Reyna*. The last things I heard before passing out were stomping and screaming, alongside the sounds of stabbing, shooting, gurgling, and most of all, *death*. *Death was everywhere.*

PART X
THE SHADOW WAR

CHAPTER 35

Have you ever woken up from a nightmare in the middle of the night? You're soaked in sweat, your heart feels like it's pounding in your head, and you have a headache that worsens with each passing second. That was exactly how I felt at that moment. I was in my father's room, lying on his bed and waking up under the crimson sheets. Yet, something seemed different. The walls were unusually bright, reflecting the unpigmented light into my eyes, which didn't help with the ache. After sensing the mystical breeze, nostalgic ambiance, and saturated, vivid hues, I realized I was inside a dream. I began vaguely remembering what had happened before, wondering if maybe it wasn't just a *dream*. My father had slashed a katana at my neck twice—no one could survive that! Was I dead?

"No, you're not dead, Krell," someone said, standing in front of the bed.

It was my mother, who magically appeared all of a sudden. I felt my eyes opening as she approached, so I held onto the bed sheets and tried my best not to wake up.

"Calm down, son," she smiled, sitting on the edge of the bed, which didn't shift its weight and confirmed what I was already thinking—it was a dream.

"I just want to stay here, you know?" I tried staying still to avoid waking up.

"You know it's not possible," she replied.

"I just don't know what to do anymore," I said, hugging her and sobbing on her shoulder. How could a dream feel so real?

"Yes you do," she comforted me, "you do."

"If I'm still alive, does that mean I still have to fight the shadows? Does it mean I have to confront my father who wants me dead? I-I can't do that!" For a brief second, I didn't want to wake up anymore—I wanted to die, "I can't do anything without you!"

"Just shut up already," she laughed quietly.

"What?"

"You haven't realized it, right?" She asked, pulling herself apart.

"No? Yes? What are you talking about?" I shook my head.

"You don't need me, and you never needed me, Krell."

"But I do! You're my motivation to move forward—to exist!" I cried.

"I shouldn't be, son," she said, taking a deep breath, "look at everything you've accomplished in your lifetime."

"Live in a castle with my abusive father?"

"Not that, Krell. You've done what no person ever thought possible. You brought together the four kingdoms and are leading an army to stop a war! Do you know how crazy that sounds?"

"It's not crazy; it's just what I was forced to do."

"You never realize your success until it's too late," my mother said, "but think about it right now. Think about all you've done—all you've accomplished without me."

"But I don't know how to move forward without you!" I sobbed.

"That's what I've been trying to tell you this whole time, son. You've done all of this no thanks to me. I've been dead for fifteen years, and you still find a way to put all your faith in me, even if you don't remember me! I died when you were only a baby, and the only fragments you have of me are paintings and portraits scattered across the kingdom. You don't know me, you don't know what I've done, and hell, you don't even know if I was a good person! So stop saying you need me because all of your accomplishments have been achieved by yourself."

"Mom," no words could describe what I was feeling.

"You're on your own, Krell, you have always been," she said at last, "so stop thinking about me and stop dreaming about me. The only help you need is over there."

I glanced at the window my mother was staring at, glimpsing the Main Kingdom's dungeons where all my friends were locked in cells. I was already waking up.

"Goodbye, Krell," she said, shedding a tear, "I love you so much."

The room began fading away until it was only my mother and me hugging each other in a void of darkness. Although I wanted to stay there forever, I knew I had to wake up for the sake of the lands. So, I opened my eyes, ready to lead an army against the shadows and survive the upcoming war. That was the last time I ever dreamt of my mother.

*****

"How am I not dead?" Was the first thing I asked after startling awake.

"That was quick," Ivy said, kneeling beside me.

Indeed, we were in the dungeons of the Main Kingdom, locked in cells that held four people each. I could see Ivory and Kharum in the cell across from mine, Kyra two cells to my right, Tyrose almost at the other side of the corridor, and Reyna sitting dejectedly at the back of my cell.

"It's a long story," Kyra said, gripping the metal bars.

"Yeah, why don't you let the elf girl tell you what happened?" Ivory yelled angrily.

"Reyna? Did she save me?" I asked, standing up.

"She did save you, but she also doomed us all!" She kicked the cell door.

"Leave her a-alone, sis," Kharum stuttered.

"Shut up!" She screamed back.

"Don't get mad!" I said to Ivory, "just explain."

"Reyna shot your father," Ivy clarified, grabbing my shoulder before Ivory could speak, "you were about to get your head shredded, so she fired two arrows at his chest, starting a fight that killed thirteen of us. And now we're here in the dungeons."

"Those were the sounds I heard..." I said to myself and then glanced at Ivory, "but she saved me. Why are you mad?

"Because she's the reason thirteen of us were slaughtered in a so-called *'peaceful protest,'*" Ivory rolled her eyes, "your life shouldn't be more important than all the others, but still, they tend to treat you like some kind of King."

"Leave him alone!" Ivy yelled.

"Oh, should I apologize because you're my Queen and I should listen to everything you say?" Ivory said sarcastically, "well, if you're the Queen, use your vines to get us the hell out of this damned place!"

"Something is preventing me from doing so," Ivy sighed, "trust me, I've tried."

"Suh-sister, come on, I want to talk tuh-to you," Kharum said, pulling Ivory to the back of the cell and away from us.

"Krell, just know that—" Ivy began.

"I'll go talk to Reyna," I interrupted, "you can go speak to that guy over there—he seems pretty cheerful."

I stared at the person lying on the corner of the cell.

"He's asleep."

"Talk to Ivory then."

"Actually, on second thought, the guy who's asleep does look pretty cheerful," Ivy chuckled as I approached Reyna.

She was sitting with her head between her knees, sobbing uncontrollably. It was harsh seeing her that way, especially after what happened the night before. Still, I sat beside her and patted her shoulder, but there was no response.

"You know you don't have to listen to Ivory," I said, "she's been through a lot, and all she does now is unleash her anger on people who don't deserve it."

"But I do deserve it," Reyna kept her head between her knees.

"Don't say that."

"I'm the reason thirteen people died," she raised her head and looked at me with irritated eyes.

"You didn't know that would happen. You saved me, Reyna, and there was no way to predict what would happen afterward."

"Do you ever wonder how everything would be better if we just died?" She asked, "we wouldn't have to bear all of this."

"As surprising as it might be, I think about it all the time," I remembered the dream with my mother and how I didn't want to wake up from it, "but it's a miracle that we're standing here at this moment. We will have to endure painful times, but when the time comes, you'll enjoy being alive. Look at me, Reyna."

I grabbed her chin and used my sleeve to wipe the tears dripping down her cheeks. I licked my fingers and cleaned the dirt on her forehead as well as the blood splattered on her neck. After I finished, she leaned into me and held me tight.

"Thank you for being here, Krell," Reyna said, then looked over my shoulder, "and also, what is Ivy doing?"

I glanced at the other side of the cell and overheard Ivy's conversation with the sleeping man, who was now wide awake.

"Your wife left you?" Ivy gasped, awkwardly smiling at us afterward.

"She cheated on me with Prius!" The man wept

"Prius? Really? Your brother?"

"Prius isn't my brother, he's my cousin! Have you been listening at all?"

"No, no, yeah, I'm listening, don't worry," Ivy said before mouthing the words "*help me*" to us.

After a long gossiping session, the man thankfully fell asleep again, giving Ivy the chance to walk away and talk to us. We began plotting an escape plan when an unexpected person walked down the dungeon's stairs: Vernan. He had no weapons at hand and no food to bring us, so it was an odd appearance.

"You..." He stood in front of my cell and took a deep breath, "the King commanded the execution of all of you in two hours. The form of execution will be... Damn it, I can't do it."

"What's the form of execution?" I asked angrily.

"I don't want to do this," he gulped and stared at me with uncertainty.

"Cut the crap. A couple of days ago you tried to murder me, so tell us what the form of execution will be," I said.

"I can't keep following orders from your father anymore, Prince," he whispered through the metal bars of the cell, "I know the shadows are here—I've seen them with my own eyes—but your father doesn't want to do a damn thing!"

"Are you serious? Are you actually...?"

"I'm done following orders," he declared bravely, "and I will free you right now if you promise to command an army against the shadows. I have lived in this kingdom my whole life, and I will not let it be destroyed."

"What's going on there?" Tyrose shouted from the other side of the dungeon corridor.

"I think they're fighting!" Kyra replied.

"They're not!" Reyna yelled back, focusing on what Vernan had to say.

I thought about his offer, but after a couple of seconds of pondering, I realized there was nothing to consider.

"Will you get us our weapons back?" I asked.

"And as many more as you want," he smirked.

"What will my father say?"

"He can't stop us," Vernan said, taking out the cell's keys, "deal?"

"Deal."

Vernan opened my cell as I laughed in disbelief and looked at him blankly. He stood in silence, wondering if I was going to attack him after everything he'd done to me, but I simply shook his hand and smiled.

"Everyone!" I announced.

"Aye, aye, captain," Tyrose chuckled.

"Grab all the weapons you need and meet me outside!" I shouted as Vernan opened every cell, liberating the light elves, "today we fight!"

"Bernard, is it? I think I've heard that name before. Kinda sounds like a kid's name," Ivy said to Vernan, handing him two bottles of zylika, "anyway, grab this, and distribute it to everyone you can. Tell them to put it on their swords, bowstrings, arrows, hatchets—all their weapons."

"May I ask why?"

"To kill the shadows. Well, not kill, but... to transform them back to normal! Remember, that's our goal—heal, not kill, right? I mean, they look very killable, but, you know.... don't do it...?"

"I do not understand you, woman."

"Just hand it out to your companions."

After grabbing my sword and bow, I walked out of the dungeons and made my way to the main plaza. Villagers gasped at my sight, screaming exaggeratingly when the other light elves stormed into the streets of the kingdom. I stood upon a podium at the center of the plaza and invited Reyna, Ivy, Kyra, and Tyrose to accompany me. Ivory was nowhere to be seen, but Kharum was clumsily walking around, apologizing to each person he bumped into.

"Get them out of there!" I heard a woman cry.

"Shut up, lady!" Vernan shouted, arriving with the other guards.

"Can I get your attention, please?" I began, but everyone started to riot against us, "how do I get their attention?"

"One, two, three, eyes on me?" Tyrose suggested.

"I've never been good with crowds," Kyra added.

"Me neither," Reyna agreed.

"Everyone, listen to him or you'll become shadow bait in a few minutes!" Ivy screamed and everyone went silent.

"Thank you," I cleared my throat, "so, yeah, the shadows are coming."

"Really, that's it?" Kyra asked.

"You've given me some of the best speeches, and you come out in front of the whole kingdom to say that?" Reyna laughed.

"Alright, I get it, shut up!" I tried whispering, yet accidentally yelled, "now, I know that was very direct, but it is the truth. In a matter of minutes, the shadows will arrive and try to take the kingdom for themselves. They've already done it to the Nature Kingdom, as well as the frost and the fire ones. Everyone who can't fight should take shelter in their house, and if it isn't safe, then ask next door. My friends Tyrose and Kharum will be at the doctor's house to treat the wounded."

"We will what?" Tyrose mumbled, looking at me, "when did I agree on that?"

"You don't know how to fight, and the kingdom desperately needs a doctor. Kharum can help you by searching for the wounded," I whispered to Tyrose, then continued, "guards, you are in charge of defending the kingdom, yet you must ensure not to kill any shadow! You will transform them back to normal with the zylika without exception! Archers, place yourself on the rooftops, and the horses will stay in the stables throughout the entire battle! We can't lose anyone! Person, elf, animal—it doesn't matter!"

"You are not our King!" Someone yelled from the crowd.

"Exactly. I am not your King," I sighed, "but will you trust the person ignoring the attack of the shadows or the one trying to help you survive?"

Everyone cheered and applauded, preparing for the incoming battle. When Vernan stood upon the podium, raised his spear, and gloriously started chanting, the cheers grew louder.

"They are coming, Prince," one of the guards warned me.

In the distance, a dark, gloomy cloud advanced towards us, destroying everything in its path. I gulped and recalled the dream I had of my mother, where she said everything I had accomplished was by my own doing—but, not really. I looked at my friends standing beside me and realized they were the reason I was still alive. Tyrose and Kharum rushed to the doctor's house, Kyra and Ivy hugged each other, and I approached Reyna, holding her hand.

"Look at everything," she smiled, staring past the steel wall, "maybe it's the last time you do."

"It's beautiful," I began to cry, "the sun rising, the trees... and the big black cloud."

Reyna placed her arm around my neck, resting her head on my shoulder and preparing for what was to come. I kissed her forehead and took a deep breath. Just as we expected, the shadows eventually arrived at the kingdom. Although I wanted to spend more time with Reyna, I couldn't. We had already commanded the army towards the shadows by then.

"May we be lucky on the battlefield," I said at last, closing my eyes, then opening them again with a burning passion, "attack!"

Chapter 36

War isn't a fun thing. If you ever hear someone saying it's a fun thing, they are wrong. When the gloomy cloud reached the kingdom, shadows tore through the houses, rushing towards the army we had built. For a moment, I thought they would overcome us in seconds, but the guards charged towards them with determination. Arrows flew over my head, swords clashed by my side, and blood was constantly splattered on my face. A shadow hurled me to the ground and tried searing its claws on my skin, yet I recalled my sword and decapitated it before anything worse happened. I hadn't looked properly at who it was—luckily, it was a trotter, but I had to be more careful about which shadows to kill and which needed to be healed with the zylika. After getting back on my feet, I stood paralyzed, trying not to gag at the bloodshed surrounding me. Why was I so weak all of a sudden? Wasn't war supposed to be glorious and entertaining? I panicked and had no other choice but to retreat. I took a step backwards when someone came running behind me and pushed me towards the massacre again. I screamed and tried sprinting away, but it seemed like each step backward seemed to be followed by being pushed three steps forward.

"Reyna!" I screamed as a last resort.

No answer. I had been separated from her.

"Stop!" I said to myself while the words *"you're on your own"* echoed inside my head, "I'm on my own... I'm on my own!"

I dashed through the multitude of guards to reach the shadows, pulling out my bow and firing an arrow at a creature's shoulder. I noticed a couple of knights struggling to free themselves from a horde of them, so I shot another bolt in their direction. Ivy and Kyra were still together—far away—but before I could even think of approaching them, a passing guard threw me to the ground. My face landed in a puddle of mud, and when I tried pulling myself up, a shadow crawled on top of me. The creature pushed my head into the mud, covering my mouth and nose. I tried recalling my sword again, but the shadow held my arm to the ground. As soon as I began drowning, the creature was launched away.

"Reyna?" I asked after taking a deep breath and wiping the mud off my face.

"Oh, it's not Reyna," a mysterious voice said.

It was *the huntress*, finishing off the shadow by stabbing an arrow into its chest and kicking it away. She looked at me briefly and began walking away.

"What are you doing here?" I pointed my sword at her.

With a swift move, she turned around, kicked the weapon out of my hands, grabbed an arrow from her quiver, and placed it right beside my neck.

"I always follow you, Krell," she said, keeping the bolt's tip on my skin, "and don't ever try something like that again. Now, please follow me, 'cause I'm certain if I leave you alone here, you'll die in less than five minutes."

"Where do you want to go?" I asked.

"I just want to lead you to some of your friends and then leave," she replied, trotting away.

"Hey, behind you!" I warned her about a creeping shadow, but she simply punctured an arrow into its chest and slit its throat.

"Duck!" She shouted at me.

"What?"

She kicked my feet, shooting an arrow at the shadow behind me once I collapsed to the ground. I had truly never met someone as skillful as her.

"Look, Kharum is on the street across from where we are, so go help him do whatever he's doing. He clearly isn't qualified to be out there alone," she pushed me in his direction.

"How do you know his name?" I asked.

"I know everything," she smirked before dashing away.

I wanted to sit down and question what had happened, but it looked like Kharum needed my help. I ran to him, slashing my sword at a few shadows on my way there. He was kneeling beside an injured guard whose leg had been half shredded.

"Kharum," I tried not to gag.

"K-Krell, I nuh-need your help! Uh-urgently!" Kharum spoke faster than usual.

"Just get me to the doctor!" The guard screeched in pain.

"I can't carry him; huh-he's too heavy!" Kharum cried.

"Don't worry, I'll help you," I said, grabbing the guard's hand.

Kharum positioned himself between the guard's arms, and after taking a deep breath, I did the same. We guided him away from the main plaza, where most of the shadows were. It seemed like the villagers had done a great job protecting themselves, as all of the houses' windows were shut and barricaded—except for one. I reluctantly looked inside and noticed blood smeared on the walls and multiple mutilated bodies lying within. I flinched and closed my eyes, trying not to think much of it, but seconds later, I dropped to the ground and began vomiting.

"Krell, duh-don't leave me alone!" Kharum stuttered, unable to carry the guard by himself.

"I can't do it, Kharum," I cried.

"Is he too heavy?" He asked.

"No, it's not that. I just can't bear any of this! All these people are dying! Not only warriors, but innocent families! The more blood I see, the more I want to hide inside the castle and forget any of this is happening!"

"Look, Krell," Kharum cleared his throat, "you are strong and fierce! This is war, and people will die, but you have to close your heart to it! You will mourn them later, but right now, you need to focus on our objective: killing these damn shadows and vanishing them from our lands! When you see the massacre around you, use it as fuel against the shadows and Osrov! Don't let it weaken you—use it to your advantage!"

"Kharum..." I panted, smiling, "you didn't stutter."

"I know," he smirked.

"Can you take me to the doctor now?" The guard missing half a leg asked.

"Oh, yeah, sorry," Kharum coughed and carried the guard by himself, "hey, I can do it! I can lift him!"

"Are you sure?" I asked as he began walking.

"Yes! I'm strong!"

"Well, take him!" I commanded, noticing the shadows approaching us from behind, "I'll keep them away from you!"

I told Kharum to focus on taking the injured guard to the doctor's house and not to get distracted by the shadows—I would handle them. When I prepared myself and menacingly stared in their direction, more began swarming the road. I thought I could overcome them, but after more than thirty of them grouped into a horde, I lost all hope.

"Are y-you sure you can take them all out?" Kharum asked, momentarily looking back.

"Concentrate on the road, Kharum!" I shouted as more shadows ran our way.

I knew my sword and bow couldn't possibly defeat all those creatures, so I tried to come up with another plan. Just as the shadows reached us, a horde of light elves from the Nature Kingdom sprinted out of a nearby alley. Erin—the deaf and mute troffe maker—fought alongside them, using a barrel of troffe to smash the creatures as his companions fended them off with logs and greatswords. I stood back, wondering if I should help them, but the elves managed to overcome the monsters, so I returned to Kharum.

"Keep going," I said, "the doctor's house is right around the corner."

As there were no more shadows around, I wrapped the injured guard's arm around my shoulders and helped him walk. By the time we reached the doorstep, Tyrose greeted and commanded us to place the defeated knight on a nearby table.

"What's up with the big guy?" Tyrose asked, arranging flasks on the countertops.

"Don't you see his leg?" I pointed at it.

"Oh, *that*," he laughed nervously, "that's a big injury."

"I kept the missing chunk from his leg," Kharum said, pulling a bloody piece of meat out of his pocket and staring at us innocently.

"You did *what*?" I yelled.

"Why would that work for me?" Tyrose added, gagging.

"I thou-thought it would help you do something," Kharum smiled awkwardly, tossing the chunk of meat onto the table.

Tyrose grabbed some materials from a nearby cabinet as I took the guard's armor off. He was already falling asleep, so I slapped his face and shouted for him to stay awake.

"I'll have to disinfect it," Tyrose said.

"Doesn't that hurt?" Kharum asked.

"It does," I replied.

"Bring it on! Bring it on!" The guard chanted, "I can hold the pain—I need the pain!"

"Masochistic," Tyrose whispered, using an alcohol-soaked napkin to clean the wound.

"The window!" Kharum yelled moments after.

Shadows attempted to break into the house through an open window. I ran towards them, but before I could strike one of the creatures, one hurled its ax in my direction, knocking me back. I screamed with my clenched teeth, aware that making noise would attract more of them. Kharum noticed my struggle and quickly devised a plan.

"Krell!" Tyrose approached me, using a piece of cloth to stop the bleeding on my chest.

Kharum grabbed the chunk of meat torn from the guard's leg and used it to distract the shadows. Surprisingly, it worked. The creatures hypnotically chased the piece of meat, so he tossed it outside and shut the window, barricading it afterward.

"I'm tired," Kharum panted, sitting on the floor, "I've al-already carried someone who weighs like twe-twenty thousand pounds, and I just fought hundreds of shadows by myself! I'm not meant fuh-for this!"

"Yeah, that must be really rough," Tyrose began, "and I hate to say it, but get your ass up and search the streets for more injured."

"What? That's not nice!" Kharum yelped.

"This is war. There's no time for manners."

"I also have to leave. I need to kill Osrov," I said, standing up.

"With that injury?" Tyrose glanced at my bloody chest.

"This'll do," I said, grabbing a bandage from a nearby desk and wrapping it around my torso.

"I can disinfect it if you'd like," he insisted.

"I feel like someone who lost half his leg is more important than someone who's been scratched by an ax," I replied, recalling my sword and walking out the door.

"Wait, Krell! If you see Ivy anywhere around, tell her to be safe," Tyrose paused, then mumbled, "and that I love her."

"I will," I smiled, leaving the house.

Kharum and I agreed to go our separate ways. I gave him one of my arrows for self-defense and advised him to avoid fighting as much as possible. Before returning to the main plaza, I caught a glimpse of the other side of the kingdom, where the steel barrier once stood. There was an extensive, gloomy nest made from the same substance Osrov could manipulate, lying over a hill. He had to be hiding inside that nest. I was heading in its direction when I heard nearby screaming. Vernan was riding a horse, galloping towards the shadows and using a giant sword to defeat them all at once. It all seemed very glorious until an arrow struck the horse, causing it to tumble. Vernan fell to the ground, the deceased mount landing on top of him, as shadows began tearing through his armor.

"Vernan!" I shouted, firing arrows at the creatures.

It didn't seem to hurt them at all, so I launched my sword in their direction and managed to scare most of them away. The last shadow remaining was killed by an arrow flying through the battlefield. It was crazy how so many deadly objects were thrown around during the war as if they were nothing.

"Kid..." Vernan mumbled weakly.

I kneeled beside him and pushed the horse away with his help. Then I noticed something horrifying: my sword—which I had tossed in his direction a few moments before—had landed on his foot.

"Holy sh—" I covered my mouth.

"It didn't chop it off, don't worry," Vernan grunted.

"How do you know?"

"Because I can still feel it," Vernan replied, resting his head on the horse to use it as cover from the arrows flying around.

"I told everyone to leave the horses on the stables! But you need to go with my friend Tyrose, now! He's set up at the doctor's house—you remember where that is, right?" I commanded, willing to carry him there.

"I won't go there. I can still fight," he breathed heavily, "and get your damn sword off my toes!"

"Oh, sorry," I lifted my hand and recalled the weapon.

"Damn it, I meant with your hands!" Vernan yelled in pain.

"Sorry," I smiled awkwardly.

"But I can keep fighting, don't worry!" He said, trying to stand up but failing.

"You can't," I touched his shoulder, "you have to go to the doctor, now!"

"This is a war I've been waiting for my entire life! I will not spend it lying in the doctor's house!" Vernan spat, grunting in pain, "now help me up."

"You can't fight like this," I insisted, "and this isn't the time or place to be arguing!"

"If I die, let me go in a blaze of glory!"

"Look, Vernan, do you want to die in two minutes because you were too stubborn to listen to me, or do you want to keep fighting for your entire lifetime and take part in dozens more battles, even more epic than this one?"

"I can't retreat," Vernan muttered, "imagine if your captain left the battlefield. What a shame!"

"Who cares what they say? It's fine to retreat, especially when someone's as injured as you are."

"I'm sorry for everything I did to you, Krell," Vernan broke into tears suddenly, "I always thought you were a good kid—giving money to the ones who deserve it. I'm sorry for all those times I argued with you at the castle and I'm sorry for not giving you another sponge when you were cleaning the toilet."

"That was odd," I whispered, "but I appreciate it. You can make it up for me by heading to Tyrose right now."

"Will you really forgive me?"

"If you go now, yes."

He immediately stood up and scratched my head as if he had never been injured in the first place.

"Win this battle for me, Krell," he said before limping away.

"I will..." I nodded, "I will."

My only objective was to reach Osrov and end him for once and for all, but I was interrupted by Ivy and Kyra, who were fighting together beside the main plaza's fountain. Kyra froze the shadows as Ivy entangled them with her vines—they were a great team.

"Look out!" Ivy yelled as she tossed a shadow in my direction, "I thought you were one of them."

"Have you seen Reyna?" I asked immediately.

"No. At least not since the war started," Kyra replied.

"There's a nest on the side of the kingdom where the steel barrier was once at. Osrov is probably in there. We need to get to him, now!" I said, fending off the shadows with my sword.

“There are too many shadow for us to get to the other end of the kingdom. We need to kill most of them before attempting something so dangerous,” Ivy continued fighting.

“Then let’s do that,” I smirked.

Ivy was adept at distinguishing between the shadows that were trotters and those that were people and elves. The trotters were torn apart by her vines, while the others were slashed by a hatchet she found at the Zumba tribe camp. In contrast, Kyra froze them all without exception. I analyzed how they worked together and used it to my advantage, pushing them near Kyra so she could freeze them or tossing them over to Ivy so she could rip them apart. After one of the shadows caught me off guard, I stepped back, impaled my sword into its stomach, and rammed it to the ground. Kyra noticed what I was doing, froze the creature’s head, and then grunted while stepping on it.

“Catch this!” Ivy shouted, ensnaring a shadow with her vines and launching it toward me.

I raised my sword and cleaved the creature in half as it passed over my head. I wanted to run away and reach the nest where Osrov was, but I knew we had to vanish all shadows before confronting him. I thought about everything he had caused—all the blood he shed, the death of the villagers—it made me so *angry.*

“Krell, what is happening to you?” Ivy asked, staring at me strangely.

My hands darkened as my body began to shake—it was happening again, but at least I knew how to control it. I closed my eyes and thought of my mother, but nothing seemed to change within me. After the dream I had of her, she begged me not to think about her anymore, so I opened my eyes and looked at Ivy and Kyra instead. Before I even noticed it, my body returned to its original state.

“You had one of those episodes again?” Kyra asked.

"Yes, but I've got it under control," I smiled, knowing the people who made me happy were standing right in front of me, "oh, and Tyrose told me to tell you to stay safe… and that he loves you."

"Oh, Tyrose," she sighed, giggling.

"Get off me, you spawns of hell!" I heard a far cry.

"Krell, we're really enjoying your company, but it seems like someone needs your help more than we do," Kyra said, pointing at the person who screamed.

Ivory was fighting dozens of shadows at a time. Did I want to go with her? No. Was she in danger and needed to be saved immediately? Definitely. So, I had to separate myself from what made me happy to help someone who absolutely loathed me. I knew she would start complaining the second I got to her, saying that she didn't need my help and could handle it herself.

"I don't need your help; I can handle it myself!" Was the first thing she shouted when I approached her.

"Knew it," I whispered to myself.

I swung my sword like a boomerang, knocking back all the shadows attacking her. When there were no more threats, she looked at me in disgust and marched away.

"Why do you hate me so much?" I stopped her and asked, "what did I ever do wrong?"

"You're the son of the King," she replied, "that's enough for me."

"My father and I are very different people—for your information—and you don't even know me!" I chased after her.

"Shut up," she said quietly.

"And now you're shutting me up?"

"Just shut up and listen," she shushed me again.

"What? The sound of blood being splattered?"

"The stables!" She yelled, running away.

I had no choice but to follow her. I had no idea what was happening, but when Ivory reached the stables, I finally realized what was going on. They were engulfed in flames.

"Come help me!" She climbed a ladder to get inside.

"Oh, now you want my help?"

"Horses are dying—yes!"

Smoke blinded us the moment we crawled inside the burning structure, but it didn't stop Ivory, who had a single goal in mind: *get the horses out*. I approached one of the mounts and patted its back as Ivory extinguished the flames on its tail. We managed to guide it out, but there were still many more trapped inside.

"Help me with this other one!" Ivory commanded, coughing.

As she ran inside to aid the remaining horses, the roof collapsed on top of her, violently crushing her in front of my eyes. I gasped and tried lifting the wood, but it was too heavy. Ivory screamed as the flames reached her body and the wooden planks mangled her chest. Her eyes began to close, but she still gasped for air and weakly called my name for help.

"I'm sorry..." I realized that despite my efforts, I couldn't get her out.

Suddenly, a wave rushed to the burning stables, extinguishing the fire and alleviating part of Ivory's pain. Then, the ground shook, and all the debris was lifted in the blink of an eye. I pulled Ivory out of the destroyed stable and ensured she was safe, but—just as she usually did—she pushed me away immediately.

When I looked behind me, I saw Ivy and Kyra fighting beside the fountain as if nothing had happened. I thought I was going insane until Ivy winked and smirked at me.

"How did you do that?" Ivory asked, "the fire is extinguished, and you pulled me out!"

"I... I have a few tricks up my sleeve," I lied, knowing damn well I didn't do any of that.

"You saved my life," she smiled at me, then looked back at the fallen stable "but you couldn't save the horses."

"The good thing is that you're fine," I said, patting her shoulder.

"My entire back is burned, but I guess I'm fine," she sighed, "it's just so hard to see the horses... *dead*."

"It isn't your fault, nor mine."

"You know, Krell," she coughed, hesitating, "you're not that bad of a person. I still hate you, but you're not bad."

"Thanks?" I said awkwardly.

"Don't ever remind me I said that," she rolled her eyes with regret, "now, are we going to keep fighting those wretches, or what?"

"Ye—" I began until something caught my eye.

On the rooftops of the various houses in the kingdom, there was a dark figure jumping through them. My blood ran cold when I realized it was the sister—the same shadow that fought us back at the land's volcano and whose sister I killed. After squinting my eyes, I noticed the sister was running straight toward the castle—the castle where my grandfather was at.

CHAPTER 37

Ivory wanted to continue fighting the shadows, but I had other plans. I stormed away, climbing the first ladder I saw to reach the rooftops and chase the sister. The thought of what she could do to my grandfather drove me to stop her before she could reach the castle.

"Where are you going?" Ivory asked, noticing I was no longer by her side.

"They are breaching the castle! Stay here to fight; I'll be back soon!" I yelled back, kicking the ladder behind me.

I was panting, jumping across the houses just like in my childhood. I flew through the gaps, dashing over the red-bricked roofs as I reassured myself nothing would happen. I could see the brawl on the streets, the bodies scattered in the alleyways, and the trails of blood smeared on the houses' walls. As Kharum said, I needed to use all those images as fuel to fight the shadows. My mind was so wrapped in that thought that I didn't notice the giant gap between the next house and the one I was standing on. I didn't have a chance to stop, so I plummeted down and landed on a haystack, which cushioned my fall. My back was aching, but I jumped out of the stack and sprinted to the castle. I couldn't stop to fight the shadows, especially when my grandfather's life was at stake. I was running beside a house when something tore through the wall and grabbed me, lifting me and destroying the roof. It was a shadow-infected trotter king—I didn't have time for it!

"Get off me!" I screamed, recalling my sword.

When the weapon flew to my hand, I hacked it at the trotter's face, but the creature moved away, and I only managed to hit its horn. My sword slipped from my hand, leaving me no choice but to rip the horn from its body and stab it in its neck. The trotter king dropped me a few seconds later. I could have stopped to ensure it was dead, but I didn't have time. I exited the house and continued sprinting toward the castle. Nothing could've stopped me.

"Please tell me you're okay," I whispered to myself.

Among all the noises that reached my ears, one caught my attention. The stained glass on the palace's wall shattered when the sister leaped inside, breaching the castle. I gasped and kept running, climbing onto a roof and jumping from house to house. I was almost there—I knew I could do it.

Although exhausted, I dashed with determination, aware there was a slight chance my grandfather had already been slaughtered by the time I arrived. With those thoughts clouding my mind, I reached the castle before I even noticed.

"How do I enter?" I asked myself, pondering.

I stood on a house's roof beside the stained glass window the sister had shattered. Clearly, she had no problem breaching the walls, but I wasn't as agile as she was, so I needed to find another way. Then I remembered an item I hadn't used in a long time.

"I've missed you," I said, reaching into my pouch and grabbing my grapple hook.

In the outskirts, the grapple hook was almost useless—people from other kingdoms and tribes needed no help when climbing—but in the Main Kingdom, it was crucial to have one.

I secured the hook on a distant ledge and ensured the rope was steady before placing my weight on it. I counted to three and flung myself forward, clutching the flimsy rope. The chord didn't look durable, but it lasted long enough to take me to the castle's stained glass window. I braced myself before letting go of the rope and landing on the crimson-colored hall.

"Ouch," I panted, injured by a glass shard impaling my shoulder.

I carefully removed it, but after realizing how much noise I made, I recalled my sword and frantically looked around, wondering if the shadow sister heard me.

"Gramps," I mumbled, focusing on my main objective after realizing there was no one around.

I ran through the hall, cautiously stepping on the carpet so my footsteps wouldn't make much noise. His room was just a few feet away, but it seemed impossible to walk with my numb legs and trembling hands.

"Please tell me you're alright," I prayed before opening the door.

He was lying on his bed, half asleep, with a bitten apple by his side. I gasped with relief, approaching him with a smile. The sister was still inside the castle, but my grandfather was thankfully still alive.

"Gramps, thank God," I touched his forehead to check for a fever.

"Krell," he laughed weakly, opening his eyes, "it looks like you've made good use of my clothes from when I was young. Although I do see they have a scratch or two—nothing that can't be fixed by a good tailor."

"Yeah, I know. I'll fix it later," I gulped nervously, "but right now we need to leave."

"Leave?" He asked, "why?"

"It's..." I wanted to tell him, but couldn't, "just follow me—"

When I tried to get him out of bed, the ground shook violently. I fell to my knees as the walls trembled and dust fell from the ceiling. I left my grandfather and walked out of the room, looking through the hall's window and noticing shadows using a catapult at the far end of the kingdom, right beside Osrov's nest. They were too stupid to be using a machine like that by themselves, which meant Osrov was controlling them. Either way, they were catapulting boulders at the castle. It would collapse in a matter of minutes, and we couldn't be inside when it happened.

"We need to leave, gramps!" I shouted, walking into his room again and noticing something terrifying.

On a far edge of the dim bedroom, partially hidden behind the curtains, I saw a pair of glowing eyes. I knew exactly who they belonged to.

"Gramps," I approached slowly, trying not to glance at the silhouette, "we need to go. Right now."

I locked eyes with the shadowy figure hiding from us. I saw as it tilted its head, then smiled, revealing sharp, deathly fangs. If I hadn't realized who it was by that point, I definitely did when she rushed out of her hiding spot and stabbed her dagger into the bed. I was lucky to pull my grandfather away before the knife reached him, but that didn't stop the sister from chasing us.

"Run!" I screamed.

With my grandfather leaning on me, I barged out of the room. The sister mercilessly ran after us before stopping and tilting her head. She began walking, realizing how slow we were.

"Who is it?" My grandfather asked, limping away from the shadow.

"Just run!" I screeched, wrapping my arms around him.

"Yeah. Just run, pigs," she scratched her dagger on the stone walls, "I'll gut you both whenever I catch you, which won't be long considering how slow your *gramps* is."

I tried walking faster, but my grandfather hindered me. Then another rumble was heard, shaking the entire palace and bringing my grandfather to his knees.

"Go without me," he panted, out of breath.

"Never!" I helped him get back to his feet.

The stairs leading to the first floor were near, but I knew it would take my grandfather ages to go down. Still, we headed that way, knowing it was our only chance of survival. Another boulder hit the castle, impacting the second floor and destroying my grandfather's bedroom.

"Can you walk by yourself?" I asked him.

"Yes," he wheezed.

I let go of him and began shooting arrows at the sister. She either dodged them or caught them with one hand and threw them back at me. Instead of weakening her, the projectiles seemed to make her stronger and faster. As a last resort, I tossed my sword in her direction, but she evaded it with ease.

"You killed my sister," she cried angrily, "the only person who ever cared about me is dead because of you! And I will make you pay."

When she jumped at my grandfather and me with her claws ready to sear into our skin, another boulder hit the castle. The sister was thrown back by the rock—it didn't kill her, but it gave us time to escape.

"Down the stairs!" I returned to my grandfather and helped him walk down.

I felt immense relief upon seeing the castle's main door, but all hope vanished when the sister jumped from the railing above onto the first floor, blocking our only exit. I screamed, turning around and leading my grandpa away from the shadow. Unlike before, the sister was now relentlessly sprinting towards us with a burning desire for revenge.

"Your room!" Gramps yelled.

As soon as I laid my hand on the knob, the sister pulled my hair and tossed me down the stairs. I fell six steps before hitting my head against the wall and getting up again. I recalled my sword and pointed it at the sister, who was grinning from atop the stairs.

"You want to fight me?" I panted, then yelled desperately, "well, go ahead! Do it! Fight me!"

"Oh, Krell," she pouted sarcastically, turning her head to my room where my grandfather was standing, "when will you learn it's not you who I want?"

"No!" I screamed.

I ran up the stairs and threw myself on top of the sister, smashing her head on the floor and attempting to stab her back. She twisted her hip, slapped the weapon away, pushed me back, and crawled toward my grandfather. Before she could pierce his chest with her dagger, I kicked her away and dashed into my room. When she tried to enter, my grandfather threw a glass decoration orb at her face. While she was stunned, I shut the door and dragged a shelf to barricade it.

"You won't hide from me!" She banged on the door.

"What now?" I asked gramps.

"Let me catch my breath," he panted.

"There's no time for that!" I bit my nails, pacing around my room.

I looked at my window, but it had been sealed shut by my father's guards, and there was no other visible way of escaping. Then I remembered the secret room where my grandfather had revealed he was "*the old hero*" and had given me the suit I was wearing. I pulled my bed out of the way and opened the hatch leading to the chamber.

"Here," I whispered, not wanting the sister to hear me.

He limped towards the hatch and dropped down alongside me. I wasn't quick enough to drag the bed to its original spot, but I managed to shut the hatch before the sister broke into the room.

"Gotcha!" I heard her say as she entered, "now, where are you?"

We both stood in silence, hoping the sister wouldn't find our hiding spot. I was surprised my grandpa didn't make a single sound, but it still didn't work. A few seconds later, the trap door opened abruptly, and the sister dropped down. The room was pitch black, so the only things I could see within the gloom were her bright eyes and beaming teeth. At that moment, I wasn't the one guiding us; my grandpa pulled my hand and dragged me away immediately. Before the shadow could even lay her claws on us, we had already found an exit—a small staircase leading to the first floor, not far from the castle's entrance.

"Come, boy," he said, running down the steps, "we need to get out!"

"Run as fast as you can, gramps!" I yelled, trying to reach the castle's main door—our exit.

"You won't escape!" The sister sprinted after us.

She was even quicker than I remembered, so I had no other choice but to let go of my grandpa and grab my bow. The only target in sight was a chandelier, but the metal hanging wouldn't break easily. I decided to shoot the straps of a banner hanging on the wall. The large red piece of cloth landed on top of the sister, and just when we thought we had a chance to escape the castle, the same banner was tossed over our heads.

"No! Gramps!" I cried, losing sight of him as soon as the red cloth landed covered us.

After everything he'd done in those last few minutes, I knew he could find the way out by himself, which was why I crawled forward without hesitation to reach the end of the scarlet cloth. I felt someone moving beside me and heard heavy breathing, which assured me my grandfather was still by my side. After dragging myself to the end of the fallen banner, I rammed towards the exit, opened the main door, and escaped the castle. I was about to run away when I realized my grandpa was no longer by my side.

"Krell," I heard a soft voice behind me.

Gramps was exiting the banner, struggling to get back on his feet. When I noticed the figure crawling below the red cloth behind him, I knew it was too late.

"No!" I cried in despair.

A sharp sound was heard before blood dripped down my grandfather's stomach, and he struggled for air. The end of the sword was visible through his chest for a split second, pulling back as soon as I screamed. He dropped to his knees and fell sideways as the sister shook her sword and wiped the blood off it.

"A loved one for a loved one," she stated, "see you soon."

She jumped through a window and disappeared into the streets. I wanted to chase after her, but my grandfather was lying on the floor—almost lifeless—so I ran over to him and held his hand, gently placing it on my cheek.

"Please, no..." I began crying, "don't do this to me."

"It's okay, grandson," he smiled, swallowing the blood so he could keep speaking to me.

"I can take you to Tyrose! He-he's a doctor; he can help you! Come on," I tried carrying him, but he was too weak to move.

"It's okay," he said.

The castle rumbled again. The catapult launched another boulder at the castle—the second floor was destroyed.

"I can't," I sobbed, "I don't want you to die."

"It's okay," he repeated.

"It's not okay!" I tossed my sword away and cursed, "it's not okay! It's not!"

"There's a war right now, Krell," he said, "you go out there and fight like the warrior you are. You're my warrior, grandson."

"I'll have no one left!" I cried.

"Think about all the life you have ahead of you," he said ln the verge of death, "but don't let my death affect you, grandson. Remember, you are the only one who can forge your path. Don't let your father intervene with your decisions."

Another rumble. The castle was collapsing.

"Get out, right now," he said with his last breath, "you will choose your own destiny."

Then he died. I watched as his soul left his body, his eyes lost their hue, his chest remained still, and his hands stopped squeezing mine. He was gone *forever.*

"Gramps," I sobbed, not knowing what to do.

The castle kept rumbling. The pillars were being destroyed, and the walls were cracking. I tried dragging my grandfather's body outside, but the roof was already caving in. I had no other choice but to leave him behind and storm out of the palace, drowning in tears. My ears began ringing as I limped through the main door and onto the kingdom's streets. I heard a muffled crash, and after smoke engulfed my surroundings, I realized the castle had fallen to the ground—my home was destroyed. I started sobbing uncontrollably, seeing all the figures hidden within the cloud of dust. One guard was fighting three shadows at once, but the creatures eventually overwhelmed him and slit his throat. I walked beside him, unable to hear his screams because of the ringing inside my ears. I noticed a woman on the side of the road with an arrow in her chest, and a man—a little older than me—stuck in the castle's debris. I kept bawling, watching every tragedy without being able to help. Then my eyes caught someone lying on the ground with blood smeared all over her colorful shirt and pale skin. It was Sof, the seven-year-old girl from the Nature Kingdom.

"No," I gasped, "no, no, no!"

I approached the little girl and glanced at her wounds, realizing she had been murdered by a shadow. Her grandfather wasn't far from her, leaning against a wall with an arrow in his neck. What broke my heart the most was that the toy I gifted her was still wrapped in her arms as if she were protecting it before she died. I hugged her tightly and closed her eyes with my fingers, carrying her away. I managed to find a nearby empty house, where I laid her on a bed and placed the toy inside my pouch. After exiting the home and closing the door behind me, the ringing inside my ears finally ceased.

"Krell," someone appeared in front of me.

"Reyna," I looked at her unemotionally.

"Krell, your head is bleeding," she touched my face, "I saw you enter the castle before it fell to the ground. I thought you... It doesn't matter anymore; you're fine."

"I'm not *fine*," I pulled away, "the little girl from the Nature Kingdom is dead."

"Oh my God," Reyna covered her mouth.

"A little girl!" I cried, "she wasn't even old enough to experience all this! I should've protected her! And now she's dead!"

"It's not your fault," Reyna tried hugging me, but I pushed her away.

"It is," I wiped my tears, "everyone is dead. I couldn't save Sof, I couldn't save the guards on the streets, the villagers, the little kids being killed by something they don't even comprehend! I couldn't even save my grandfather!"

"Oh, Krell," Reyna gasped.

"My entire family is dead! I don't have anyone anymore!" I screamed, flooded with tears, "no one!"

"You have us," Reyna said.

"Stop," I trembled.

"What? Are you going to forget everything we've been through?"

"Just stay here," I wiped my tears, then frowned, "keep fighting these things."

"What are you gonna do then?"

"Kill the sister," I glanced at the nest on the other side of the kingdom, "and kill Osrov."

"All alone?" She asked.

"I don't need your help," I said without even looking at her.

"You will die!" She yelled, but I pretended not to listen.

Although she kept screaming at me not to leave, I ignored her. I simply recalled my sword and started walking towards the nest Osrov and the sister were most likely at. I knew I would kill them both that day—nothing in the lands could have stopped me.

Chapter 38

Vengeance is a bittersweet feeling. When you take revenge and see the person who hurt you the most die, it feels good—powerful. But afterward? That's another story. You become consumed by guilt the moment you realize the barbarities you've committed. Well, then I'd have to enjoy it while it lasted.

After leaving Reyna behind, I marched away to stop the war for once and for all. The endless things I could do to make the sister and Osrov suffer were satisfying to think about as I made my way to their nest on the other side of the kingdom. I tried killing as many shadows as I could before arriving, warming up in preparation to meet the sister again. A horde of them ran my way in a crooked line, but with a single swing of my sword, the creatures fell to the ground, lifeless. I stepped on top of them, staring at the nest, hypnotically mumbling as my eyes twitched with rage. When I noticed another shadow in front of me, I gripped his head and stuck it inside the flooded fountain in the main plaza. He tried getting out of the water, but I kept pushing his head inside, grunting with anger.

"Krell," I heard a voice from afar.

I ignored it and continued pushing the shadow's head into the fountain. If I could just keep him in place for a few more seconds, maybe he would finally die.

"Krell!" I heard the voice again, louder.

I couldn't stop—I was doing the lands a favor by killing that shadow. The creature was already drowning when something pushed me away, launching me to the other side of the plaza. I stood up in pain and grunted, noticing Ivy a few feet away from the fountain, standing petrified and glaring at me oddly.

"What the hell, Ivy!" I ran to her after realizing she used her vines to fling me away.

"Krell, listen to me—" Ivy tried to calm my temper, but as soon as I reached her, I slapped her face.

"Hey!" Kyra appeared behind her and pushed me away.

"She almost killed me!" I shouted.

"Krell, you're not doing well," Kyra stepped back, holding Ivy's hand.

"Yeah, of course I'm not doing well! My entire family is dead!" My voice cracked, "and I'm gonna kill those responsible."

"We're sorry, but we can't let you go," Ivy ignored the slap and comforted me.

"Why?" I cried.

"Because you almost killed an elf!" Kyra pointed at the shadow lying on the ground beside the fountain, "you were drowning him and weren't planning on stopping!"

I was so consumed by rage that I hadn't noticed I was drowning an elf instead of a shadow. While pushing his head into the flooded fountain, I even noticed his pointy ears, yet I decided to ignore it.

"It's okay, Krell," Ivy rubbed my cheek, "but you can't go to Osrov right now. We need to wait."

Deep down, I knew what she said made sense, but I couldn't accept it behind the cloud of fury.

"I'm so sorry," I said unemotionally.

I pulled away and stepped back, turning around and continuing my path to the nest. I was going to kill Osrov and the sister—I needed to do so.

"Krell, no!" Ivy shouted, but I didn't listen.

"Let him go," Kyra whispered to her, "he'll learn for himself."

I limped through the stone streets, hearing the screams of a woman from a house's second floor. Shadows pushed her off the balcony, but I didn't stop to help. I kept staring at the nest, completely ignoring my surroundings. Last time I hurried somewhere, my grandfather died. Maybe if I had arrived at the castle sooner, the sister wouldn't have been able to hide inside his room. Maybe if I had fought the sister instead of cowardly running away—or maybe if I had let her kill me instead—my grandpa would still be alive. As much as I wanted to blame his death on the sister, it was truly my fault.

"Krell! Thank God you're here!" Kharum cried for help upon seeing me, "there's an injured man, buh-but he's too heavy, and I nuh-need to carry him to Tyrose. Come huh-help me!"

"You can handle it yourself," I said without batting an eye.

He stood in silence, trying to carry the injured man alone before eventually failing. I barged into an empty house and ran upstairs, exiting through a hatch and jumping onto the roof. Below me, there was a nympho—probably a survivor from the Nature Kingdom—fighting seven shadows at once. I ignored his struggle, and moments later, screams and roars were heard, followed by the sound of blood splattering. I closed my eyes for a second and then opened them again, focusing on the nest.

"Osrov... Osrov..." I whispered to myself.

The nest was less than thirty feet away. I grinned and chuckled, already imagining the look on Osrov's face when he realized I hadn't died inside the castle. The last few streets before reaching him were empty, probably because he had already exhausted all his forces.

At last, I reached the nest, perched on a hill just outside the Main Kingdom and a few feet beyond the fallen steel barrier.

"I'm going to kill you," I mumbled.

There was no door on the nest, so I walked around it for a few seconds, searching for an entrance. I tried tearing it apart, but a sticky substance clung to my skin whenever I attempted it. It seemed as if the nest was alive and had a mind of its own. I decided to recall my sword and slash through the goo, gradually revealing the ample, dismal interior. It was much bigger than I expected: a simple, circular, gloomy cavern with a strange beaming light in the center. After focusing on the blinding figure, I noticed Osrov standing within it, hovering above the ground.

"Rah!" Someone screamed behind me.

It was the sister, wielding two swords and leaping in my direction. She slammed them to the ground, knocking me back and hissing as I rolled away and crawled backward.

"You recognize these blades?" She asked, sharpening them against each other, "one is mine, and the other belonged to my sister. You know, the one you murdered?"

"You killed my grandfather and my father!" I shouted, standing up.

"Your grandfather, yeah, but your father? That's a new one added to the list."

"The catapult destroyed the castle," I said, recalling what had happened, "he was inside."

"Then blame it on Osrov, not on me!"

The sister slashed both blades at me, but I parried with my weapon and countered. She stepped back, circling me and giggling maniacally just like her late sister. The way she used the two blades felt as if she was fighting alongside her. She replicated her moves almost identically—I was essentially fighting the two shadow sisters at once.

"What, you want to take a break?" She asked after I stopped fighting.

I charged at her, grabbing her legs and lifting her over my head, but she slammed her elbow into my shoulder and climbed my body, wrapping her legs around my neck. She began squeezing, and when I retreated to a nearby tree, she jumped off and kicked me away.

"You surrender?" She asked, licking her teeth.

"I'll fight until I die," I panted.

"It won't be long now," she grinned.

She threw one of the swords in my direction, but I stepped aside, causing the blade to get stuck on the log behind me. I shot an arrow at her stomach and attempted to stab her afterward, yet she evaded and hacked the remaining sword at my feet, knocking me down. As I tried to crawl away, she sat on my back and pulled my hair, swiftly placing her sword on my neck. She was ready to slash my throat, but I recalled my weapon and smashed its hilt into her face before anything happened. She tumbled back and screeched in anger while I got back on my feet and raised my sword over her chest. I was about to kill the sister when a shadow tackled me to the ground and began scratching its claws at my face. Before I could try freeing myself, a sharp blade pierced the creature's head, killing it.

"Let's keep it even," the sister said after stabbing the shadow.

I thought she would give me time to recover; however, she pulled me up and tossed me to a nearby tree, where one of her swords was still stuck in its log. I hit myself with the weapon's handgrip before turning around and noticing the sister's malign intent. She shoved her blade at my stomach, but I was lucky to step away and rip the weapon from her hands.

"No more weapons, huh?" I panted, tossing the sword aside.

"I don't need any!" She screamed, pushing me away.

Despite being unarmed, the sister still overpowered me and hurled me against Osrov's nest. The sticky substance from the gloomy cocoon ensnared my arms and tangled my feet, covering my entire torso in seconds. I was stuck on the nest's wall, unable to move, with only my head exposed.

"Leave his face free," the sister commanded the substance from the nest, controlling it at will, "I know exactly how I want to kill him."

She approached the tree and pulled her sister's sword from the log, glaring at me with vengeance. She charged at me as I shut my eyes, bracing death. The blade was about to reach my neck when the sticky substance from the nest shielded my head. The sword struck the goo, which was too thick to penetrate, and the sister was knocked back, stunned.

"Damn it, I told you not to cover his head!" The sister screamed.

Then, the thick matter released my limbs and set me free. The sister stood paralyzed for a few seconds, and I knew it was my only chance, so I pushed her against the nest and took her weapon from her hands. The sticky substance began tangling the sister, trapping her body in the same defenseless position I was once in. It was as if the nest was reading my mind and responding to my thoughts.

"You're one of them now," she mumbled, trembling.

I hadn't noticed it before, but apart from the sister's head, there was another uncovered circle in the middle of her stomach. The goo was avoiding it, almost beckoning me toward it. I knew exactly what I needed to do. The sister glanced at me oddly and then looked down in horror.

"No," she cried, screeching in fear, "no, no, no! Please, no!"

Instead of hearing the sister's screams, my mind kept repeating the sound of the blade that stabbed my grandfather. I was reminded of him lying on the ground with blood dripping down his chest, as well as the last words he uttered before passing away. With no more hesitation, my weapon pierced the sister's stomach. Her eyes widened, shedding a single tear as the nest released her and she dropped to the ground. It was strange seeing the sister cry—she looked just like a human. For a moment, I completely forgot she was a shadow, seeing my grandfather's expression on her face instead.

"You..." She looked into my eyes, terrified, "you will be... You are..."

"I'm what?" I asked.

"You will be the beginning of it," the sister struggled to stay awake, "a death in the family. The death of the lands. The beginning of a war. The rise of the Gods. Mark my words, Krell... You are the... You're..."

"I'm what? I'm what!" I shook her arms desperately.

"The old God... Mo... Gana..."

Before I could ask further questions, the sister closed her eyes and turned to ashes. I didn't pay much attention to the words she mumbled before dying, so I simply stood up, shook my arms as shivers crossed my spine, and stared directly at the nest in front of me, which had already opened itself for me. I nervously stepped inside and noticed how the entrance sealed behind me.

"Osrov?" I called his name.

The inside of the nest was circular, and the same sticky substance from outside covered the walls and floor. The cylindrical light beam at the center of the nest remained there, with Osrov's figure inside. The moment I touched the ray of light, I felt my skin melting and my hand disintegrating. I yelped and looked at my fingers, realizing nothing had happened.

"Come inside," Osrov's voice called to me.

With no other alternative, I stepped inside the light. The pain I felt was indescribable, but thankfully it didn't last long. Within the mysterious beam, there was no agony; instead, I felt a strange sense of... *peace*? I opened my eyes upon entering, observing the beautiful oasis that surrounded me. The sky was pink, the sun bright—but not to the point of burning my eyes—and I was standing on a shallow ocean that reached my ankles. I looked around in awe, noticing the dark figure standing behind me: Osrov.

"Krell," he bowed as I tried recalling my sword, but it wouldn't come back to me, "that doesn't work here. We are inside your mind."

"Why are you in my head?" I asked, breathing heavily.

"Because we are connected. You and I are both shadows," he replied, taking a step forward, "now, now, I'm very sorry about what happened back at the Fire Kingdom, but you know that when a man is under attack, he has to defend himself, right?"

"What is this place?" I ignored his apology.

"You know, I've had this talk with all the shadows. I've spoken to every single one of those beautiful creatures you see on the streets," Osrov grinned, "this is a place where you can choose to be wherever you want to be."

"Elaborate," I stepped back, intrigued.

"You know how the Khan works, right? When people become shadows, all the negative aspects of them emerge and create another version of themselves—a version some may call *evil,*" he explained, "but if negativity creates the shadow, where do you think their positive aspects go? Here."

"What, a half-inch tall ocean?"

"No," he chuckled lightly, "right now, your mind is inside the Khan."

"What? And where is the Khan?" I frowned.

"The chamber in which we—" he paused, then laughed, licking his rotten teeth, "*I* first found it. But it doesn't matter where it is. All that matters is that the shadows are connected through it. The mind of every single shadow is inside the Khan. The Khan creates a world of their choice in which they can live."

"And what if the shadow dies?" I gulped.

"Then their mind stays alive inside the artifact."

"I'm not buying it," I shook my head, "take me out."

"It's not that eas— "

"Take me out!"

"You have to—"

"I said..."

As I puffed and angrily marched towards Osrov, he grabbed my head and pushed me away. I flinched and fell into the water, but when I opened my eyes again, I wasn't in the same oasis anymore. I lay on a bed with warm, white sheets and the coziest pillow I had ever rested my head on. I panted and stood up, pinching myself to see if it was a dream.

"Ouch," I said, realizing it wasn't.

"Breakfast is ready!" I heard Kyra's voice from another room.

"Kyra?" I mumbled, standing up from the bed and opening the bedroom door.

I seemed to be inside a wooden cabin with a spacious living room and three bedrooms. Kyra was cooking in the kitchen, and when I approached her, Ivy emerged from another room wearing a white shirt and beige pants.

"Smells delicious," she said, hugging Kyra and grabbing a plate.

"I had the craziest dream!" Tyrose yawned, entering the cabin.

"Was it dogs chasing you again?" Ivy asked, giggling.

"Yeah, for some reason."

"And what are you doing, Krell?" Kyra looked at me after some seconds of silence, "come eat."

I was paralyzed but still managed to move my legs to the table, even if the rest of my body remained stiff. What the hell was happening? It looked like we were living together as a family. Ivy and Kyra seemed to be getting along, and Tyrose had definitely grown a few inches. Had the Shadow War ended already?

"Wait for me!" Reyna trotted to the kitchen and kissed my cheek.

I was too confused to say anything else, so I simply sat at the table and remained motionless. After Tyrose noticed there was no plate in front of me, he served me a loaf of bread and a portion of acorn soup.

"Acorn soup? From Kharum?" I asked, confused.

"Yeah," Kyra sat down and blew on the steaming soup, "thank God he gave me the recipe!"

"It smells delicious, *Ky*," Ivy laughed.

"*Ky*?" I asked.

"Yes, *Ky* for Kyra..." She looked at me strangely, then chuckled, "are you okay, Krell? Did you have some of our special novo juice last night? We told you it was off-limits until you turned eightee—"

"I'm fine, don't worry," I interrupted, taking a sip of the hot soup.

There was a small chat at the table. Reyna announced she would go hunting with me later that evening, and Tyrose began complaining about wanting to join us. When they looked at me for my opinion, I simply nodded. Then, Kyra and Ivy revealed they had been working with Ivory to move further north where we could continue living.

"I'm sorry, where are we right now?" I asked, eyebrows furrowed.

"We made alliances with the Quora tribe, remember?" Reyna grabbed my hand, "are you sure you're doing alright?"

"And what about the Main Kingdom?"

"Oh, don't worry about them! Your father said he allowed you to move with us and that he'll take good care of your grandad while you're away," Tyrose replied.

"Gramps is alive?" I dropped my spoon, "and my father? Is the castle still standing?"

"Of course they're alive, Krell!" Ivy laughed, "at least now I'm certain you took some of my special novo juice last night!"

"I know it's hard to move out for the first time after living in that castle your entire life, but you've gotta start getting used to it," Kyra said, "trust me, the Main Kingdom is in good hands. The villagers will be alright!"

"What about Osrov and the shadows?" I asked.

The table went silent. They continued eating the bread and slurping the soup, but no one answered my question. I pulled myself out of the chair and shook my head, realizing what was happening.

"You're not real," I mumbled.

They all looked at me and then at each other. In a far corner of the cabin, my sword lay, so I carefully ran over to it and pointed it at them. They all gasped and stood from their chairs, stepping back.

"Krell, you're freaking us out," Reyna breathed heavily.

"You're not real," I repeated, "you hear me, Osrov? I know it isn't real!"

Suddenly, I was back at the oasis with Osrov standing in front of me, panting in anger with a scythe in his hands. Out of all the weapons he could have wielded, that seemed like the deadliest one. Luckily, my sword didn't disappear when I was transported back to the shallow ocean, so he wasn't the only one with a weapon at hand.

"I gave you everything you wanted," he grunted, "your deepest desires were standing in front of you, and you threw it all away!"

"I won't live inside your fake fantasy," I replied, my eyebrows knitted in rage.

"Then you might as well not live at all," he took a deep breath before charging at me.

With what seemed like one step, he swung through the water, throwing his scythe upwards and nearly decapitating me. I tossed my sword at his face and then recalled it, slashing it across his chest. After taking a few steps back, I carefully attacked him. He was too smart, which was why my neck was grabbed with the scythe and my body was slammed to the ground. I thought he would try choking me, but he stabbed the scythe into my back and twisted it.

"How about now, kid?" Osrov laughed while I screamed.

It was clear he wanted to make me suffer; the weapon impaled me slowly and painfully. I clenched my teeth and abruptly pushed the scythe away, rolling and weakly standing up.

"I'm going to kill you," I panted.

He wrapped the scythe around my neck and pulled me closer. I felt the blood spilling down my spine, but when he had the chance to sever my head, he leaped back and waited for me to recover. I glanced at him in confusion when he kicked my leg, dropping me to my knees. Again, he had the opportunity to murder me, yet he simply punched my shoulder and stepped on my chest.

"Kill me," I commanded him.

He grunted and ignored my words, letting me go and waiting for me to recover. Instead of trying to fight him again, I simply tossed my sword aside and spread my arms.

"Kill me," I repeated.

"Why are you asking that?" He stuttered.

"Because I'm in front of you," I said with a shaky, yet confident breath, "murder me."

He didn't say a word.

"Exactly," I smirked, walking in circles and forcing Osrov to follow my lead, "you can't kill me here, right? You just want me to give up so I can live inside that fake land again? Well, I won't go back!"

"Either way, you can't escape," he smiled malevolently.

"Oh, I already figured it out," I stopped walking and lifted my hand.

My sword flew to my palm, tearing apart any obstacle in its way. That "*obstacle*" was Osrov, who stood between the weapon and me. His face was sliced in half, which would have normally killed him, but none of it was real.

I was jolted back to the real lands so forcefully that I hit my head with the nest's wall when the beam of light expelled me. Osrov emerged seconds later and, unsurprisingly, he was still alive.

"You thought I couldn't figure out your little game? Or the Khan's little game?" I wiped my runny nose, "now we can actually fight here instead of inside a twisted reality."

"You are smart," he began, "the Khan had no other choice but to let us out. You see, it isn't accustomed to death. But you're right; we really needed to figure this out with a fight to the death."

He no longer had his scythe, just his bare fists and a lot of rage. I knew I had gotten the best of him inside that fake oasis and was certain he had shown his limits back at the Fire Kingdom. With all my past experience, I knew exactly how to kill him. After chasing him with my sword, he blocked with his forearm, just as I expected. We locked eyes, and he was so focused on my expression that he didn't notice my plans. I dropped the sword and caught it with my left hand, gripping it tightly so it wouldn't slip out. More determined than ever—and without him expecting it—I stabbed the sword into Osrov's chest, twisting and pushing it so hard that we flew to the nest's wall. He gasped for air and tried aiding himself with the sticky substance from the nest, but it began pulling itself apart, opening an exit for us. He fell backward and was about to roll down the hill into the Main Kingdom when I stopped him and tossed him aside. He tried pulling the blade out of his chest but didn't have enough strength, so he simply lay on his back and looked at the morning sky.

"I guess I'll never see my... my kingdom," he stuttered as I approached him.

"You won't," I pulled the sword from his body and looked at the battlefield.

I wanted to see how the kingdom was faring against the shadows, but I was greeted by someone walking up the hill: my father. He was unharmed, wearing the same scarlet robe he always wore, with the golden crown still atop his head. I recalled how he almost murdered me before the war started, so I knew he was still a threat.

"Lower the sword, my son," he said with a proud and cordial tone, "I'm not going to do anything to you."

"Fine," I said and dropped the weapon, "I thought you were dead, you know? When the castle fell, I—"

"I know. I was able to escape, but your grandfather... he couldn't," he lowered his head, noticeably sad.

"How do you know he's dead? The castle crushed his body," I asked.

"Some villagers pulled him out," he said, "I'm so sorry, Krell. I knew you were very close to him."

"I was," I said, holding back tears.

"But I am so proud of you," he continued, "you killed Osrov and led a whole army against the shadows! You have accomplished so many things!"

"And you didn't bother saying that before you went ahead and tried killing me?" I shook my head.

"I thought you were leading a rebellion against me, but when I saw the shadows, I knew I was wrong. And I am so terribly sorry about it," he approached, "don't you think you could give your father a hug?"

It felt wrong doing such a thing. Why would I forgive someone who tried to murder me? Before I could even reject the embrace, his arms were already wrapped around me. It was something I never thought possible—my father finally saw me as his son. The hug was short and odd, especially when some liquid began soaking my clothes. I thought my father might have spilled something on my shirt, but it was a unique sensation as if it came from inside my body. When I pulled away from his arms, I heard a sharp sound.

"Fool," I heard him mutter.

I looked at my chest and noticed the dagger's hilt protruding from my body. I spat blood and fell to the ground, leaning sideways as my father stepped on me and pulled the knife out. Blood stained the grass, running down the hill while I gurgled and began closing my eyes. I fought to stay awake by staring at Osrov, who lay a few feet away in the same position as me.

"You can't even do what you're supposed to," my father kneeled beside him, "you're weak, Osrov."

"P-please, no..." Osrov said weakly before my father pushed his hands against his chest.

Osrov's darkness began draining out of his body and entering my father's, who twitched and screeched as he absorbed the power. After sucking every last drop of dark magic from the Shadow King—and leaving his colorless, deceased body behind—my father turned towards me and laughed.

"You are..." I spat blood, falling unconscious.

"I am Henrius Kovner," he said, "the goddamn Shadow King."

Chapter 39

Reyna

I had been searching for him for far too long. He couldn't have crossed the shadow-infested kingdom in search of Osrov, right? I tried my best to remain calm by assuring myself nothing had happened to him, but as soon as I noticed the shadow cocoon glowing in an odd pattern from afar, I knew something was wrong.

"Krell isn't with you?" I approached Ivy and Kyra, who were defeating the last remaining shadows in the main plaza.

"Not since he slapped Ivy," Kyra replied, rolling her eyes.

"I'm fine," Ivy interjected, "that kid's gone through a lot."

"Yeah, and that *'kid'* is fighting the Shadow King as we speak!" I sighed with desperation, "I will go find him right now."

"I'm coming with you," Ivy said, following my lead.

"It's not like I have any other choice," Kyra added, trotting behind her.

I was almost certain the war was over—we were definitely winning. All that remained was to kill Osrov and cure the remaining shadows. However, as easy as it might have sounded, killing the Shadow King wasn't an easy task, especially for someone like Krell. I couldn't believe he was fighting that monster all by himself.

"That looks like a good path," I said, pointing to an alleyway leading to the kingdom's edge, "we just need to cross that alley and then take the street to our right. We'll reach the shadow cocoon in no time."

"Anything to avoid the plaza," Ivy continued walking.

A couple of shadows crossed our path, one from the Main Kingdom and the other from the Ah'Lah'Rra tribe. I mercilessly killed them both with my daggers, stabbing one's neck and gashing another's chest. Before I could continue following the path to the cocoon, a shadow crawled out of a window and looked at me. I recognized his face—he had the same pointy ears as me, along with a musty beard that almost reached the ground.

"Reyna, are you okay?" Kyra asked, approaching me.

"Dad?" I mumbled after a moment of realization.

I could have used the zylika to turn my father back to normal, but as I stepped closer, his voice echoed in my head. I recalled the moments he screamed at me after my brothers' deaths, remembering when he locked me out of the camp for three weeks. Ivy and Kyra stepped back, not wanting to intervene, but when I looked deep into my father's eyes, my body froze. I thought he would remember me—even as a monster—but he jumped at me and flung me to the ground without hesitation.

"Reyna!" Ivy shouted, ready to aid me.

Surprisingly, the struggle ended in seconds. I gently pushed my father away and noticed the dagger stuck in his chest. Without realizing it, I had stabbed him. I gasped and crawled away, silently sobbing as the zylika began turning his body back to normal. Not wanting to look at him, I stood up and stared at Ivy and Kyra, who were speechlessly standing a few feet from his body.

"I hated him either way," I snorted, wiping my tears.

"What?" Ivy asked, paralyzed.

"He was an asshole," I replied, not knowing how to mourn his death, "let's just leave. We must find Krell."

"Are you sure?" Kyra asked, patting my shoulder.

"I'm fine," I pulled away and followed the road, quietly crying.

Yes, I hated him, but did he really deserve to die? I tried not to think about it too much, knowing he was a horrible person.

Yet, I still couldn't wrap my head around the fact that I had murdered my own father.

"Holy..." Ivy gasped, carefully looking at the small hill where Osrov's cocoon was perched.

"Is that...?" Kyra squinted her eyes, then gasped.

"The King," I muttered.

Krell was unconscious, lying in his father's arms as he carried him inside the shadow cocoon. It was a brief glimpse, but I could have sworn Krell's clothes were stained with blood. When the King approached the cocoon, it magically opened its walls as if the darkness obeyed him.

"He was bleeding," Ivy remarked.

"We need to get to him, now!" I shouted, running up the hill.

I was sprinting with Ivy and Kyra behind me when a trotter king crossed the street we were on. It walked slowly and was late to notice us, but when it did, it made sure the entire kingdom heard. The creature roared and charged our way, slamming the log in its hand to the ground.

"Ivy, use your vines to trap him!" I commanded, "try to find me an opening!"

Ivy and Kyra had spent enough time with me that they already knew what to do. Ivy shook the ground and jerked vines around the trotter's legs as Kyra froze it in place, giving me the chance to leap at the creature and stab my dagger into its back. When I thrusted the second dagger at its neck, the trotter king grunted and tore through the vines, smashing the ice and rising again.

"Jump off!" Ivy shouted, but I was too scared to do so.

I tried gashing the trotter's spine with the dagger; however, it violently shook, attempting to throw me off. As a last resort, I blindly grabbed an arrow from my quiver and stabbed the creature's back. When I realized it was an explosive arrow, it was already too late.

I was thrown to the ground as my clothes caught fire and my bow broke in half. Normally, I would lay defenselessly and wait for help, but Krell was in terrible danger. So, I stood up, extinguished the fire on my shirt, and wiped the dirt off my face.

"Reyna!" Kyra covered her mouth, "are you alright?"

"I'm fine," I struggled to say.

I hadn't noticed it, but the trotter king had been killed by the explosion. I might have been flung away, but the arrow did its job correctly after all.

"Are we going to pretend she didn't fall off a trotter king and onto stone ground?" Ivy whispered to Kyra.

"If she doesn't cry about it, she's fine," she replied.

We were just a few minutes away from the cocoon. I hoped Krell was doing alright, but after seeing his abusive father carrying him inside that dismal place, I knew something was off.

"We'll find you Krell," I said to myself, looking directly at the cocoon, "we have to."

*****

I woke up inside the shadow nest, strapped at the center with a rope tied around my arms and legs. I remembered it all too well—my father had stabbed me. Blood was still dripping down my stomach, and I felt the sharp pain of my skin tearing apart each time I breathed. I tried not to glance at my wound, so I bit my lip and stared at the person standing in front of me. It was my father: Henrius Kovner. *No...* I couldn't call him *father* anymore. That thing was not my father.

"You're awake," he said, standing a few feet away, leaning against the wall of the nest, "I expected you to be out for at least a couple of hours, but three minutes? Good thing I was able to tie you up, or you would've caught me off guard."

"Get me out of here," I gasped for air.

"Don't get ahead of yourself," he replied, licking his teeth, "I strapped you down so I could talk to you, son."

"Yeah, and you also stabbed me so you could talk to me?" I shook, trying to free myself.

"That wasn't part of the plan, but I knew that if I didn't do such a thing, you would never have listened to what I had to say," Henrius paced through the room.

"Who are you?" I gulped.

"The Shadow King," he smirked.

"Yeah, I heard you once, dumbass," I raised my voice and grunted in pain, "what I'm asking is how yo—"

Before I could finish the sentence, he took a step forward and slapped my face.

"You think that's a proper way to speak to your father?" He aggressively grasped my chin and pulled me closer.

"You're not my damn father," I said through clenched teeth.

His eyes widened, clearly threatened by my words. He let go of me and stuck three fingers into my stomach wound, twisting them with a macabre grin.

"Stop, stop!" I screamed, unable to push him back.

"Have you learned now?" He asked, keeping the fingers inside.

"Go to—"

"Have you learned it?" He continued, twirling through my insides.

"Yes!" I begged for mercy before he stopped.

"You knew Osrov, right?" He began speaking as if nothing had happened.

"Yeah," I panted, looking at him with disgust.

"Then you know there was another explorer traveling with him when he opened the Khan," Henrius said, "I was that man."

"You and Osrov...?"

"I left the kingdom to go on an expedition with him. No one knew about it. Only we and your mother, who wasn't very pleased with the idea. We traveled across the seas and crawled into a cavern, finding the artifact we had heard so many legends about: the one and only Khan. The power we felt within it was something we had never experienced before. We knew it was the only way to heal the lands. Then, the war began."

"If you were King and wanted to expand the Khan's power, why did you even command an army against the shadows in the first place?" I asked, confused.

"Your mother was the one who led the army," he revealed, "that's why I had to..."

"What?" I mumbled, "that's why you had to do what?"

"The point is that afterward—"

"What did you do? What did you do to my mother!" I cried, "did you kill her? Did you kill mom?"

"I did what I had to do," he replied unemotionally.

I gasped and began sobbing, glancing at my father with repugnance. My entire life, I had been living under the same roof as the person who murdered my mother. I had been sharing a home with the one behind it all.

"You're a monster," I bawled.

"When I killed your mother, the war hadn't even started," he continued, ignoring me, "other people made sure the kingdom won the war. They even created the prison on the west shore of the lands where the shadows were kept for more than a decade! I tried liberating them for years! I had to live a miserable life, knowing the Khan was the only way to make everyone in the lands happy!"

"By making them happy, do you mean turning their bodies into monstrous creatures and trapping them inside an artifact to live a fake fantasy?" I cried.

"You don't understand right now, Krell," he shook his head, "you think I'm the bad guy of the story, don't you? You think I killed your mother because I wanted to? Well, no! But I would sacrifice anyone just to have people see a new horizon. Even the dead shadows' minds are still inside the Khan, where they continue to live their best life."

“Being inside an artifact—trapped inside your own mind—isn’t living your life!” I yelled, “you could’ve reconstructed these lands by becoming a better ruler instead of obsessing over this madness! People are dying on the streets because of you! Children are getting killed because of something you unleashed!”

“If they rejected the Khan, it’s fair for them to die,” he said monotonously, “and I can see you aren’t interested in living the life you have right now, but what if I told you there’s a better alternative? I know you want to become a leader like me.”

“You really want me to be the ruler of those poor things?” I shook my arms in an attempt to free myself.

“You know, I could have released the shadows from their prison many years ago, but I chose not to. I knew one day you’d rule by my side, and I had to wait for you to grow up so you’d understand what it meant for our legacy. You will become the lord of the lands alongside me. Everyone will look up to you as a King! Think about that for a moment, Krell. Don’t you want to become someone greater? Don’t you want to rule the lands beside your father?”

I stood in silence for a moment, processing his words and wondering what my response should be. He killed my mother, caused the death of grandpa, and led an army of monsters to murder thousands more.

“So, what do you say?” Henrius asked with a mischievous grin.

“I say...” I breathed heavily, “I say that I’d rather die than spend another second by your side.”

He sighed in dissapointment, stepping back and leaning against the nest’s wall. He gripped the sticky substance and ripped a chunk of it out, creating a sword made of the same viscous matter.

“I was always by your side,” he shook his head, “I commanded Osrov not to kill you so you could rule alongside me. Who do you think controlled the nest to help you kill the sister? Who do you think saved you from getting stabbed by her? I did that! And this is what you decide to do? You're a joke, Krell."

He raised the weapon over his shoulder and was about to strike when someone opened the nest with a small dagger. Reyna stepped inside, too focused on getting the goo off her hair to notice Henrius at first. After glaring in his direction, she gasped and stood still as Ivy and Kyra emerged from the same hole she had arrived through. They all stared directly at him without saying a single word. The silence was deafening. Henrius briefly looked at them, then returned his focus to me, tilting his head and smiling.

"Reyna..." I mumbled with a shaky breath.

Henrius grunted and slashed the sword at me, but before it reached my skin, Ivy launched him away with her vines, trapping him against the nest's wall. Reyna quickly approached me, trying to untie my arms, but she was distracted by a blaring sound on the other side of the nest. Although we thought the vines would hold Henrius for a while, he cut through them and freed himself immediately.

"Untie Krell while we distract him!" Kyra commanded Reyna.

As soon as she finished speaking, Henrius smashed the hilt of his sword into her face. Ivy spread her arms before realizing her powers were no longer working. The entrance of the nest was sealed, blocking Ivy's connection to the outside—she couldn't use her plants anymore. Henrius bumped his head with hers and began walking toward Reyna and me.

"Behind you!" I warned Reyna while she untied me.

Her reflexes were marvelously quick; she turned around and stabbed one of her daggers into his shoulder. Ivy grabbed him from behind and pulled him away, giving Reyna the chance to untie my arms.

"Help me with the others," she breathed heavily, pulling the rope on my legs.

"Ouch!" I exclaimed after bending over.

"What is that!" She covered her mouth and stared at the wound on my stomach.

"I'm fine," I lied, "he stabbed me, but I'm fine."

"As soon as I set you free, you're gonna get the hell out of this nest and go to the doctor's house, alright?" She said while untying my feet, "you can't fight with a wound like that."

"I'm not going to leave you alone," I insisted, pulling myself free, "this is my father we're talking about. I will fight by your side."

She was about to reply when Ivy was launched over our heads. They were clearly not strong enough to fight Henrius by themselves, but after Reyna successfully untied me, I knew we had a chance against him.

"You think you and your group of inhumans will be enough?" Henrius laughed as we surrounded him, "well, I'm the goddamn Shadow King!"

Kyra dashed at him, slashing her sword at his thigh and crossing to the other side of the nest. I shot an arrow, impaling his arm, and when he tried pulling the projectile out of his skin, Ivy charged toward him and hacked her hatchet at his chest. We were outnumbering him, but when Reyna raised her dagger to stab his shoulder, Henrius grabbed her neck and began squeezing. She tried freeing herself, but I was the one who came to the rescue by firing an arrow into his neck. That would have easily killed any normal person, but he wasn't a normal person anymore.

"Come at me!" He screamed, ripping the arrow out of his neck and sadistically smearing the blood over his face, "keep coming!"

When Ivy struck her hatchet at Henrius again, he moved out of the way and kicked her back, shoving her to the ground. Kyra attempted a similar move before blood began dripping down her shoulder. I knew I couldn't risk going near him, so I shot arrows at a distance. However, he caught them all and flung them back at me. Reyna followed my lead, but even if we fired our bows simultaneously, he would catch both arrows and send them flying back like boomerangs.

"What about now? Do you wish you had accepted the offer?" He asked, walking towards us.

I stepped back, shooting as many arrows as I could, yet he deflected every single one. Kyra intervened, but Henrius slapped her face and slammed her to the ground. He was getting dangerously close, so I recalled my sword and stabbed his chest. Obviously, it couldn't have been that easy. He painlessly yanked the sword out of his skin and smashed its hilt into my face.

"Leave him!" Ivy shouted from behind.

She leaped at Henrius, managing to wrap her arms around his neck, but he turned and—with my own sword—impaled her. The weapon pierced her stomach as Henrius shoved her against the wall of the nest. Ivy gasped and screamed, collapsing to the ground before Kyra and Reyna approached her.

"Ivy!" Kyra kneeled beside her.

Shock washed over me as Henrius stared and smirked. I could almost hear his voice taunting me about the consequences of not accepting the Khan. I cautiously recalled my sword, ready to aid Ivy, but Henrius grabbed my neck and hurled me away. Expecting to hit the nest's wall, I was surprised when I tore through it, flying outside and crashing into a tree far from where I stood before.

"Her screams," Henrius reached my location with a single jump, "the screams of that girl remind me of your mother's screams when I butchered her."

I got back on my feet and glared at the nest, which was more than two-hundred feet away. But I couldn't focus on the distance between the nest and me, especially with Henrius stepping in my direction. I raised my sword and aimed it at him. He didn't seem bothered by it and simply walked in circles.

"How could you have killed her?" I asked with the sword in front of me.

"When someone doesn't agree with my vision, fate comes for them," he said.

"Fate is murder?"

Without him expecting it, I slashed my sword in his direction, hoping it would reach him. However, he evaded the attack and kept walking in circles around me.

"I always took care of your mother," he continued, unbothered, "I knew she would come around sooner or later, but when I realized she was planning to murder me? I couldn't let her live."

"She wanted to kill you?"

"She did, even leading an entire academy for that sole purpose!" He explained, "after I noticed her malevolent intent, I had no choice but to lock her up in hopes she would join me one day."

"You put her in a cell!" I clutched my eyebrows and charged at him again.

"I was going to have a talk with her and eventually free her!" Henrius dodged and continued, "but then I saw her talking to a *huntress* from the cell's window."

"A *huntress*?" I asked, unable to understand what she had to do with my mother's death.

"In fact, I got so mad that I had to pull out my sword and..." He smirked, deliberately trying to provoke me, "she put up a great fight, I'll tell you that."

"You're sick," I twitched.

"But you wanna know what the worst thing is?" He started laughing, "moments after killing her, I heard muffled crying from below our bed. Lorette hid you there. She hid you from me!"

I wanted to cry, knowing one of the last things my mother did was hide me from that monster I once called "*father.*" All the stories I heard about the Shadow War weren't real. My mother died soon before it even started, and from the information I gathered, she commanded an army against the shadows before passing away.

"Lorette didn't care about me anymore!" He screamed, "each time I spoke to her, she would reply with: *'but is that safe enough for Krell?'* or *'what does that mean for the future of our son?'* All she cared about was you! So I followed her legacy. She wanted you to become a great warrior and ruler, so I gave you a portion of my power soon after her death, knowing that when the time was right, you'd rule by my side. And now it has all gone to hell!"

He gnashed his sword through a tree, severing it as he screamed with rage.

"Just because you think that what I'm doing is wrong?" He was so angry I wouldn't have been surprised if he destroyed another tree, "well, let me tell you, everything you've done in these last couple of days has been for nothing. Everything you've fought for and all you've accomplished will be for nothing. Without you ruling by my side, your entire life is bullshit!"

I had never heard my father curse before, which made me realize—once again—he wasn't my father anymore.

"I gave you a piece of me! I sacrificed a part of my power to see you grow! Thankfully, now that I know you won't be following my legacy, I recovered that fragment of darkness by absorbing it from Osrov. And you're next."

"All you care about is power," I muttered after listening to his sickening monologue, "you don't care about making the lands a better place; you just want to rule them!"

"So what?" He asked, chuckling, "power is a privilege that can help accomplish many things."

"The goal and purpose you hold are greater than the power you have," I resisted the urge of slashing my sword at him.

"If you really believe that, then tell me..." He began, "can *goals and purpose* do this?"

He tossed his sword away and dropped to the ground. I thought he was going to crawl toward me, but instead, his body grew twice its size. Smoke swirled around his chest as claws appeared in place of his hands, and his head transformed into that of a beast. Somehow, Henrius used dark magic to transform into a lion-like creature. The only thing not engulfed in dark, somber smoke were his eyes, which beamed with a blood-red glow.

"Run," Henrius' actual voice emerged from the creature's fangs.

He didn't have to tell me twice. I sprinted into the forest, stepping on crunchy leaves and pushing away branches blocking my path. The beasts' paws slammed the ground at a faster pace than mine as I panted and tried dashing in zigzag to confuse him. I couldn't afford to look back, but I felt the creature's breath on my neck. If I was honest, I could also smell it.

After running for what seemed like an eternity, I started recognizing my surroundings, realizing I was following the trail to the Zumba tribe camp. I knew the lion would butcher me the second I stepped inside that camp, so I thought of something that could be of greater help: the *shackflyer.*

The beast cast his claws at me, managing to rip a piece of my clothes off. Luckily, I pulled away and continued running, noticing the *shackflyer's* tail from afar. Seroph saw me and moved his tail up and down as if he were waving at me.

"Seroph, be careful!" I shouted, knowing the beast could easily kill him.

I bolted up the few steps to get inside the *shackflyer,* bursting through the door and locking it behind me. The beast was only a few seconds from reaching the entrance, so I pushed a shelf in front of it and stepped back, recalling my sword and breathing heavily as the creature banged on the door. He eventually rammed into the shack, gripping his claws on the shelf and throwing it aside as he roared and looked me in the eyes. I knew I had to stand my ground to survive, so I didn't run away. We charged at each other, and before he could lay his claws on me, I leaped and stabbed his head.

"Augh!" My father yelled from within the shadow beast, reminding me he was the one controlling it.

The lion shook in pain as I drove the sword deeper into his skull. In an attempt to free himself, he galloped outside and clamped his fangs on my arm, launching me away. He was about to strike again while I lay defenseless, but Seroph's tail slammed the beast to the ground.

"Thanks!" I smiled at the *shackflyer* and dashed to the beast trapped under his tail.

About to stab his head once again, I realized it hadn't worked last time. The beast was twice the size of Henrius, so if he were inside, his body should have been in the creature's torso. With that in mind, I pierced the beast's chest, and moments later, the lion turned to ashes.

"You fool!" Henrius' image reappeared

With a sword that seemed to appear out of nowhere, he slashed at Seroph's tail, freeing himself as the poor creature cried in pain and flew away. He leaned on a nearby tree—clearly injured—and caught his breath, looking at me with rage.

"Was that really everything your *'power'* did?" I pouted sarcastically.

"I'll show you my real power!" he grunted, running after me.

Closer than before—and without a four-legged beast chasing me—I dashed to the Zumba tribe camp. The gate was still open, and some of the tents remained unzipped, so I stealthily crawled into one and hid behind a small table. I hadn't realized it upon entering, but after stepping on one of the many acorns scattered around, I noticed I was inside Kharum's tent. I was reminded of the time I spent with him before raiding the Main Kingdom and how I was cracking acorns to feed the light elves. I almost started crying after realizing our main goal at the time was to convince my father. Who would have known he'd be the one trying to kill us all.

"Where are you, boy!" He screamed, clashing his sword against the metal gate of the camp.

I tried not to breathe too loudly, but with all the wounds—especially the one on my stomach—it was impossible. I briefly looked at it and noticed how awful it truly was. The adrenaline stopped the pain, but looking at the open wound made the agony return.

"I can hear your breathing," Henrius stood a few feet away from the tent I was in, "and I will give you five seconds to come out."

I gasped, panting in desperation and clutching my stomach in pain. Without hesitation, I blindly shot an arrow in his direction, yelling at him to go away.

"You almost got me with that one, Krell," he laughed.

When I heard footsteps approaching, I crawled to the back of the tent. I thought he would crawl inside to drag me out, but he slashed his blade at the shelter and began tearing it apart.

"Go away!" I cried as the sword crept closer.

I knew that if I didn't want to be chopped into pieces, I had to get out of the tent, so I lay with my chest touching the ground and crawled to the entrance. The blade scrapped against my back, scratching my skin, but I clenched my teeth and pushed forward. Just as I was about to reach the exit, a hand grabbed my hair, lifted me, and tossed me aside.

"Come on! Let's finish this!" Henrius yelled.

I furiously charged at him, aiming below the waist with my sword, but he paired and launched me backward. While I was still recovering, he jumped forward and aggressively cut open my knee. I tried to defend myself, but he spun and slashed at my stomach twice. I felt the tip of the blade pierce my wound and scratch my insides, but I couldn't fight back. I limped away and tried climbing a ladder to the second floor of the camp. As soon as I placed my hand on the stair, Henrius wrapped his arm around my neck and pulled me back. I rolled away, but that didn't stop him from stabbing my hand and slamming the sword into the ground.

"Stop!" I cried as the weapon tore through my palm.

I knew Henrius would take advantage of my hand being pinned to the ground with his sword, so I had no other choice but to pull myself apart, cutting my palm in half. I screamed in agony and crawled away with a chunk of my hand hanging, trying not to vomit as I held it together.

"You're bleeding out," Henrius laughed, picking up the sword, "it's a matter of time before you die."

"And I'll fight every second I have left," I trembled.

There was a glass box on the wall behind him. It was one of those rectangular, transparent display cases where a weapon would be stored. The one I was staring at held a dagger, but I didn't want to get the tiny knife inside. I was planning something else.

I shrieked, pushing Henrius into the display case and smashing his face against the glass. His lip was cut open and his cheek grazed, but I wasn't satisfied with that, so I recalled my sword and raised it over his head. Before I could even attack, he grabbed a shard of glass from the display case and stabbed it into my stomach wound. My heart pounded as blood dripped down my legs, and I struggled to hold myself together.

"I have never seen someone cling to their life this... *fiercely*," he chuckled, amused, "as if you even had one worth holding onto. You could just accept your fate and die."

With my sword at my father's feet, I recalled, but something strange happened when the weapon was mid-air. The force pulling it toward me failed as if someone else was calling it away. Henrius raised his hand and took the sword for himself, chuckling as he gripped its hilt and drove the blade into the ground.

"This tiny thing?" He laughed, examining my sword.

"How are you...?" I wanted to finish the sentence, but the more I spoke, the more blood I lost.

"I've known that magic for years now," he said, "and I know exactly how to destroy it."

I watched as he bent the weapon in half. It was destroyed, and although I kept my hand in the air hoping it would return, nothing happened. He had destroyed it.

"No!" I screamed as blood rushed down my stomach; I was dying.

"And look at what else I have for you," he smiled.

He reached into his pocket and took out the dagger from the display case we had just shattered. I had no way to protect myself, so I simply prepared for what was about to come. Henrius stabbed my stomach twice, hugging me with his left arm so I wouldn't escape. I tried not to scream—I wanted to make my death glorious—but with the last thrust, he spun me around and kicked the back of my leg. After dropping to the ground face first, I heard the sound of a blade charging toward my back, so I rolled around and caught the dagger with my bare hands. Henrius tilted his head and twisted the knife while I still held it, cutting open my remaining palm. One of my hands had a chunk of flesh hanging, and the other was almost completely skinned. With no strength left, I tried to stop the dagger, but Henrius was too strong. He rigidly stabbed the knife into my chest until only the hilt protruded from my body—the rest was inside.

I closed my eyes—dying. *No! I needed to stay awake.* I couldn't fall asleep. I couldn't die. I didn't want to. I crawled backward in search of help, but there was no one—and nothing—around to aid me.

"Now, this is how I love for it to end," Henrius giggled, stepping in front of me, "you're slowly dying at the feet of... of..."

"Of a monster," I spat blood.

"I'm not a monster!" He shouted, yet he still couldn't find another way to complete the sentence.

"Kill me," I mumbled, deciding I didn't want to feel the pain anymore.

"Kill you?" He laughed, "you think I will kill you out of pity? I'm not like that, Krell, and you know it. I'm going to wait until you bleed out. I want to see the life drain from your eyes. I want to watch as the spasms and flinches crossing your body cease, as well as the tears dripping down your cheeks. I will sit down and enjoy the view."

I hadn't realized spasms and flinches were crossing my body—I didn't even know what was happening to me anymore. I was slowly fading away.

"And you want to know what the worst thing is?" Henrius began, "it's that I invited you to rule these lands alongside me, and you refused. We could've accomplished what no other human had ever done—rule the lands—but you chose not to! 'Cause you know what? I forged my own path, and you simply chose the way of the hero. You thought everyone on these lands would worship you just because you were their savior? Well, no! People don't care who saves them; they just care that they're safe. They would've never looked up to you. One thing that I know is that people don't enjoy seeing the hero rise; they enjoy seeing them fall, fail, and die! That is when people start to worship you! They treat you like crap while you're alive and then treat you like a God when you're dead!"

He was so angry that he punched a hole through a wooden pole.

"I suppose the only sad thing now is that you'll never see the empire I'll build," he sighed, looking at my chest as if wondering if I was already dead, "you surely won't last long, so I've got to ask... any last words?"

For the first time in my life, I was scared of death, knowing that in a matter of seconds, I would cease to exist. I had to choose my last words—waste my final breath on some stupid speech. Because I didn't know what to say, I surreptitiously looked back at the shelf I was leaning on, noticing a full jar of novo juice in one of the open drawers. I scrapped the idea, knowing I had no time to open the flask and smear a single drop of juice on each of my wounds. Then I was reminded of Reyna's words.

"Quick tip, don't use it on your eyes—it will blind you," I remembered Reyna chuckling as she said.

"I wasn't planning to..." I could even recall my reply.

Focusing on Henrius—who was still waiting for me to die—I took a deep breath and said my *"last words."*

"Go to hell," I panted.

I reached behind me and grabbed the jar of novo juice, gripping it with my weak hands and using my last bit of strength to smash it on Henrius' eyes. The flask shattered upon impact, covering his face with the purple, thick liquid as he tumbled back and screamed. I managed to lean forward and crawl to the fractured jar, smearing a few drops of the healing liquid on my torso and hands.

"Ah! My eyes!" He screamed, clawing at his face with his nails.

I bravely pulled the dagger from my chest and stabbed Henrius with it. He fell to the ground, leaning against the same shelf where I had been just moments before. My body ached from the healing juice, but it didn't compare to the pain Henrius was experiencing. I staggered to a nearby desk on weak knees, using it to support my weight.

"I can't see!" He cried, "I can't see, I can't see! What did you do!"

He continued screaming for a while before finally calming down and accepting his fate. I watched as he reached for the dagger impaling him, but I kicked his arm away and started crying, wiping my nose and walking in circles.

"I can't see, Krell," he said despondently.

"You brought this on yourself!" My voice broke as I shouted, wiping my tears and frowning, "you could've been so much greater, yet you decided this!"

"I wanted to heal the lands," he replied.

The juice washed off after a few seconds, revealing the purple skin around his eyes and his night-black eyeballs looking in another direction. He was completely blind.

"You didn't want to heal the lands; you just wanted power!" I searched the drawers and eventually found a bandage, "and look where it has led you!"

"Now I can't see my empire..." He wanted to cry; however, his eyes weren't functioning properly anymore.

"There was a time when I looked up to you!" I confessed, wrapping the bandage around my gashed hand, "you were a hero to me! But you threw it all away!"

"I didn't want it to end this way," he snorted.

"You killed your wife, your own father, and were about to murder your son!" I cried, "do you think that's something to be proud of? No! You're a disappointment!"

"Just kill me, son," he said unemotionally, "I can't live without my eyes."

"I..." I wanted to drop down and keep crying, "I'll make sure you receive the best help once you're locked away in the dungeons."

"No! Krell, no!' He screamed, "I'll come back again! Even if I'm blind, I'll escape and become the lord of the lands! I'll return!"

I kept sobbing, kneeling by his side and making a tough decision that could either save the lands or doom them forever.

"I'm so sorry," I closed my eyes and wrapped my hands around his neck.

Recalling what he did to Osrov after stabbing me the first time, I squeezed his neck and began absorbing the power from his body. The darkness drained and entered the tip of my fingers as I grunted and panted heavily. It was a powerful—yet strange—sensation. My father weakly wheezed and glanced at the sky, unable to push me away. I knew I had finished transferring the darkness into my body when the tingling in my hands ceased. He had no power any longer—he didn't pose a threat to the lands anymore.

"You've done the wrong thing," Henrius said, looking in my direction after hearing my loud breathing.

"Prince Krell, we're here to help you!" Two guards rushed through the camp's gate.

"Thanks," I said, wiping my nose and standing up, trying to get accustomed to the power within me, "take him to the dungeons and don't let anyone see him."

"May we ask why?" One of them inquired.

"He's a threat to the lands," I gulped, "take him away."

They didn't hesitate and immediately dragged him out of the camp, following my orders as if I had greater power than Henrius, the King.

"You don't know what you've unleashed!" Henrius yelled while being taken away, "you will be the doom of these lands! The prophecy will come true! When the lion falls, the snake rises."

I didn't know what to make of his words. He seemed to want to tell me more, but the guards carried him away before he could. I was panting and about to sit down when someone crossed the camp's gate.

"Krell!" Reyna exclaimed with relief upon seeing me.

"Reyna, you're here," I smiled.

"It's..." Her voice cracked as if she were sobbing, "it's Ivy."

Shivers went down my spine as my smile faded, and I dashed to the shadow nest on the hill beside the Main Kingdom. Those two simple words were enough to make me cry. There was an opening to the nest, where I squeezed inside and noticed Ivy lying on the floor with pale skin and a bloody stomach.

"You'll be fine, Ivy," Kyra was kneeling beside her, comforting.

"Ivy," I gasped, "you're..."

"I look like crap, don't I?" She coughed, "I'll live, don't worry."

Reyna entered the nest seconds after, looking at Kyra in fear and shaking her head.

"You didn't find novo juice?" Kyra gulped, "that was our last option."

I stood in silence, knowing I had wasted the last jar of novo juice by defeating Henrius. Apart from feeling guilty for blinding him, I felt even guiltier knowing that Ivy was on the verge of death because of me.

"Don't worry about me," Ivy took a deep breath, "worry about those creatures out there. Krell, did you kill Henrius?"

"I defeated him. I didn't kill him, but he's not a threat anymore," I replied, "but I don't understand—why are there still shadows out there? I defeated Henrius and absorbed his power. How are the shadows still alive?"

"It's more complicated than that, Krell," Reyna sighed.

"That thing you see..." Ivy paused to catch her breath.

"Slow breaths, Ivy, slow breaths," Kyra held her hand.

"The thing in the center," she continued, pointing at the beam inside the nest—the oasis I fought Osrov, "that light holds the power of those creatures."

"The connection to the Khan," I whispered to myself, "if someone absorbs the power out of that thing, the shadows will no longer have a connection to the Khan, which means that they'll—"

"Transform back to normal," Ivy stole the words from my mouth.

"I'll do it," I declared.

"Krell, no," Reyna protested, "you'll die."

"I know I'll die, but if I sacrifice myself, the shadow within me will perish too. That means all shadows in the lands will die. If we want to stop this war, we need to sever every single connection to those creatures. I will do it. End of discussion."

"You won't die!" Reyna argued, "I will do it!"

"Don't be stupid, I will!" Kyra pushed us aside.

Three people were willing to sacrifice themselves for the lands. We were all arguing about who would do it, even approaching the light beam at the center of the nest, ready to absorb its power.

"I'll do it," Ivy muttered quietly.

"You won't do it, I won't let you," Kyra said without batting an eye.

We continued fighting over who would be the one to take their own life to banish the shadows from our lands. I knew I was the one who had to do it—there was no other outcome. If I didn't absorb the power from the light beam, a fragment of darkness would remain on the lands, and who knew if anyone would try to take advantage of it. We were so focused on each other that we didn't notice when Ivy stood up and weakly limped towards us.

"I said I will do it," she took a deep breath, "I'm dying anyway, so..."

"You're not dying," Kyra hugged her, "don't say that again."

"We'll find something to cure you," Reyna reassured her.

"It's poisoned," Ivy snorted, "I can feel it expanding through my body."

Kyra covered her mouth and took a step back, not knowing how to react. The only way to cure poison was through novo juice, which meant we were out of options.

"You all have a reason to live," Ivy cried as she approached us, "Krell, I have no doubt you'll be the greatest King these lands will ever know. Reyna, you are the fiercest, most skillful elf I have ever met. And Kyra... you are the greatest person I've ever come across in my entire life."

"You won't die," Kyra sobbed, "I won't let you."

"If any one of you decides to sacrifice yourself, two people will die today, but if I do it, only I will," Ivy trembled, "it's stupid."

"And if I don't do it, a piece of the shadows' darkness will remain in these lands," I argued with her.

"And you will take the best care of it," Ivy walked around me and stood beside the light beam at the center of the nest.

"I won't let you do it," I held my ground.

"Well then," she hesitated briefly, then locked eyes with me, "I'm sorry."

With one last effort, Ivy raised her hands and pushed me to the nest's wall. Vines tangled my hands and hugged my chest, trapping me as Reyna and Kyra flew by my side. Ivy glanced back and shed a tear before limping to the light beam, ready to absorb its power.

"Ivy, no!" Kyra screamed and struggled to herself, but the vines pressed her firmly against the wall.

Ivy placed both hands on the light, gripping it as she moaned in pain and silently cried. I couldn't see her expression, but I noticed how her pale skin brightened and her hair lost its blood-red color. It seemed as if she was becoming a shadow for a split second when dark smoke engulfed her body and her limbs began contorting. Reyna stared in awe, watching Ivy slowly decaying, but Kyra pushed the vines away in an attempt to rescue her.

"Stop! No!" Kyra eventually pulled herself free and desperately rushed to Ivy.

It was too late—the light beam exploded, and the nest vanished into thin air. Kyra and Ivy were launched away, rolling down the hill before hitting the fallen steel barrier.

Ivy had successfully absorbed the nest's power, releasing the shadows from their deadly curse and freeing them from the Khan's fake fantasy. A part of me thought Ivy hadn't perished during the process, but when I glanced at my wrist, those hopes ceased. The tikh bracelet fell off my arm, which could have only meant one thing—Ivy died. I puffed and got to my feet, limping down the hill and noticing the two figures lying on the grass.

"Answer me, please," Kyra bawled.

She sat beside Ivy, running her hands through her hair, trying to comfort her even though she was no longer alive. Her gleaming crimson hair had lost its hue, and her clothes were buried in ashes—the last trace of humanity on her face was her beautiful smile.

"Oh no," I exclaimed, rushing over when someone patted my shoulder.

"Don't," Reyna said, trying not to cry.

Kyra appeared to be having one last special moment with Ivy. She embraced her lifeless body, kissed her, and began confessing all the things she had never shared. My eyes overflowed with tears, so I didn't notice Ivy's palm, which bloomed a beautiful rose with blue petals. Kyra gently plucked it from her hand and placed it in her hair, smiling bittersweetly.

"I'll miss you so much," she cried, hugging her again, "I'm so sorry for everything, Ivy. I love you."

From the streets of the kingdom, Tyrose sprinted toward us with a preoccupied look on his face. He stepped over the steel barrier, and when he saw Reyna and me standing on the hill, his worries increased.

"What happened!" He yelled desperately, "why did the bracelet just fall off?"

It took him a while to notice Ivy's body, but when he did, he dropped to the ground, crying and hyperventilating. Each time he raised his head to look at her again, he bawled harder. Tyrose slowly crawled towards Kyra and kneeled beside her, rubbing Ivy's cheek and examining her corpse.

"Ivy, why?" He sobbed, "I love you, Ivy."

Hearing those words from Tyrose made me cry even harder. Reyna squeezed my hand and rested her head on my shoulder, frowning as we stared from afar.

"I've loved you my entire life," he held Ivy, "I knew you didn't feel the same way for me, but I... I never stopped loving you! I'm so sorry."

Reyna kept holding my hand as we slowly approached Ivy's body.

"If I had only been here for you," Tyrose's tears fell on her body, "if only I had been better. If only I had spent more time with you, maybe you would've realized how much you mattered to me."

Then, as Tyrose pulled himself apart, Ivy's body began shifting into something else. Tree roots grew from her fingernails, and autumn leaves started falling from her hair, matching its crimson color. We all stood up and stepped back, watching as her body slowly transformed.

"What is happening?" Reyna asked.

"It's a tree," Kyra said, smiling instead of crying.

Indeed, it was a tree. Like a seed, it grew on top of her body, shielding her torso and eventually reaching her head. I looked at her beautiful smile one last time before the roots sheltered her limbs and she disappeared from plain sight. Hazelwood sprouted around her, growing over thirty feet tall. Branches cracked out of the log, along with beautiful red leaves that reminded me of her lips and hair. At the center of the tree, there was an abstract shape resembling her eyes and facial traits. Ivy wasn't just inside that tree—Ivy *was* the tree. In another form of life, Ivy was still with us. And she would forever be.

Chapter 40

Epilogue

It had been two days since the war ended, and we were still rebuilding the kingdom and recovering what had been lost. Last I checked, more than 400 people went missing after the battle, but the number decreased as hours passed. Being the new King of the Main Kingdom was overwhelming—I hadn't slept since the war ended, and my attention was scattered. I was either helping sheltered children return to their families or assisting guards in rebuilding homes. Unfortunately, the castle couldn't be saved after it collapsed, and although pieces of debris were collected, it would take months for the palace to be restored. Still, that was the least of my worries. I was more focused on helping the villagers rather than satisfying my own needs. After the agony the kingdom endured for sixteen years, I had to be careful not to repeat my father's mistakes. Speaking of him, it's important to note he no longer holds power over the lands. After being blinded by the novo juice and taken away by the guards, I had to ensure he spent the rest of his life in the dungeons.

Although no official announcement was made, everyone in the kingdom knew what he did and who he truly was—mainly because of the rumors. However, the one thing they didn't know was that he was still alive. For the safety of the villagers, I had to keep that a secret. So, apart from my friends and a couple of guards, everyone in the lands thought I killed my own father, who was actually lying in the old dungeons of the kingdom.

All light elves from the Nature Kingdom—including Ivory and Kharum—were planning to rebuild their kingdom after Ivy passed away. Kyra and Tyrose said they would stay in the Main Kingdom until things were settled in theirs, and for the first time in a long while, I decided anyone could live within our walls. It didn't matter if they were a light elf or a nympho—everyone was allowed to live in the Main Kingdom from that moment forward.

That evening, Ivy's ceremony would take place. Kyra, Tyrose, Reyna, and I gathered to send our tikh bracelets flying on a hot air balloon so we could reunite in another life. I didn't believe in reincarnation, but Ivy certainly did, which was why the event was organized in the first place. I arrived before the ceremony started as I had a special gift for her: a letter. I looked at the piece of paper one last time before crumpling it and placing it below the tree she had turned into when she died. In my head, I pictured her inside that log, curled up and watching our every move. Realistically, she was dead, but I still liked to imagine otherwise.

"What are you doing?" Reyna approached me from behind.

"Nothing," I sighed without looking at her.

"Don't worry, Krell," she held my hand and smiled, "I also wrote her a letter. I gave it to her yesterday."

"I just want to believe she's still with us," I said.

"She is," Reyna glanced at the tree, "that is Ivy."

I carefully examined the tree and grinned, hearing voices in the distance. I turned around and noticed Kyra and Tyrose laughing as they walked through the streets of the kingdom, making their way to us. It was the first time any of them cracked a smile after Ivy's death.

"Do you have the bracelets?" Kyra asked as soon as she arrived, dropping her light smirk.

"Of course," I replied, showing her mine.

"And I've got the balloons," Reyna added.

She handed each of us a hot air balloon and a match, instructing us to light the candle at its center and place our tikh bracelets over it. Kyra hesitated for a moment before doing so and bittersweetly releasing the balloon alongside us. They ascended into the sky, passing by the crimson leaves of the tree and reaching the clouds. No one spoke afterward. We all watched in awe as the balloons disappeared from plain sight. Ten minutes went by before Reyna patted my shoulder and silently left. I stayed for a few moments, then followed her into the kingdom. Tyrose stood in front of the tree for more than twenty minutes before bowing and walking away, sobbing quietly. But Kyra stayed there all day and night, standing on the tree's roots until dawn. Even when I went to sleep that night, I could still see her from afar, motionlessly glaring at the tree. That became her daily routine—at least one hour a day, she'd stand in front of the tree, even having conversations with it. I hadn't thought about it at the moment, but Reyna was correct. Ivy was still alive—in another form of life—inside that log. At first, I felt terribly sorry for Kyra, but I shouldn't have been. After all, she never really lost her best friend.

1 Year and 7 Months Later

I was sitting on the castle's terrace, looking down at the beautiful kingdom as I sipped a warm cup of troffe. I was relieved the villagers didn't see me as someone superior; they would rather think of me as a normal person enjoying an evening on their balcony. I was lost in my thoughts, staring at the rebuilt kingdom and wondering if I had the courage to do what I was planning. I took another sip from my cup before hearing two knocks on the door.

"Hey, Krell," Reyna walked into my room.

"Reyna!" I exclaimed, surprised to see her, "how long has it been? It's felt like forever since I last saw you!"

"It's only been a month," she chuckled.

"I haven't seen you in so long!" I said ecstatically, wrapping my arms around her.

"I know," she sighed, "I've been spending more time with the Zumbas lately. You know, my family."

"I get it," I said, "and the offer is still in place! You and your tribe can come by whenever they want! I still have that piece of land on the edge of the kingdom, and you know you're safer there than on the outsides."

"I appreciate it, Krell, but I think my tribe's happy where they are," she said with a smile, examining my room, "but today is the coronation, remember?"

"Oh, crap," I gasped, looking in the mirror and fixing my messy hair.

"I'm surprised it took this long," she remarked, "after Ivy's death, I thought it would take less than three months for them to choose a new Queen, but *almost two years*?"

"You think the new Queen will be as good as Ivy?" I asked.

"Ivy did illegal clashes in her kingdom, so I don't think the new one has much competition," she laughed, "but she is kind of a—"

"Asshole?" I finished her sentence.

"I was gonna put it another way, but yeah," she giggled, grabbing my hand, "so, shall we go to the coronation?"

"I'll catch you in a second," I said, pulling away.

"Why? What do you have to do?" She asked, tilting her head.

"I just need to get changed," I lied.

"Oh, alright," she began walking away before turning around and sarcastically adding, "see you at the coronation, *my king*."

I chuckled and patiently waited for her to exit the castle. It might have seemed obvious, but I wasn't going to change my clothes at all. I ran downstairs and opened a door leading to the basement of my reconstructed castle. I had ordered the architects to build an extra room for a certain someone—that way, no one could ever realize he was still alive. I hurried down the spiral stairs and stood in front of the cell at the end of the corridor. As I gulped and prepared myself, I noticed a set of statues covered with a white blanket beside the cellar.

"I've never seen you before," I said to myself, uncovering the first of three statues.

It was a sculpture of a lion with a crown atop his head, sitting on a log with various animals below, worshipping him. A large snake was hissing in the beast's direction, along with four mice who seemed to be whispering something to the serpent. The carving below the statue read: "*The bastard holds his throne as seeds of rebellion are sown.*"

I tilted my head and licked my teeth in confusion, approaching the next statue and unveiling it. The lion was nowhere to be seen. Instead, the serpent slithered through the grass, followed by the four mice. The sentence below read: "*The outsiders now advance, seeking a future, a hopeful chance.*" I glanced back at the lion from the first sculpture, noticing the strange resemblance to the beast my father transformed into when I fought him during the Shadow War. Were the statues narrating our path?

I uncovered the last statue, squinting as I processed the image before me. The serpent wrapped around the lion's neck, stealing the crown from his head as the beast furiously roared. Another thing I noticed was the dead mouse lying beside the snake. Below the gruesome sculpture, a sentence was carved: "*The crown now claimed, a gown soaked red: a golden age ahead.*"

I frowned and stared blankly at the three statues, wondering if they were created to narrate our path in recruiting the kingdoms during the Shadow War. I was clearing my mind and approaching the cell when something caught my eye. Separated from the original set of sculptures was another. I gently pulled the colorless blanket away and gasped as my blood ran cold.

The lion was munching on the serpent's head, reclaiming the crown as the three mice lay lifelessly by his side. Below the statue, there was a much shorter sentence composed of only five words: "*The end descends on all.*"

Who was responsible for crafting all those sculptures, and how dare they make such an awful "*prophecy*" of what they thought would happen in future years? I threw the blanket over the statue and concluded that no one knew my fate, and I was the one who'd carve my own destiny. Still, it was pretty unsettling to see myself depicted as a serpent who got his head munched by my own father—who also murdered my three friends.

"It's not real," I whispered to myself.

"It's not real?" Someone repeated from inside the cellar beside me.

Henrius placed his head between the cell's bars and grinned macabrely. The sizzled purple skin on his face wrinkled as his smile grew bigger, and his night-blind eyeballs stared into my soul. He was creepy enough already, but after the novo juice burned his eyes, he was utterly terrifying.

"Shut up," I stepped back, startled.

Curiously, his eyes seemed to follow me as I moved away as if he could actually see me. I cautiously approached his cell and slowly extended my finger towards his face, wondering if I could catch him off guard. When I was about to touch his nose, I stopped, realizing how stupid the idea was.

"Just a little closer and I would've bitten that goddamn finger off your hand," he laughed maniacally.

"What? How did—"

"How di... how di..." He wheezed, then coughed, "I can see everything now. I can see you, within you, behind you, what's at your side, what's above me... I can see everything, including those four statues."

"The novo juice healed you," I began to realize, "it improved your eyesight."

"Not just improved," he said, keeping his head between the bars, "I transcended being a human. I can hear the voices... they tell me things..."

"What do they tell you?" I asked, indulging his stupid game.

"They warn me that something terrible is about to happen," he replied, laughing, "something that will devastate the lands. All life will cease. *The end descends on all.*"

"You know what?" I said, walking away and shaking my head, "you're crazy."

"I will rise again and kill all of you!" He screamed, gaining my attention once again, "and as the prophecy says: it will come."

I tried ignoring him, but it was impossible. The sound of trumpets was heard from outside the castle, followed by cheering—the coronation was starting. I had to leave immediately, yet I couldn't stop listening to what he had to say. So, I kneeled before his cell and asked, "What is coming?"

With a slow murmur, his blind eyes looked at me.

"Kumblesgard."

TO BE CONTINUED IN...
The Kingdoms:
Rise of the Old King

Dictionary

- **Ah'lah'rra Tribe** - A sadisctic tribe of murderous elves known for committing horrendous crimes and killing thousands every year. They have had many battles with the *Quora tribe* and *Zumba tribe*. No one should ever cross their territory.
- **Dark Elves** - A species of elves banished from the *Main Kingdom*, believed to be extinct since the *elvish revolution*.
- **Echoes** - Monsters that started *Kumblesgard* and—by far—the deadliest creatures to ever set foot on the *lands*. They are said to be trapped inside the *land's volcano*. Legends say they will rise once *Kumblesgard* begins again.
- **Ember** - A small stone made of magma. When crushed, a radiant explosion warms everything around it.
- **Elvish Revolution** - Before the *Shadow War*, a dark elf led a revolution to overthrow the King and rule the *Main Kingdom*. After the troops fought back and killed him, all *dark elves* were exiled from the kingdom, seen as a threat.
- **Fire Creatures** - Inhabitants of the *Fire Kingdom*. They have volcanic rock adhered to their skin and are said to be taller than the average human.
- **Fire Kingdom**- Built within the *land's volcano* and surrounded by a lava lake. Home of the *fire creatures*.
- **Frost Kingdom** - Home of some *light elves*, including their Queen: Reva. The kingdom lies beneath *Trotter Mountain* and is protected by the *Trotter God*, who stands at the entrance and kills anyone who dares to enter.

- **Khan** - One of the most dangerous artifacts in the *lands.* It holds the power of the *shadows* and is the reason the *Shadow War* started.
- **Kumblesgard** - Catastrophic event that happened centuries ago, before the kingdoms were created. The *echoes* were creatures who started the war after the *titans* sent them to consume the *lands.* The *lands* won the war and supposedly trapped the *echoes* inside the *land's volcano.* The event is said to happen again sometime soon, and although legends mention prophecies found in sea caverns far from the *lands,* it is not confirmed to be true.
- **Lands** - The place we all live in. There are three types of lands: the *lands below,* the *lands above,* and the *lands between.*
- **Lands Above** - The place we live in, right above the *lands between.* The lands above are surrounded by a large sea. In that sea, various caverns and islands lie, hosting different civilizations.
- **Lands Below** - The lands below are the most mysterious of the three types of *lands.* There is a civilization living there, but no one has heard of it since the first *Kumblesgard,* leading people to believe it was destroyed.
- **Lands Between** - The place where the things that enter never escape. There is not much known about the *lands between* as they have never been properly researched. However, if anyone takes a wrong turn in a cave leading to the *lands below,* they can get stuck in the lands between forever.
- **Land's Volcano** - Home of the *fire creatures* and the *Fire Kingdom,* which was built inside the volcano and covered with a concrete crust. The volcano is surrounded by a lava lake that prevents trespassers from entering. It has been inactive for several centuries but is said to erupt once *Kumblesgard* begins again.
- **Light Elves** - The habitants of many tribes around the lands, as well as the *Nature Kingdom* and *Frost Kingdom.*

They are known for their bright skin, dark horns, and colorful runes on their arms.

- **Main Kingdom** - The kingdom where every magical creature and person once lived. After the *Shadow War* ended, the magical creatures were exiled from it. Fifteen years later, the place is mostly known for its extreme poverty, powerful forces, and rich monarchy.
- **Nature Kingdom** - Home of most of the *light elves*. It was once swarming with many more creatures, but after the *Trotter War*, most went extinct. The Queen of the kingdom, Ivy, used her abilities to create a colossal vine wall to protect her kingdom after the war.
- **Nympho** - Creatures that inhabit the swamp area of the lands. Their two horns and rock-hard bodies make them deadly for outsiders.
- **Quora Tribe** - A peaceful tribe located near the *Main Kingdom*. They are known for being enemies with the *Ah'lah'rra tribe* and allies with the *Zumba tribe*.
- **Shackflyer** - Serpent creature from the *Nature Kingdom* that has a shack on its back. It serves as an effective means of transportation for large groups.
- **Shadows** - Bloodthirsty creatures that emerged from the *Khan,* initiating the *Shadow War.*
- **Shadow War** - A conflict that began when the *shadows* were released from the *Khan*. The battle occurred in the *Main Kingdom*, resulting in Queen Lorette's death and the exile of magical creatures. The *shadows* were imprisoned at the *lands'* edge, with the King ensuring there was no possible way for them to escape.
- **Tabron** - An explosive device used by bounty hunters.
- **Tikh Bracelets** - Worn by various elvish tribes, including the *Zumba tribe*. Elves don these bracelets at six years old, each representing a member of their tribe. When that

member dies, their bracelet falls off. At the funeral, the tribe members send it flying on a small hot air balloon so that in the person's next life, they can reunite once again. Reincarnation is a shared belief among elves.

- **Titans** - Colossal inhuman beings who rule the *lands* without any relation to a kingdom. They are said to be three in total, representing nature, ice, and fire.
- **Troffe** - Sweet beverage served throughout the kingdoms.
- **Trolems** - Creatures made of rock with a heart that powers its entire body. The only way to kill them is by destroying their heart.
- **Trotters** - Reincarnation of *echoes.* Less deadlier, but can be a menace in groups. They are made of volcanic rock and have a leader: the *trotter king.*
- **Trotter God** - The father of all *trotters* and the voice of the *echoes.* Many believe it is a legend, but there have been numerous sightings at *Trotter Mountain's* peak.
- **Trotter King** - Leaders of *trotters* and very powerful species. They are made of molten rock and, like all other *trotters,* aren't living creatures.
- **Trotter Mountain** - A place swarmed with *trotters* and the supposed home of the *Trotter God.* Inside the mountain, the *Frost Kingdom* lies.
- **Trotter War** - A conflict between the *Trotter God* and the *Nature Kingdom*, instigated by Reva, the Queen of the *Frost Kingdom*. After Reva stole a precious artifact from the *Trotter God* and blamed it on Ivy, the Nature Queen, *trotters* invaded her kingdom. The war concluded when Reva returned the artifact, though she never confessed to stealing it.
- **Vanes** - Currency of the *lands.*
- **Zumba tribe** - One of the first tribes to form after the *Shadow War* ended. They are said to possess a great secret.

- **Zylika** - A rock found in the *Nature Kingdom*.

Made in the USA
Columbia, SC
03 July 2025

3b6cc7d4-e127-4f25-946d-27d1e2287050R01